BLACK EYES ALL OF THE TIME: INTIMATE VIOLENCE, ABORIGINAL WOMEN, AND THE JUSTICE SYSTEM

Reform measures to reduce domestic violence in Manitoba's Native communities have led to fewer criminal charges, less vigorous prosecution, and shorter jail terms for Aboriginal offenders, but with questionable results for their women and children victims.

This book arose out of a 1995 Winnipeg study involving twenty-six Aboriginal women. Their compelling, and at times harrowing, accounts of the abuse that they experienced and witnessed, first as children and later as wives and mothers, make it all too clear that any plan to implement 'diversion' of offenders must first take into account the victims' suffering and their needs. Jail terms for partners and fathers may allow families time for healing, and the threat of criminal prosecution may quell violent outbreaks. Lax responses from an inconsistent criminal justice system often put Native women at risk.

Drawing on the experiences and views of the women affected, *Black Eyes All of the Time* analyses how this pervasive cycle of violence evolved and suggests possible solutions involving both the dominant Canadian justice system and Aboriginal traditions.

ANNE MCGILLIVRAY is a professor at the Faculty of Law, University of Manitoba.

BRENDA COMASKEY is a research associate at Research and Education for Solutions to Violence and Abuse (RESOLVE), University of Manitoba.

ANNE McGILLIVRAY AND
BRENDA COMASKEY

Black Eyes All of the Time: Intimate Violence, Aboriginal Women, and the Justice System

UNIVERSITY OF TORONTO PRESS
Toronto Buffalo London

© University of Toronto Press 1999
Toronto Buffalo London
Printed in the U.S.A.

Reprinted 2004, 2011, 2012, 2015

ISBN 0-8020-4206-6 (cloth)
ISBN 0-8020-8061-8 (paper)

Printed on acid-free paper

Canadian Cataloguing in Publication Data

McGillivray, Anne
    Black eyes all of the time : intimate violence, aboriginal women, and the
justice system

    Includes bibliographical references and index.
    ISBN 0-8020-4206-6 (bound)   ISBN 0-8020-8061-8 (pbk.)

    1. Indian women – Crimes against – Manitoba.   2. Wife abuse – Manitoba.
3. Family violence – Manitoba.   4. Criminal justice, Administration of –
Manitoba.   I. Comaskey, Brenda.   II. Title.

    E78.M25M25 1999   364.15′553′0899707127   C99-930915-3

University of Toronto Press acknowledges the financial assistance
to its publishing program of the Canada Council for the Arts and
the Ontario Arts Council.

University of Toronto Press acknowledges the financial support for
its publishing activities of the Government of Canada through
the Book Publishing Industry Development Program (BPIDP).

I HONOUR all the brave women who, with courage, opened their hearts to speak the truth. And I HONOUR the women responsible for bringing these stories to the attention of all Nations, for their hard work and dedication.

The stories from these courageous women tell us of their trauma, their fears, their hurt and pain. They tell us of their mental, physical, and emotional abuse, of their years of suffering from their male partners. The children carry these same feelings, for many have witnessed this shame. IT MUST STOP.

The research and the personal stories revealed on the pages of this important document need to be told. This work will be a great contribution and, we hope, be instrumental in bringing about more effective support – for example, through more safe houses, more counselling, fairer judicial decisions, and, most important, traditional healing methods incorporated in all systems and set up to include the whole family.

ELDER MAE LOUISE CAMPBELL
WINNIPEG, MANITOBA

Contents

FOREWORD by Judge C.M. Sinclair   ix
PREFACE   xi
A NOTE ON TERMINOLOGY   xiii

Introduction   3

1 Intimate Violence Today   8

2 The Historical Context   22

3 The Experience of Intimate Violence   53

4 The Criminal Justice System   84

5 Thinking about Reform   114

6 Rights and Relationships   147

APPENDIX: THE WINNIPEG STUDY   173
BIBLIOGRAPHY   183
INDEX   195

Foreword

In traditional Aboriginal societies, women were the equal of men and were entitled to be treated with respect. In fact, in Aboriginal matriarchal societies, women were the ultimate holders of political and social power, with responsibilities expressed in teachings handed down from mother to daughter. One of the saddest influences of the years of contact between Aboriginal and European people in North America has been the denigration of the status of women in Aboriginal societies, as a result of or in conjunction with assaults that occurred against Aboriginal cultures generally.

European societies spoke about and dealt with women in much different ways than did Aboriginal societies at the time of first contact, and, with the increasing power of European nations in North America, that view prevailed.

Too many Aboriginal men have been raised in the belief that the inappropriate and inaccurate images of Aboriginal women that they see in movies, books, comic strips, and television accurately reflect the relationship between Aboriginal men and women. Too many Aboriginal men, having lost contact with their own cultures, have failed to see and accept the importance of family relationships to our future generations and the impact that their behaviour towards their partners has upon their children.

At present, the average life span for Aboriginal people in Canada is considerably lower than that for the rest of the population, and the birthrate is also considerably higher. These factors will have tremendous implications for society unless steps are undertaken to ensure that the social and personal problems related to long years of oppression are recognzed and addressed.

In the *Report of the Aboriginal Justice Inquiry of Manitoba*, vol. I, *The Justice System and Aboriginal People* (Manitoba 1991a), Associate Chief Justice A.C. Hamilton and I recommended that steps be taken to address the plight of Aboriginal women caught in intimate violence, particularly in remote and rural Aboriginal communities where resources to protect them from ongoing abuse were virtually non-existent. Additionally, we made recommendations to Aboriginal leaders, calling on them to take steps to ensure that the women of their communities were no longer subjected to the harmful treatment resulting from the improper handling of domestic violence by a predominantly male Aboriginal leadership.

More important, however, we called on society at large to understand the terrible situation that had evolved in Aboriginal communities as far as women were concerned and to take steps to assist these communities generally, and women specifically, to return to their rightful place in Aboriginal society.

Black Eyes All of the Time marks an important step in the process of recognition and action. The stories that are revealed here by the victims of abuse are compelling and instructive. No greater testament to the impropriety of past actions to undermine Aboriginal societies exists than the words of the women in these stories. No greater impetus for action exists than our realization that this behaviour can no longer be tolerated.

JUDGE C.M. SINCLAIR
WINNIPEG, MANITOBA

Preface

We are grateful for the contributions to the study on which this book is based, made by Marg Assiniboine-Myran (Elizabeth Fry Society); Lucille Bruce (Native Women's Transition Centre); Jackie Lavallee (Ikwe-Widdjiitiwin); Kathy Mallett (Original Women's Network), who originated the study; and Sharon Perrault (Ma Mawi Wi Chi Itata Centre Family Violence Program). Staff at these agencies contacted potential respondents, administered consent forms, and provided space for project coordination, safe spaces for interviews, and follow-up support and counselling. We thank in particular Norma Binguis, Velma Cockcroft, Virginia Cooke, Colleen Dell, Gwen Gosek, Verna McIvor, and Maureen Morrisseau. Donna Everette and Kathy Whitford conducted the interviews with sensitivity and insight.

Sid Frankel, then co-director of the Manitoba Research Centre on Family Violence and Violence against Women (now RESOLVE), located at the University of Manitoba in Winnipeg, has been a stalwart supporter, advising us on research planning and methods and reviewing manuscripts at various stages. Linda Mills (University of California at Los Angeles) and Elizabeth Comack (University of Manitoba) commented on the study's design. Jo-Anne Parisienne prepared an annotated bibliography of works on indigenous women and intimate violence as a basis for the study, with the support of a grant from the Manitoba Research Centre. The E.K. Williams Law Library, University of Manitoba, donated office space and computer services for data analysis. Rod Ward of National Typewriter donated audiotapes and a tape eraser for use in interviewing.

Funding for the 1995 study was granted by Heritage Canada and the Seventh Generation Fund. The Manitoba Research Centre sponsored the study. The Ethics Committee of the Faculty of Law, University of Manitoba, granted ethical approval. We are grateful for their informed criticism and support.

The Manitoba Legal Research Institute sponsored the help of law students Rekha Malaviya and Dorothy Tanaka in checking the manuscript and assisting with publication tasks, as did Cary Clark.

We dedicate this book to the twenty-six women who shared their experience and insights with us, in the hope that things will change and others will be spared suffering at the hands of partners, family members, and 'the system.'

A Note on Terminology

Canada is the original homeland of dozens of culturally and linguistically diverse peoples to whom a variety of legal entitlements accrue depending on historical circumstance, registration, and treaty. 'First Nations' refers to original peoples inhabiting the Americas prior to contact, in a general sense to their descendants, and in a legal sense to registered bands and reserves. These peoples have their own names – Cree, Dakota, Dene, Ojibwa, Sioux, and so on – and belong to fifty-three nations speaking dozens of distinct dialects that fall into eleven language groups. The largest language group, Algonkian, includes at least two Cree dialects and is spoken by about 100,000 people; the smallest, Kootenay, is spoken by about thirty. Huron (central Canada) and Beothuk (Newfoundland) languages are extinct (as are the Beothuk people, shot for sport by European fishermen on shore leave).

The term 'Aboriginal,' meaning literally 'from the beginning,' denotes those of First Nations descent, including the Inuit of northern Canada; registered or 'status' Indians, most of whom are also 'Treaty'; non-registered Indians descended from those not registered in the early days of the Indian Act or deregistered under a variety of provisions in the Indian Act (out-marriage for women, military service for men, voluntary enfranchisement); and Métis, descendants of Canadiens and Indian partners, who constitute one or more distinct cultures. 'Métis' also refers to those of other Euro-Aboriginal descent, although some prefer to be called 'Half-breed,' equivalent to 'Creole.' 'Indian' as used here refers to registered Indians under federal aegis. 'Tribal council' is a term used by the federal Department of Indian Affairs to designate associations of band councils for the administration of federally funded but provincially governed child-protection and family-support services.

'Intimate violence' refers to any and all forms of maltreatment committed in relationships of intimacy, trust, and dependence. Violence against women and girls is defined in the *Platform for Action* (1995) Address at the Fourth World Conference on Women in Beijing (1995) as 'any act of gender-based violence that results in, or is likely to result in, physical, sexual or psychological harm or suffering to women, including threats of such acts, coercion or arbitrary deprivation of liberty, whether occurring in public or private life' (section D: 113). We add to this definition violence against children. 'Intimate violence' refers to acts that violate physical, financial, sexual, psychological, emotional, and/or spiritual integrity. Such acts shade one into another on a continuum of violence. The term embraces wife battering, battered woman syndrome, wife abuse, spousal assault, child battering, child abuse, child sexual abuse, family violence, domestic abuse, domestic assault, and domestic violence. It is a breach of the relationship of deep trust presumed to exist among family members, between intimate partners, between caregivers and children, and, ultimately, between any adult and child.

'Colonization' refers to circumstances in which a dominant group undertakes to modify or eliminate the laws, customs, and belief systems of a community rendered unable to resist effectively. Colonization is a 'pervasive structural and psychological relationship between the colonizer and the colonized' which is 'ultimately reflected in the dominant institutions, policies, histories, and literatures of occupying powers' (LaRocque, 1996: 11). It involves the colonizer's taking over a community's social structures, governance, and administration and often imposing a different religion and world-view. This may have meant, as in Canada, the United States, Australia, and New Zealand, its taking control of childhood through such systems as residential schooling, child apprehension, and out-group adoption. Domination invites resistance, which may occur at the micro level of tactics, in the form of small acts against the dominator, or at the macro level of politics and insurrection, in struggles towards mutual cultural accommodation.

'Euro-colonial' designates people of European origin or descent colonizing a country already populated. 'Alterity' or 'Othering' and 'other' refer to processes or results of differentiation that make a people, culture, or 'race' seem alien, deeply different from or even opposite to one's own. These processes also apply on an individual level, as messages of difference are absorbed into the definition of the self. Here the concept refers to Euro-colonial politics and the politics of the imagination that construct 'Indianness' as alien to 'whiteness' and inimical to colonial goals.

BLACK EYES ALL OF THE TIME

I just think it's a normal life to live like that, black eyes, all of the time. I go out in the store like that. I didn't care, because – it's a life ... I was just black and blue, all the time.

Introduction

One does not go uninvited into the private spaces of another. This book originates in an invitation from Original Women's Network of Manitoba to design and conduct a study that would ascertain the opinions of Aboriginal women violated by partners on the question of whether Aboriginal men charged with domestic violence–related offences should be diverted from the criminal justice system. The involvement of Aboriginal women's agencies offered non-Aboriginals a rare research opportunity to speak across cultures about intimate violence against women and to investigate intimate violence in childhood – a dimension almost routinely excluded from studies of spousal assault. To consider the childhood origins of violence and victimization is not to mitigate criminal responsibility but to understand how violence begets violence and to underscore the importance of childhood both in its own right and as a situation that produces adult victims and violators.

We designed a structured, open-ended format for interviews in consultation with Aboriginal women dedicated to the healing and empowering of victims of intimate violence. Our steering committee and the agencies that they direct opened their files to us, contacted women, provided safe spaces for interviewing, and helped us design and refine the study. We conducted interviews in Winnipeg in the summer of 1995. The report *Intimate Violence, Aboriginal Women and Justice System Response: A Winnipeg Study* (McGillivray and Comaskey, 1996) was finalized in the summer of 1996 in consultation with the steering committee, for the use of the Aboriginal women's community in seeking justice reform. Aboriginal Ganootamaage Justice Services of Winnipeg, a diversion project, decided its first case on 29 September 1998 (*Winnipeg Free Press*, 29 Sept. 1998). In this book, we return to the original data and expand upon the criminal justice context. We explore more deeply the impact of colonialism on gender, childhood, and intimate violence in Manitoba's Aboriginal communities. We consider rights claims to be free of violence against women globally and locally, in the context of indigenous self-determination.

We are writing at the intersection of cultures and disciplines. Our selection from the vast literatures on intimate violence, criminal justice, and the history of Euro-colonial relations with First Nations is guided by what respondents told us. Themes that emerged in the data – the life stories of the women interviewed and their interpretations of these experiences – framed and constrained our selection of source materials. In our discussions of Aboriginal childhood, we draw on the work in progress of Anne McGillivray and Russell Smandych on the colonization of Aboriginal childhood. We have tried to avoid the jargon of our own disciplines – law and sociology. As jargon is in the eye of the beholder and stands in, if awkwardly, for complex concepts developed within a theoretical or disciplinary framework, this is not always possible. Where jargon – colonialism, othering, genocide – speaks to the complex yearnings of the dispossessed, it may be dismissed as mere polemic. Yet the context of colonialism recalls the origin of *polemic* in the Greek *polis* or *head* of the city-state and the smoothing of – making *polite* – the *politics* of resistance.

Our research lends support to the polemics of self-determination – the havoc wreaked on indigenous peoples by such Euro-colonial policies as the reserve system, residential schooling, and child welfare, themselves in turn wrecked on Certeau's 'dark rock' of culture and resistance (Certeau, 1984: 18). Polemic is a smoothing of the way from resistance to accommodation. This is the larger political engagement of Canada with its Aboriginal peoples. Where culture itself provides the excuse for perpetrating intimate violence and for failures in the system's response, silencing those who try to speak out, the violated become another 'dark rock' in the political stream, offering a small but tenacious resistance to resistance. This micropolitic frames our study. It propelled the originating question and guided our search for explanation in the historical record, in intimate violence statistics, and in policy of the justice system. Most centrally, it emerges from the data.

We report the words of respondents as fully as possible. Oral history brings immediacy and minimizes reporting bias. Quotation respects the authority and the authorship of the person telling the story. The telling of a life story respects the one who lived that life, but the lives of women in our study could not be reported. Change of name is a thin disguise, and altering anything else is an untruth that distorts data. We disaggregated the interviews, in that we do not follow the sequence of each originating interview but organize material according to topic and theme. This disaggregation was a boundary condition of consent – an assurance to respondents that they could not be recognized in any use of these interviews. In view of the number of respondents being stalked by former partners, this strategy proved wise. We regret the resulting fragmentation of their histories and the lack of full narrative account. Yet disaggregation and maximum use of quotations produced another narrative, rich and interconnected, in which accounts resonate to produce a composite experience and difference is not effaced. Throughout the book, we have used italics to highlight the words of the respondents.

We await corresponding studies that investigate the childhood experiences of men who violate intimates. The work of Lonnie Athens on dangerous violent offenders is among the few such studies available. We acknowledge the presence of intimate violence in same-sex relationships and recognize that this factor too is an area in need of research, particularly within culturally closed communities. As the subject did not arise in our interviews, it is not investigated here. We do not know whether alternative justice processes now being explored in Aboriginal communities, the return of powers of dispute resolution to First Nations, or the establishment of First Nations justice systems will decrease or eliminate intimate violence and rebalance gender relations in Aboriginal communities. These changes are part of a larger political process now under way in Canada – one in which, we hope, Aboriginal women and children will play central roles.

For reasons of protection, we cannot introduce the twenty-six women who made this work possible. They all share the experience of intimate violence. The reader can see that they have also shared other experiences – motherhood, poverty, isolation, connection to the reserve, violence in childhood. What follows here is an aggregate picture, based as closely as possible on the median of reported experiences.

She is a thirty-three-year-old woman of Indian status, born and raised on a prairie reserve. Of her two or more children under the age of eighteen, at least one is in the care of others. She has not completed high school, and her annual income is under $10,000. She has been a victim of intimate violence since early childhood. She grew up witnessing the abuse of other children and women, including her own mother. She has herself lived with two abusive partners, becoming involved with the first while she was in her mid-teens. She last experienced intimate violence about three years ago. Although she has a peace bond or restraining order against her abuser, and charges laid against him have been settled, she is currently being stalked and harassed or still fears that he may come back into her life. She is not now in a committed relationship with another partner.

As a child, she experienced physical, sexual, and emotional abuse at the hands of family members and neighbours. She was physically and emotionally abused by her mother and sexually abused by a male relative. For a long time, she did not recognize that what was being done to her was wrong; she even thought that she deserved it. She told few people about these things, thinking that no one would believe her or help her or that there was nothing unusual about her situation that would merit help. She tried to protect herself in various ways. If social services were available, she did not know about them. In adolescence and adulthood, she was humiliated by her partner and frequently and severely assaulted. She received injuries requiring hospitalization. Her children often witnessed her abuse. To gain her compliance, her partner injured or threatened to injure her children and threatened to deprive her of custody. He bribed and sweet-talked the children to turn them against their mother or to lie to investigating agencies. She did not contact police until numerous acts of violence had occurred. Concern for her children and fear of death prompted her decision to leave her partner. When she left, she sought shelter services and counselling from Aboriginal women's agencies in Winnipeg, as there was little or nothing available to her at home.

Her partner's violence brought her into contact with the criminal justice system. He pleaded guilty and received a short sentence – not enough, in her view, to 'pay' for what he did to her, not long enough to give her a period of safety to rebuild her life. Despite having racist and insensitive encounters with police and with lawyers, who did little for her and did not understand her situation, and no input into his sentence, she believes that the justice system is there to protect the innocent and to punish wrongdoers, even if it did neither very well in her case. She knows that jail does not help the guilty party but believes that he needs to be taught a lesson. She values punishment and wants longer jail terms for such crimes. She thinks that counselling and treatment should be available in jail. She is not particularly impressed with diversion from the justice system or with alternative measures, given the politics of reserve communities, but feels that they might be worth a try as long as the sentencing process is fair, he learns a lesson and gets effective treatment, and she is kept safe from him.

To outline the book's contents, chapters 1 and 2 provide a frame of reference for Aboriginal women's experience of intimate violence. In chapter 1 we consider the statistical picture of violence against Aboriginal women and children in Canada compared with intimate violence generally. In chapter 2 we look at the historical context – the ethics of cross-cultural research in the context of alterity, the 'othering' of the Indian through the production of images of Aboriginal women and children in the course of Euro-colonial contact, the past 'solutions' to the 'Indian problem' in the reserve system and residential schooling, the emerging counter-vision of Métissage, and cultural devaluation as 'spirit murder.' In chapters 3 and 4 we report and analyse the responses of participants in the 1995 Winnipeg study, which allow us to depict the dimensions and the imposed subjectivity of intimate violence and the criminal process. Chapter 5 surveys respondents' recommendations about diversion and other reforms arising from these discourses. Chapter 6 looks at intimate violence as an issue of human rights in international law and at grassroots levels in women's cultures throughout the world.

After 1870, government strategies of removal and assimilation, intended to create an unobstructed political, social, and agricultural space, intensified with the opening of the Canadian west, disrupting gender balance and transmission of culture to children. The reserve, the residential school, and the post-1960 system of child welfare imposed and internalized messages of alterity and further devalued culture and female gender. This history begins to account for the rate, risk, and frequency of intimate violence as it has affected Aboriginal women in Canada. Sarah Carter (1996: 55) argues correctly that any approach stressing subjugation and cultural decline 'ignores the motives, interests, and understandings of Aboriginal people themselves, and overlooks the degree of cultural continuity.' A desirable approach is one that looks at mutual interactions and influences and takes a more nuanced and comparative view of the lives of Aboriginal women in the colonial context.

However, this is not the approach that we take in chapter 2. Our concern there is rather with non-nuanced images of difference produced in Euro-colonial accounts and with state projects that totalize and reify culture and manipulate cultural images of Aboriginal women and children.

1

Intimate Violence Today

In the reserve just, like, everybody had black eyes, walking around, all the ladies, all black. I thought that's the life ... Nobody don't say nothing.

Violence and Everyday Life

The normalization of intimate violence is a major barrier to the protection of women and children. Intimate violence is an open secret in societies throughout the world, and Canada is no exception. Even so, variations in rates, forms, circumstances, excuses, and explanations are important. For Aboriginal women, it may be, as the Canadian Council on Social Development (1991) observes, 'the exception rather than the rule to know of an aboriginal woman who has not experienced some form of family violence throughout her life.' The Royal Commission on Aboriginal Peoples (RCAP) observes that intimate violence 'has invaded whole communities and cannot be considered a problem of a particular couple or an individual household' (Canada, RCAP, 1996b: 57). 'In too many Aboriginal communities, or among subgroups within Aboriginal communities, violence has become so pervasive that there is a danger of it coming to be seen as normal' (75).

For respondents in the present study, normalization has already taken place. The frequency, variety, and severity of violence reported by respondents stand in startling contrast with the sense that it is an ordinary part of everyday life.

It seems to be what's normal for you – getting a licking once a week, every other day, every day.

I thought it was normal to be hit ... – to hit or be hit.

Of course, each and every one of us grew up in a violent home. I guess they thought it was normal.

It's still happening quite a bit. It seems like it's a norm, a normal thing.

There was never any comfortable feeling and I guess a lot of it was my upbringing, and it was just a way of life for me. At least now, when I look back and think about it now it was just a way of life, the feelings, being uncomfortable and stuff ... When you grow up with stuff like that, you think it's normal.

I didn't like seeing abuse as I was growing up, and I didn't want that for my kids or anybody else's kids. I don't like seeing alcohol when there's adults there while the children are playing around. They think it's normal or something. They don't want to break the chain. Until one of the kids do break that chain.

Well, I think the problem is widespread. It can't be addressed until people say there is a problem. It takes time, a long time, to unlearn the behaviour and violence.

If violence by one in a position of intimate trust – parent, partner, family member – is perceived as the community norm as well as the relational norm, the difficulty in responding to it increases. How can one be in special need of help if the same thing is happening to everyone else? Normalization of violence in childhood had a strong influence on whether respondents sought help as children and as adults:

I didn't know I needed help. I thought it was normal.

I didn't think anybody would believe me.

I never asked, because I thought no one would understand.

I tried to get help from my family but all they did was ... they laughed at me.

[T]he first time I was sexually abused, I was only twelve and he was thirty. The whole reserve said I deserved it. They shunned me. They talked about me and made me feel like dirt. They made me feel worthless.

I guess because all of the abuse got in my way, my mother, what she did to me. I was afraid to ask for anything because when we were kids, when we asked for help or whatever, we were turned down. We were hit. I guess that is what got in my way for asking for the help I needed.

The reserve where I lived, there was nothing – I didn't know anything at all – if I could ask for help.

I think about half-way through this, all the violence, all those years of violence, I started thinking to myself, 'Something is not right here.' I knew even deep down in me something was wrong. I was still incapable of reaching out for help.

Challenging the norm is frightening, and escape may mean the abandonment of everyday life. For those in geographically or culturally isolated communities, it may mean community shaming, banishment, and the abandonment of one's culture, people, kin, even one's children. There may be other repercussions against the complainant by an abusive partner and his supporters. Normalization confounded help-seeking by children and women (chapter 3) and the system's response (chapters 4 and 5).

While some community members are now more aware of intimate violence as pervasive and problematic, others deny its existence. This denial is true of all forms of intimate violence, but it has been most spectacularly apparent in child sexual assault. 'No, we don't have sexual abuse. We don't have an alcohol problem. We don't have child neglect here,' a respondent to the royal commission puts it (Canada, RCAP, 1996b: 64). The 1988 suicide of a thirteen-year-old Ojibwa boy, Lester Desjarlais, became the subject of the longest inquest in Manitoba history (Giesbrecht, 1992; McGillivray, 1997c). First Nations leaders were criticized as being in denial both of their own childhood experiences of sexual abuse and of the fact, extent, and damage of sexual abuse in their communities. Paediatrician Charlie Ferguson, testifying at the inquest, described the boy's community as 'infested with incest.' Chiefs and councillors exercised band powers to interfere in the work of intertribal child protection agencies, banished workers, and returned children to abusive environments. These actions were motivated, the inquest concludes, by both denial and nepotistic protection of relatives and supporters who were sexually abusing children. The provincial Ministry for Child and Family Services also came under attack for failing to intervene; the reason given was that the minister feared being labelled 'racist.'

Privacy surrounds and protects relations of intimacy. The first step in seeking change is a shift in self-definition. Generally, one must define or accept a definition of oneself as 'battered' or 'beaten' or 'abused' before one can initiate or effectively participate in a healing or restorative process (McGillivray, 1987). Victims' self-definition may be compromised by media portrayals of abuse that bear little relevance to their experiences of violation. Help-seeking may be further compromised by police views of battering as somehow consensual or ideas about 'worthy' and 'unworthy' victims. These stereotypes also confuse judicial response, where the victim does not match cultural images of the battered woman as passive, helpless, and sweet (Merry, 1997; Shaffer, 1997) and accord with Emma La Rocque's observation that 'Sadly, there are insidious notions within our own communities that we as Native women should be "unobtrusive, soft-spoken and quiet"' (LaRocque, 1996).

The problem is more intense for children. Parents may have impossibly high expectations for their children's conduct, which do not match their actual developmental ability and needs. Parents may expect them to be *seen and not heard*, to integrate the parents' definitions of behaviour, to demonstrate loyalty to parents, and to accept assault as a normal part of childhood. Children lack the physical strength and social status effectively to resist violence against themselves or against mother or siblings. Law and social convention severely limit their autonomy. This humiliating powerlessness, as much as the internalization of violence and images of violence, results in violence against intimates or others in adulthood (Alice Miller, 1983; Athens, 1989). *They don't want to break the chain. Until one of the kids do break that chain.*

Although intimate violence is universal, it is culturally constructed. Where violence against women and children is normalized within an isolated community, thresholds – personal, familial, and community, as well as those of law-enforcement and social services – tend to shift. The meaning of intimate violence is different for victims, families, offenders, and the community. The justice system further restructures meaning in ways that may ignore victims' ambiguity, their continuing relationship with the offender, and the shame of public disclosure. The psychological impact of the violence leaves a residue that may impair perceptions of the victim's credibility (chapter 4). Cultural and geographical distance from policing, child-protection, and victims' services also complicates response. Access to help for women and children living on a reserve may be further compromised by band politics and powers of banishment (Giesbrecht, 1992; McGillivray, 1997c).

The extended family networks characteristic of Aboriginal communities heighten the fear and shame of revealing abuse. Such revelations 'are likely to reverberate through the whole kinship network,' and family members may 'collude with the perpetrator to deny and cover up the situation' (RCAP, 1996: 68–9). Collusion may take place within the political structure of the reserve (chapter 3). Gender and generation also influence how people understand intimate violence. The increased dialogue of late around the effect of colonization on intimate violence in First Nations communities suggests that younger women may more quickly identify abuse than older women, as these discourses are 'more in their psyche' (273). By inference, boys are less likely than girls to report abuse. Sexual abuse of boys by men is silenced by the shame associated with homosexuality, while that by women is confused with 'coming of age' sexual fantasies. Physical abuse may be absorbed as an alleged contribution to the boy's masculinity. The new discourse is thus less 'in the psyche' of men and more readily denied.

The Extent of Intimate Violence

We should look at intimate violence affecting Aboriginal women and children in Canada within the context of such behaviour generally. On a global scale, domestic violence is the most prevalent form of interpersonal violence, with abuse of women and girls 'substantially' present in eighty-four of ninety cultures studied (Levinson, 1989). Despite two decades of changing mores and of legal and policy reform, Canada is no exception. According to the Violence against Women Survey (VAWS) conducted by Statistics Canada in 1993 (Rodgers, 1994), 29 per cent of Canadian women had experienced physical or sexual violence in a marital relationship, and 15 per cent were exposed to it in a current relationship. Sixty-three percent of the women reporting violence had experienced more than one episode, and 32 per cent reported more than ten episodes. Fifty-one per cent had experienced at least one incident of physical or sexual abuse after the age of sixteen (Johnson, 1995a: 131). In 1994, 33.8 per cent of 49,870 offences against women in Canada were committed by a spouse or ex-spouse. Most frequently reported were 'level-one' (the least serious) common assault (29,106), level-one sexual assault (6,487), and assault with a weapon (4,865). Other sexual offences, abduction, robbery, and criminal harassment accounted for the remaining 7,718 (Canada, Statistics Canada, 1995). In its study of 420 women, the Canadian Panel on Violence against Women found that 27 per cent of women are physically assaulted in an intimate relationship (Canadian Panel, 1993: 11). Thirty-six per cent of women feared for their lives during the attacks. One-half of such assaults were accompanied by sexual assault, and one-fourth by death threats. Over half reported rape or attempted rape; of these, 40 per cent were raped at least once, and eight in ten knew the perpetrator. The population of 273 shelters (serving 78,429 clients in 1992) was surveyed on 31 March 1992 (Canadian Panel, 1993: 10). The majority of residents were between the ages of twenty-five and thirty-four. Almost half their children were under the age of five. One-quarter requested police intervention, but charges were laid in under half of these cases.

It is important to note that the VAWS excluded Yukon and Northwest Territories and homes without telephones, effectively excluding many Aboriginal women. The rate of intimate violence against Aboriginal women is consistently higher than the VAWS figures by a factor of three. Eight in ten Aboriginal women witnessed or experienced intimate violence in childhood, and the same number have been child or adult victims of sexual assault (Ontario Native Women's Association, 1989; Kiyoshk, 1990). Between 75 and 90 per cent of northern Ontario's Aboriginal women are assaulted in an adult relationship. Aboriginal women typically endure thirty to forty beatings before calling police. Physical injury is the leading cause of death of Aboriginal women on reserve (Dumont-Smith and Labelle, 1991). Statistical relationships between intimate violence and the death of women in geoculturally remote populations require further investigation. Aboriginal women and children living in Canadian inner cities are similarly exposed to high levels and rates of intimate violence (La Prairie, 1994: ii).

Canadian children experience high rates of sexual and physical violence. In the largest study of its kind, researchers at McMaster University and the Clarke Institute for Psychiatry in Toronto surveyed 10,000 Ontario residents over the age of fifteen in 1990–1 to determine the prevalence of a history of childhood physical and sexual abuse in the general population (MacMillan et al., 1997). They chose a self-reporting questionnaire as most likely to elicit disclosure. Over 31 per cent of the boys disclosed physical abuse, as did over 21 per cent of the girls. Almost half of these, 10.7 per cent of boys and 9.2 per cent of girls, were severely physically abused. Girls were three times more likely than boys to be sexually abused: 12.8 per cent of girls and 4.3 per cent of boys reported childhood sexual abuse. Severe sexual abuse was disclosed by 11.1 per cent of girls and 3.9 per cent of boys. Prevalence rates are similar to those reported in culturally similar countries using similar definitions of abuse. As girls grow older, the prevalence of sexual abuse, the occurrence of childhood physical and sexual abuse together, and severe abuse decline. There is no significant change for boys.

The study most often identifies biological fathers as physical abusers, with biological mothers second. Sexual abusers were most often 'other persons' outside the family, unrelated by blood or marriage, with persons inside the family second. The study defined sexual abuse as adults exposing genitalia more than once to a child, threatening to have sex with a child, sexual touching, attempting sex, and having sex with a child. It defines physical abuse as pushing, grabbing, shoving, and throwing objects, but only if these acts occurred 'sometimes' or 'often,' and kicking, biting, punching, hitting with an object, choking, burning, scalding, and physically attacking. It defines childhood as 'when you were growing up.' It did not distinguish between situations of family, mixed-family, and alternative (foster and institutional) care. Data collected on corporal punishment (slaps and spankings) will form the subject of a separate report.

Rates of violence reported to police or child protection agencies are low compared with those reported in studies such as the McMaster–Clarke study. An abuse rate of only 21 per 1,000 children was found in a 1993 random survey of the files of fifteen Children's Aid Societies in Ontario (Trocme et al., cited in Johnson, 1995a). Nico Trocme reviewed 2,400 files from Ontario child protection agencies and found that boys were physically abused slightly more often than girls and that 59 per cent of the affected children were abused before the age of three. Fifty-six per cent of victims of sexual abuse are between eight and eleven years of age. Of all cases of violence against children under the age of nineteen reported to the criminal justice system, physical assault accounts for 46 per cent and sexual assault for 43 per cent (Johnson, 1995a). One-fifth of all reported assaults are committed by immediate family members, and in the majority of cases perpetrators are known to children – two in three cases to boys, four in five cases to girls. Girls are twice as likely as boys to be assaulted by a family member. The study did not account for the increased probability of sexual assaults being committed by strangers, casual acquaintances, or 'dates' as children age.

One in every five assaults reported to police in Canada in 1996 involved a child, and the offender was most often a family member, according to the Canadian Centre for Justice Statistics (*Winnipeg Free Press*, 8 Nov. 1997). Fifty-four per cent of 420 abused women had at least one experience of sexual abuse before the age of sixteen, with 24 per cent of such incidents being attempted or completed intercourse (Canadian Panel, 1993: 9). The Canadian Centre for Justice Statistics did not examine other forms of childhood abuse and exposure to violence towards other family members in childhood.

The studies cited above are retrospective, dependent on memory and respondents' interpretations. Prospective or longitudinal studies, which follow respondents into the future, are considered more reliable. The first such study of the treatment of children in Canada began in 1994 (Johnson, 1995a). Researchers will follow 25,000 children intensively from birth to age eleven and every two years from twelve to eighteen.

The risk of violence is heightened for Aboriginal children, as it is for Aboriginal women. Children in foster, extended, or 'varied' family situations are at higher risk of all forms of abuse. Prolonged child–parent separation and institutional care jeopardize the child's acquisition of parenting skills, learned by observation, and increase risk not only to that child but also to his or her children in subsequent generations. Aboriginal children were and are far more likely to experience parental separation and institutional care than are non-Aboriginal children. Indian residential schooling exposed over 100,000 children to physical, psychological, and sexual abuse and denied them the experiences of culture, parenting, and the development of child-rearing skills and norms (Manitoba, 1991a; J.R. Miller, 1996; RCAP, 1996a; McGillivray, 1997c). Between 1920 and 1960, 375 of every 1,000 status Indian children attended a residential school. Rates approached 100 per cent in western provinces (Armitage, 1995; J.R. Miller, 1996). In 1936, for example, 44 per cent of Manitoba's Indian children, 77 per cent of Saskatchewan's, and 98 per cent of Alberta's were enrolled in a residential school (Armitage, 1995). When the system of residential schooling was abandoned in the late 1960s, the child welfare system had begun to take over, apprehending Indian children in the prairie provinces in record numbers (McGillivray, 1987, 1997c). By 1975, 62.9 of every 1,000 status Indian children were in institutional or state foster care, primarily because of 'neglect.' Rates fell to 38.9 children per 1,000 by 1990 but remain four times the Canadian average (Armitage, 1995: 206). It is estimated that up to 50 per cent of cases of child abuse reported to Manitoba agencies arise in foster homes (McGillivray, 1997c).

Violence in childhood and violence in adulthood are correlated. Children exposed to violence against their mother by her partner are three times as likely if they are male to use violence against an adult partner, and if they are female to enter an abusive relationship (Gelles, 1979, c.f. Athens, 1989; Straus, Gelles, and Steinmetz, 1980; Rabin, 1995). Women who use violence against a partner are most likely to be acting in retaliation or self-defence, but the 'choice' of such relationships may be influenced, constrained, or dominated by violence witnessed and experienced during childhood. Boys who witness intimate violence against their mothers are ten times as likely to repeat the cycle with their partners. Boys who are physically abused are up to a thousand times more likely to use violence in adulthood against a spouse or child. The fact that a child has experienced or witnessed abuse does not condemn the child to abusing as an adult or entering an abusive relationship, but it does heighten the risk significantly.

VAWS data show that children witnessed violence in 39 per cent of cases of assault on their mothers (Bala et al., 1998). The figure rose to 61 per cent in cases in which the mother was injured, suggesting that children are more likely to see serious incidents. Children witnessing violence triggered women's decisions to leave – 60 per cent of women whose children saw or heard violence left the relationship, compared with 32 per cent of women whose offspring did not. Whether the violence is seen or heard, even a single incident can cause post-traumatic stress disorder in children. The mother's abuse may impair her parenting capacity, making her colder and more coercive with her children. The worst outcome occurs where a child both witnesses abuse and is abused. Twenty-five per cent of men who physically abuse partners also do the same to offspring. Children also may be hurt in an attempt to protect their mother, infants may be dropped and otherwise 'accidentally' injured, and an abuser may kidnap children, use them to control the spouse, or, in the most serious of cases and usually in the context of marital breakdown, kill his children and spouse or kill his children and himself. Children growing up in households where there is violence against their mother experience behavioural problems, nightmares, and lowered self-esteem. Boys become more aggressive, and girls more depressive. Both are more likely to become involved in abusive relationships as adults – boys as abusive and girls as abused. Young people who stop living with the abusive parent experience substantial improvement, especially when they receive therapy. Although any family member may be a victim or instigator of violence, children under fifteen and women are most frequently violated and most severely injured (Dumont-Smith and Labelle, 1991). In the absence of healing and insight, an intergenerational cycle of violence emerges as child victims grow up to become adult victims and abusers.

Records on intimate violence remain incomplete because of under-reporting and the sporadic notation of kinship and ethnicity. Even so, Canadian studies are consistent in reporting much higher rates of intimate violence against Aboriginal women and children than the population norm. If violence against women and children is endemic, that against those who are Aboriginal would appear to be an epidemic.

Studying Culture, Exploring Alternatives

The study of Aboriginal peoples in Canada has exploded in the past decade. Major studies and inquiries – among these the reports of the Canadian Bar Association (1989), *Locking up Natives in Canada*; Manitoba's Aboriginal Justice Inquiry (AJI) (Manitoba, 1991a, b); the Law Reform Commission of Canada (Canada, LRCC, 1991); the Donald Marshall Inquiry in Nova Scotia in 1993; and the Royal Commission on Aboriginal Peoples (Canada, RCAP, 1996b) – disclose the personal and communal damage done to Aboriginal peoples by the criminal justice system and draw on the broader context of colonialism and culture. All found discrimination against Aboriginal people in the criminal process and massive over-representation of Aboriginal people in carceral institutions. All agree on the desirability of approaches based on traditional cultural values of healing, restitution, and reintegration. They propose as alternatives circle and community sentencing within the courtroom context; diversion via alternative measures such as mediation, peer and elder counselling, and healing circles; increasing the numbers of Aboriginal police, lawyers, judges, and other personnel in the justice system; First Nations' administration of justice, in which all court personnel would be Aboriginal; and First Nations justice systems that would make as well as administer law.

Some 3 per cent of the Canadian population and 6 per cent of the Manitoba population are of First Nations origin. On average, 19 per cent of admissions to penal institutions are Aboriginal men, but in some institutions, particularly in the west, the rate approaches 90 per cent (Statistics Canada, 1991). In Manitoba, well over half of those incarcerated are Aboriginal people (Griffiths and Verdun-Jones, 1994: 633). Rates of incarceration are higher for Aboriginal women, who account on average for 50 per cent to 90 per cent of the women held in provincial penal institutions and 20 per cent of those in federal institutions.

The high rate of incarceration of Aboriginal peoples is typical of colonized countries (Greer, 1994). The silence surrounding the brutal gang rape and murder of Helen Betty Osborne, an Aboriginal high-school student in The Pas, Manitoba, has come to symbolize the inadequacies of mainstream response to violence against Aboriginal women and girls. Yet the cultural disorientation, lack of rehabilitation, and anger that accompany criminal justice and penal experiences for Aboriginal offenders may themselves escalate both public and intimate violence. Alternative approaches in Aboriginal justice have begun to appear in Canadian reserve communities (chapters 4 and 5). An urban diversion–peer counselling program has been developed in Toronto (Aboriginal Legal Services, 1992), managed by Aboriginal Legal Services of Toronto working with the Crown Attorney's Office and the Native Courtworker Program. The goal is community reintegration for offenders. The accused is invited to appear before a peer or elder group in return for charges being dropped. Failing to appear or failing to comply with the counsel given by the group does not result in the charges being reinstated, but that person will not be given a second chance with the program. Original Women's Network, in consultation with the Aboriginal Council of Winnipeg, has initiated a similar project. Provincial prosecution policy (discussed in chapter 4) requires that charges be laid in all cases involving intimate violence by a partner. Under a similar policy in Ontario, the Toronto program does not accept such offenders. Should Aboriginal men charged with crimes of violence against intimate partners be diverted from the justice system, or should provincial prosecution policy apply? What do Aboriginal women in Winnipeg want?

In contrast to the deterrence-based criminal justice system, which focuses on the offender's guilt, Aboriginal dispute resolution looks to reintegrative, community-based solutions (Green, 1998) and is concerned with restitution and atonement rather than punishment (Canadian Panel, 1991: 167). Such resolutions may be problematic for Aboriginal women. Experiences of culture, colonization, and violence are not uniform, nor can it be assumed that Aboriginal women subjected to intimate violence will view 'cultural' solutions in the same way as Aboriginal men or First Nations political leaders. There is a 'serious lack of research on Aboriginal women, particularly Métis, Status and non-Status women not residing on reserves' (Canadian Panel, 1993: 156). Although some studies include interviews with Aboriginal women or reflect consultation with them (Ontario Native Women's Association,

1989; Canadian Council on Social Development, 1991; Manitoba, 1991; Dumont-Smith and Labelle, 1991, cited in Canadian Panel, 1993; Canada, RCAP, 1993, 1996), they may interpose interpretive layers between their voices and the conclusions reached. Few studies get directly at experiences and insights of abused women, report with a minimum of editorial interference, or use themes emergent in the data to construct theory. McIvor and Nahanee (1998: 68) assert that 'there are pressing needs for knowledges about violence against Aboriginal women ... [that] should be built on Aboriginal women's experiences.' Autohistory – one's history as told by oneself, or the history of a people as told by the people – is integral to understanding intimate violence as at once embedded in community practice and as individually experienced. A study foregrounding Aboriginal women's histories of intimate violence would, we felt, link child and adult experiences of violence and generate information on justice issues.

A central question facing researchers is the legitimacy of cross-cultural research. The stereotype of such research is the voiceless and unknown 'other' who is given voice and identity by the researcher. Gayatri Chakravorty Spivak (1988, quoted in Fine, 1994: 75) writes that researchers must 'stop trying to *know* the Other or *give voice* to the Other and listen instead to the plural voices of those Othered, as constructors and agents of knowledge' and as 'primary informants' on Othering. 'Domination and distance get sanitized inside science.' Investigating the conditions of Othered groups may be seen as a form of oppression and cultural colonization, a theft of cultural capital, even where that capital resides in someone's pain. Academics and other privileged observers who identify themselves with the goals and norms of another culture contribute to a social hierarchizing of cultural values by co-opting and suppressing distance and difference. 'The Bororos of Brazil sink slowly into their collective death and Levi-Strauss takes his seat in the French Academy,' as Certeau (1984: 25) observes. Yet, as Michelle Fine (1994: 80) writes, '[we] all have genders and races, classes, sexualities, dis-abilities, and politics [and] if poststructuralism has taught us anything, it is to beware the frozen identities and the presumption that the hyphen is real, to suspect the binary, to worry the clear distinctions.' Researchers must 'work the hyphens' of these multiple identities in order to get at the self.

'Violence against Aboriginal women must be seen through the eyes of Aboriginal women' (Canadian Panel, 1993: 150). Research must anchor 'the legal, moral, and cultural sanctions attached', in 'the context of the relationships and settings in which it takes place' (20). The participation of Aboriginal women in all stages of research in the present study provided an opportunity to 'work the hyphens.' The model reflected in the study design is that of community-based participatory research (St Denis, 1992). After considering other methods – workshops and 'yes–no' and short-answer questionnaires – we chose a qualitative method to capture the context, richness, individuality, and originality of women's experiences and insights. Expertise in the naming and meaning of intimate violence and in assessing responses to it must belong to the respondents. To correct for biases in selection of interview subjects, and to balance the confidentiality that bars readers from investigating the data for themselves, we interrogated the information by referencing related research, interpreting data within a defensible conceptual framework, and using direct quotations from the interviews (cf. Thornton, 1996, on investigating discrimination and alienation in the legal profession through the experiences of disaffected women). Community-based participatory research is responsive to disempowered communities by emphasizing collaboration and women speaking for themselves, yielding research that is 'for and with' Aboriginal women rather than 'on or about' them (St Denis, 1992).

We developed a two-stage interview format combining open-ended and probing questions. Women were to name and define their experiences rather than be confined to a standard 'violence checklist.' We selected respondents from agency files, and initial contact was made by agency workers. We developed precautions for preserving confidentiality and protecting respondents. Interviews took place on the premises of the sponsoring agency or anywhere else where respondents felt safe. Follow-up counselling was made available, and lists of services and resources were compiled and given to respondents. In order to assess recent justice reforms, we focused on violence occurring within five years prior to the interviews. Only those who had undergone treatment and counselling were to be interviewed: research should not evoke unresolved pain. One respondent had not completed a counselling program, we later learned, and attempted suicide a few hours after her first interview. Although we do not know what role any intervening events may have played, it was clear in retrospect that her interview revealed suicidal ideation in childhood and adolescence. We suspended research until she was found and her safety assured. She declined the second interview (see Appendix). Two respondents had been abused by a partner eight and ten years before the study but entered shelters because of recent abuse of children – physical abuse of a grandchild, in one case, and sexual abuse of daughters by their father, in the other.

Aboriginal women with agency experience, who are fluent in Ojibwa, conducted one-on-one interviews. Although interviews took place in English, subtle language usage could be interpreted and a level of comfort achieved by all parties to the research. We selected twenty-five respondents from agency files. Two volunteer test interviews were included at the respondents' request (granted as the final questionnaire was changed only in minor ways). Twenty-six women completed the first part of the interview, and twenty-five, the second part. Each part took one hour on average to complete.

We structured the study around areas of inquiry – intimate violence in childhood, partner violence in adulthood, intervention and support, responses of the police and justice system, and system reform and alternatives. We took data apart – disaggregated them – to ensure that respondents would not be recognized. This is frustrating, as narrated case histories carry a special immediacy, but it was essential in view of the continuing danger that we anticipated respondents might face. This wariness was confirmed by respondents' reports of harassment and death threats at the time of the study. The first interview explored demographics and dealt with the first three areas of inquiry – violence in childhood, violence in adulthood, and support and intervention (chapter 3). The second interview explored the fourth and fifth areas, namely the justice system's response – policing, prosecution and lawyers generally, the court process, victim support, sentencing, and protection orders (chapters 4 and 5) – and reform through alternative programs (chapter 5). Finally, we place all this in a global context (chapter 6). With the invitation, support, and direction of Aboriginal women, and by enhancing opportunities for women to speak of their experiences in intimate and alien systems, we have tried to 'work the hyphens.'

2

The Historical Context

Civilizing the Indian: Colonialism, Gender, and Childhood

Intimate violence in Aboriginal communities must be seen not only in a comparative statistical context (as above), but also within the history of Euro-colonial relations with First Nations in the colonies that now make up Canada. Colonialism creates extreme dynamics of domination and subjectivity, which readily translate into the more intimate relations of abuser and abused. Colonialism has shaped the nature, severity and rate of intimate violence in indigenous communities. It has influenced internal and external evaluation of the violence and created an environment in which it thrives as learned behaviour, transmitted across generations, silenced by culture. The reduction of women's roles in tribal economies and politics, the 'decentring' of motherhood in mission schooling, and the patriarchy embedded in the Indian Act, in its regulation of band membership and electoral privileges, are entwined with the targeting of childhood for 'civilization.' Residential schooling and out-group adoption separated children from mother, clan, and culture. This past continues to speak, in the dynamics of intimate violence in Aboriginal communities.

Women's roles and social status as embedded in Euro-colonial relations with First Nations and legislated in the Indian Act accorded with nineteenth-century Anglo-Canadian law and social structures. Under English law, women were legally subject to their husbands. They did not control or participate directly in trade, contract, government, or decisions about residence, nor did they have a prior claim (or indeed any claim) to their children. Extended separation of children from parents for residential schooling was the norm for the middle- and upper-class

English and Canadians who developed Canadian Indian policy. Abuse, humiliation, and corporal punishment were not unknown in the institutions that schooled the children of the wealthy and housed the children of the poor. Discourses surrounding education, protection, and civilization of children in the nineteenth century were centrally humanitarian, yet schooling and child protection 'failed dismally' for Aboriginal children (Kimelman, 1985). What went wrong? At the heart of the question is the cultural devaluation implicit in projects of cultural conversion.

Cultural and gender devaluation are visible in the targeting of the bodies of Aboriginal children and women for sexual exploitation and other forms of violence. 'When I see my sisters in the prisons, on the streets, and in their walking coffins, I see where the battle has taken its greatest toll. I see the scars,' elder Jeannette Armstrong (1996: xi) told the National Symposium on Aboriginal Women of Canada in 1989. 'My utter disgust is for those who feed on the wounded. Who abuse them further with their bodies, their eyes, and their unclean minds.' Cultural devaluation plus the devaluation of children and women in the dominating culture invites predation and exploitation from all sides.

Cultural and gender devaluation is clearly present in documents produced across five centuries of European manipulation of the meaning of Aboriginality in furtherance of Euro-colonial goals. Indians were allies in war, guides in exploration, partners in trade, souls to convert, populations to assimilate through agriculture and education or relegate to geopolitical margins to clear the path of settlement (J.R. Miller, 1989; Buckley, 1992; Fleras and Elliot, 1992). The post-1850s focus on childhood as the primary site of citizenship and normalization offered a solution to the 'Indian problem' (McGillivray, 1997a, c). If adulthood means ways that are set, childhood offers a clean slate for the writing of culture. Colonialism introduced or exacerbated variables associated with high rates of physical and sexual assault and abuse. These include substance abuse as a coping mechanism, acute poverty and welfarism ('fare-wel,' it is called in a self-deprecating Aboriginal wordplay) within a rich society, racism, erosion of parenting skills, learned patterns of intimate violence, and infantilization of adults as wards of the state.

Aboriginal people have brought this history to public attention in academic and literary writings, in the law courts, and in testimony before commissions and boards of inquiry. Less well understood is how historical processes of colonization and cultural devaluation further devalued children and the gender and status of women in the affairs, economies, and daily life of their communities. Gendered racism and the marginalization of women within their own communities as well as in the larger society carry messages of subjectivity that are internalized in childhood. How one is defined by the 'other' is a vector of the definition of the 'self.' This process – from cultural devaluation through gender devaluation from beyond, and then from within, one's culture, leading to devaluation of the self via the internalizing of racist and sexist messages – begins to explain how intimate violence becomes normalized, not only in the family (where 'we' as a couple or family may be different) but also in the community (where 'we' as a community are different). The problem of definition is acute in isolated communities.

'Othering' the Indian – Images of Alterity

The powerful sense of otherness that pervades European accounts of contact with New World people is central to the impact of the historical process of colonialism. 'Writing the Indian' by explorers, traders, captives, missionaries, settlers, artists, dramatists, poets, novelists, and government inquiries has produced images of difference that have preoccupied Europeans for over 500 years (McGillivray, 1999). Whether accounts were sympathetic, indifferent, or hateful, whether they advocated military partnership, trade, conversion, extermination, peaceful co-existence, or assimilation, otherness is central. It is the drawing card for public readership, the face and justification of humanitarianism, and the backdrop against which Euro-colonial interests are played out.

As one of us has earlier written (McGillivray, 1997c), culture in a post-colonial context is about the construction of otherness and the inscription of difference in policy and law – a specular relationship in which each is alien, to the other. A 'high' or 'original' culture is claimed to have been lost or debased. A 'debased' culture, having for its other lost its utility, romantic, economic, or otherwise, must be transformed. The experience of culture and of cultural colonization lies in what Certeau has called the practice of everyday life. Here 'culture' is less about artefact or text than about *a way of using* imposed systems [that] constitutes the resistance to the historical law of a state of affairs and its dogmatic limitations ... that is where the opacity of a "popular" culture could be said to manifest itself – a dark rock that resists all assimilation' (Certeau, 1984: 18). Everyday life 'bring[s] to light the clandestine forms taken by the dispersed, tactical, and makeshift creativity of groups or individuals' on a small and daily scale to constitute the 'dark rock' of resistance. Tactics of resistance insinuate themselves 'into the other's place, fragmentarily, without taking it over in its entirety, without being able to keep it at a distance' (xix). Tactics are shaped by and in turn inform strategy. As a result of the carving out of defined and possessed cultural locations, strategies of assimilation are revised, discarded, and reinvented, creating possibilities for new tactics of resistance.

We need the other in order to make ourselves. This is most obvious in race and gender discourses, but it has its greatest impact in preconscious formative levels in infancy. Otherness is central to both social ordering and the making of the personality (Caudill, 1997). The self ('I') is constructed with and by the other, the internalized image ('me') that others have of us. For psychologist Jacques Lacan, the formation of the ego begins at between six and eighteen months of age, when, in the 'mirror stage' of infant development, the child internalizes her image as reflected back to her by others. She is now bound to the social structure, her contact with the world forever mediated by this image. The image is not static but is reinterrogated, challenged, and reinforced throughout life in the 'misrecognitions and identities of the Ego in its everyday relations to others, and ... its relation to the unconscious, to the determinative Other' (Caudill, 1997: 81). The subject produced from this socializing process is 'a subject of the unconscious,' bearing the residue of childhood. Subjectivity is the constitution of the self by the other. This idealized image or subject is the subject of law. Socialization into the dominant ideology is explained by unconscious processes in the subject. The rational, autonomous, choosing self supposed by law is decentred and split. For Aboriginal people in daily life, as victims of violence or as its instigators, as subjects of law, extremes of otherness profoundly condition subjectivity.

Patricia Williams (1991) draws on Lacan's subject in *The Alchemy of Race and Rights* (Caudill 1997: 79–80). Williams writes that 'blacks look into the mirror of frightened white faces for the reality of their undesirability [and the] distancing does not stop with the separation of the white self from the black other. In addition, the cultural domination of blacks by whites means that the black self is placed at a distance even from itself. [Blacks are] conditioned from infancy to see in themselves only what others, who despise them, see.' Where the internalized other is distorted by extremes of otherness – by misogyny, racism, intimate violence – then legal, social, and self-evaluation of the domination and abuse are also distorted. Emma LaRocque (1993: 74) writes that 'as a result of disintegrative processes inherent in colonization, Aboriginal peoples have subconsciously judged themselves against the standards of white society.' They internalize the 'White Ideal' as defined by Howard Adam in his 1975 *Prison of Grass* – 'the standards, judgements, expectations and portrayals of the dominant white world.'

Negotiating identity may be a lifelong process for those deeply othered – a struggle at the extreme boundaries of self-disclosure, race interpretation, and state penetration. Of her adopted Latina sister, Michelle Fine writes, 'Her life has been punctuated by negotiations at the zippered borders of her gendered, raced and classed Otherhood.' Identity 'is partly the relationship between you and the Other. Only when there is an Other can you know who you are ... Racism is a structure of discourse and representation that tries to expel the Other symbolically' (Fine, 1994: 72, citing Hall, 1991). Otherness makes a 'simple binary distinction between us and them.' This distinction lets us deny 'the dangers that loiter inside our homes' (Fine, 1994: 72). The other becomes a scapegoat, yet the stranger against whom children are warned is most often a family member or family intimate, and women socialized to fear assault in the streets are at far higher risk of assault by an intimate partner. The danger ascribed to the other in fact lurks within the home.

At the heart of colonialism is culture as 'race.' Here the other is largely imaged as oppositional to the colonial observer. Patricia Monture-Okanee writes, 'It is the status of "otherness" or "outsider" and the corresponding consequences where the feminist mind and the perspective of Aboriginal women are shared' (1992: 256). The contradiction between feminist thinking and the experiences of Aboriginal women may lie in the fact that while 'Aboriginality' is identified as a problem category 'Whiteness' is insufficiently problematized. If the contradiction is expressed, Monture-Okanee suggests, it can be overcome. Each perspective can then inform the other. This mutual informing of feminist thinking and indigenous experience has driven community-based approaches to intimate violence and international human rights discourse (chapters 5 and 6).

Otherness and its imaging spectacularly focused on New World First Nations from first contact on (McGillivray, 1999). Columbus took New World captives to Europe as proof of discovery. Frobisher displayed Inuit captives from the Labrador coast in London in 1556 and 1557 as proof of the existence of a North-West Passage, believing that his captives were Mongols from the Asian steppes (Sturtevant and Quinn, 1987). He exploited their image by exhibiting them before paying crowds to raise money for future voyages. Displays were short-lived.

The first of his captives died of unknown causes. The hunter taken on the second expedition died from injuries inflicted aboard ship; the young mother taken with him died of a 'pox,' perhaps a cold or influenza; and her baby, wetnursed by a countrywoman, outlived his mother by only a fortnight. Shakespeare (1611) drew Caliban from contemporary depictions of enslaved Carib Indians and the response of Londoners to the Frobisher exhibitions – 'when they will not give a *doit* to relieve a lame beggar, they will lay out ten to see a dead Indian' (*The Tempest*, Act II, Scene 2).

The Jesuit Lafitau, missionary to the Iroquois in New France from 1712 to 1717, offers what may be the most accurate and sympathetic of early portrayals of First Nations. His *Customs of the American Indians Compared with the Customs of Primitive Times* (1724) includes numerous observations of women, childhood, and rites of passage. Women 'are careful not to give their children to others to be nursed. They would think that they were cheating themselves out of the affection due a mother and they are much surprised to see that there are nations in the world where such a practice is accepted and sanctioned' (356). Children whose mothers die are kept within the immediate family circle and wetnursed by aunts or even grandmothers whose milk, long 'dried up,' returns. Children are depicted as well cared-for, deeply loved, given great freedom by comparison with children in Lafitau's France, sharing in and enduring hardships that strengthen them for the hard lives of their people. Games, work, feasts, observances, and rites of initiation prepare children for adult responsibilities.

Harsh treatment of children, it was believed, would cause children to return to the spirit world. Severe shaming might provoke them to commit suicide by eating water hemlock, Socrates' poison. 'No one moreover, would dare strike and punish them,' Lafitau writes. 'In spite of that, the children are docile enough, they have sufficient deference for the members of their lodge, and respect for the elders from whom one scarcely ever sees them emancipated; a thing which indicates that in methods of bringing up children, gentleness is often more efficacious than punishments, especially violent ones.' This was an extraordinary response for a European and a cleric. The Jesuit Lejeune, ministering to the Quebec Montagnais in 1633–4, was so appalled by the lack of corporal punishment that he devised a strategy for mission education requiring removal of children to a distant site far from parental influence (Bull, 1991; McGillivray, 1997c). Children would be given a period of freedom in which to become dependent on European clothing and comforts and learn to abhor Aboriginal ways as 'filth.' There would follow a 'disciplinary regime' and induction into Christian ways. Lejeune's strategy of separation and discipline would come to fruition two and a half centuries later, by a different route.

Lafitau does not cite Lejeune (whom he quotes elsewhere) in his discussions of childhood and corporal punishment. Nor does he mention church doctrine or, except by negative inference, European corporal punishment. In his departure from powerful contemporary European wisdom that corporal punishment of children is fundamental to inculcating spiritual, filial, and state obedience, it would seem that he is favourably impressed by Aboriginal child rearing. However, children's participation in the community torture of captives troubles even Lafitau's cultural relativism (McGillivray, 1999). Lafitau's observations of childhood are echoed in many Euro-colonial accounts. Certain practices are viewed favourably by some, disparagingly by others. Father Hennepin, writing in 1699, explored mission possibilities in the western regions of the New World. He observes the lack of corporal punishment of children, the unusual freedom given them, and the fond care shown by parents and especially mothers (Smandych and McGillivray, 1998). While Lafitau admits to good results from these practices, Hennepin, like Lejeune, is appalled.

The treatment of women in First Nations societies frequently appears in negative terms in Euro-colonial accounts. Much of this negativity can be attributed to European notions of femininity and gender. Heavily burdened women walking with children behind men on horseback, for example, seemed to Europeans a sign of disrespect and the use of women as beasts of burden. Yet this arrangement leaves men ready to fight off attack or catch dinner. Some First Nations believed that women were naturally stronger than men and more fit to carry heavy loads, while European societies saw women as weak and fainting. Missionaries from early contact to the nineteenth century report ministering to women beaten by their husbands. Such practices as cutting off the noses of women suspected of adultery are mentioned by Lafitau and others. Emma LaRocque (1993: 75) writes, 'Many early European observations as well as original Indian legends (e.g., Wehsehkehcha stories) point to the pre-existence of male violence against women.' LaRocque argues for a reconsideration of legends and traditions in light of women's status and treatment, arguing that 'culture is not immutable, and tradition cannot be expected to be always of value or relevant in our times' (1996: 14). This stance is echoed by women who told the Royal Commission on

Aboriginal Peoples that 'tradition' is often structured to serve the interests of political leaders, at the expense of women and children (RCAP, 1996: 66).

Violence against women was not introduced by Euro-colonial contact, nor did matriarchal and matrilineal cultures necessarily preclude it. 'We know enough about human history that we cannot assume that all Aboriginal traditions universally respected and honoured women,' LaRocque (1996: 14) observes. 'It should not be assumed, even in those original societies that were structured along matriarchal lines, that matriarchies necessarily prevented men from oppressing women. There are indications of male violence and sexism in some Aboriginal societies prior to European contact and certainly after contact.' Maltz and Archambault (1995) ask 'how violence was used to intimidate, control and embarrass when it was brought home from the battlefield, to what extent man the hunter and man the warrior was also man the wife beater and man the rapist' (247–8). Violence, they write, was 'clearly' present in early pre-contact societies, but the image of pre-contact practices of violence against women is 'unflattering' to Aboriginal groups. Further, the high valuation placed on autonomy in First Nations cultures may have implied unwillingness to intervene in circumstances of violence against women in intimate partnerships. Patricia Monture-Okanee (1992: 256) observes that one notable difference is that 'Aboriginal women do not share with Canadian women the history of *legally* sanctioned violence against women' (emphasis added).

While there may be disagreement on whether First Nations experienced or countenanced intimate violence in partner relationships, there is wide agreement that contact with European culture exacerbated it (Klein and Ackerman, 1995; LaRocque, 1996). This influence begins with economic and social change brought by European contact (Fiske, 1991; Carter, 1996), missionary work and its imposition of European religious values, and the devaluation of culture and femaleness in the intensified cultural conversion projects, policies, and laws of the nineteenth century.

The official documentation of indigenous cultures produced by missionaries, explorers, and early anthropologists requires careful reading. Although the cultural relativism exemplified by Lafitau was the anthropological norm by the latter part of the nineteenth century, culture and cultural meaning remain distorted. In particular, observers ignored or misunderstood women's social roles, status, and contribution to the economy (Carter, 1996; LaRocque, 1996; Payment, 1996; Peers, 1996) and the impact of trade, conversion, and colonialism on women and children (Fiske, 1991; Smandych and Lee, 1995). There is growing evidence that Aboriginal women experienced these processes differently from Aboriginal men. There is also evidence that women resisted trade and mission involvement, recognizing the damage that this would cause to gender balance and women's control of the close links between culture, cultural survival, and childhood.

Jo-anne Fiske (1991) examines the early influence of mercantile capitalism and missionary efforts on gender roles and prestige among the Tsimshian of the west coast. Where women control resources and property, they hold key decision-making roles, and where women dispense patronage they build personal followings and exert political influence, as was the case in pre-contact Tsimshian society (509). Higher-ranking men and women had the resources to elevate their status further through potlatch – the ceremonial redistribution of wealth and names. Europeans traded with men and used women as mediators. This arrangement devalued and diminished women's status, wealth, and potlatch. As trade became solely a male opportunity, some women were forced to turn to prostitution in order to acquire trade goods and alcohol. Prostitution, as an individual trade associated with shame, disease, and high rates of infant mortality, further devalued women in European eyes. Tsimshian men benefited from preferential treatment by traders and missionaries and came to share the European view of women. 'Thus, from the outset of the mission, women faced systematic and unrelenting castigation for "sinful," "shameful" and "depraved" behaviour, a moral judgment that distinguished them from their male peers' (524). European denunciation of polygyny (a woman's having multiple marital partners) and polyandry (the reverse) and of women's economic autonomy further eroded women's status. Gender devaluation, Fiske concludes, resulted in the increase of marital discord and violence.

Euro-colonial accounts generated a variety of images of the Indian. Rousseau's noble savage links Aboriginality with childhood and the good natural or primitive state. Anti-primitivist accounts portray the Indian as subhuman, fierce, animalistic, weak in character. The 'noble savage' image cut two ways for state policy. Inherently noble, the Indian could be saved by protective sequestration and tutorials in civilization or be allowed to die a mourned but inevitable death in the face of progress and of a superior culture that the Indian could neither attain nor resist. Alternatively, his childish nature left him obstinate in his savagery and unsalvageable – although something might be done with his children, if they were removed early from his influence. Images of Aboriginal women share in this essentialized portrait of the Indian. If she could not be an Indian princess, the romantic and sexualized woman of the wilderness reimaged in Disney's Pocahontas, then 'the she-Indian' was a squaw – an early corruption of the Cree *isquao*, 'woman' – slovenly and immoral or, alternately, a workhorse and drudge exploited by her lazy husband (Carter, 1996; LaRocque, 1996; Christine Miller and Chuchryk, 1996; Payment, 1996). By the latter part of the nineteenth century, she was the bad mother, uncivilized and uncivilizing. Her motherhood must give way to the civilizing environment of the industrial or residential school and, later, the foster or adoptive home. Images of women that had little to do with either the realities of subsistence-level reserve life or women's real skills were manipulated in state, public, legal, medical, and economic discourses to justify a variety of programs and strategies (Carter, 1996).

Images were also manipulated in the popular genre of the captivity narrative, tales told by Euro-colonials of their capture by Indians. Indian captivity ante-dates European contact. Capture of settlers intensified as a result of European wars fought in the New World. Euro-colonial captivity narratives were made to serve a variety of discursive purposes – spiritual instruction, cultural differentiation, support for imperialist and expansionist policies (Carter, 1997; McGillivray, 1999). They depict Aboriginal women and children variously as savage, cruel, and filthy or as skilled, resourceful, and brave, with women essentialized as princess or squaw, their motherhood as loving and tolerant but as lacking in discipline. The captivity narrative branches off into the anti-primitivist nineteenth-century 'Indian-hater' genre valorizing the rugged frontiersman and his one-man Indian war. Despite the persistence of Euro-colonials' belief in the superiority of their mother cultures, assimilation was a one-way street. Benjamin Franklin writes in 1753, 'When an Indian child has been brought up among us, taught our language and habituated himself to our Customs, yet if he goes to see his relations and makes one Indian Ramble with them, there is no perswading him ever to return.' Conversely, 'when white persons of either sex have been taken prisoners young by the Indians, and lived a while among them, tho' ransomed by their Friends, and treated with all imaginable tenderness to prevail with them to stay among the English,' they soon return to their Indian families (McGillivray, 1999). Crèvecoeur writes in his *Letters from an American Farmer* (1782) that captured Euro-colonial children became 'so perfectly Indianised' that their parents did not know them and older ones 'refused to return.' He concludes that 'there must be in the Indians' social bond something singularly captivating, and far superior to anything to be boasted of among us; for thousands of Europeans are Indians, as we have no examples of even one of these Aborigines having from choice become European!' There is much speculation as to why abducted Euro-colonial children and youth cleaved to First Nations cultures. Accounts of assimilated captives who returned, such as those of Pierre Radisson and John Tanner, portray their adoptive families, cultures, and in particular their mothers with affection and respect (McGillivray, 1999).

In *Capturing Women*, Carter (1997) situates the manipulation of cultural images of women in the prairie west in three Canadian captivity narratives that cemented public opinion of Indians and Métis in support of post-1870 dominion Indian policy. The Canadian edition of the narrative of Ontario-born Fanny Kelly (1872), captured by Sioux on the Missouri Trail, ran to six printings. Preface and footnotes stress the benevolence of Canadian Indian policy compared with U.S. wrongs and invite Canadians to find it 'unimaginable' that this could happen in Canada. But it did, during the 1885 Riel uprising. Theresa Gowanlock and Theresa Delaney, the only white women in Frog Lake, were widowed and taken captive by renegade Cree from Big Bear's band, in an attack that left nine settlers dead. The accounts of the two women, published jointly as *Two Months in the Camp of Big Bear* (1885), draw on established captivity tropes of threatened ravishment, heinous Indians, squaws, and squalor. The novelized account differs in central aspects from statements given to press and public (Carter, 1997: 49). The Theresas had reported good care and the protection given them by Métis men, for example, but *Two Months* depicts Métis in a 'sinister' light. The threat of ravishment, an underlying theme, 'carried the clear cautionary message that unions between white and Aboriginal were abhorrent, particularly as such unions created the menacing Métis.'

Gowanlock's depictions of women and children are vicious even for the captivity genre (McGillivray, 1999). Gowanlock writes, 'An Indian boy is a live, wild, and untamed being ... full of mischief and cruelty to those he hates ... I never saw in their character anything that could be called love'; nor did they laugh unless cruelty aroused 'the little fragment of humour' (Gowanlock and Delaney, 1885: chap. 14). 'Like father, like son; the virtues of young Indians were extremely few.'Aboriginal women are beaten, disorganized, dirty drudges. 'In travelling, the Indians ride, and their squaws walk and do all the work, and they pack their dogs and have "travores" on their horses, upon which they tied their little children, and then all would move off together; dogs howling, and babies crying, and Indians beating their wives, and carts tumbling over the banks of the trail, and children falling' (1885: 36). Not only are the Indians 'vicious, treacherous and superstitious,' but they are also 'childlike and simple' (43). They are 'the happy murderers of defenceless settlers, the despoilers of happy homes, the polluters of poor women and children. They did all that, and yet they are called the noble "red man." It might sound musical in the ears of the poet to write of the virtues of that race, but I consider it a perversion of the real facts. During the time I was with them I could not see anything noble in them, unless it was that they were *noble* murderers, *noble* cowards, *noble* thieves' (43).

As Carter (1996) shows, white women were iconic in the settlement of the prairie west. As 'the civilizer and the producer of the race,' women of Anglo-Celtic origin were actively recruited (8). In popular and state discourses of white women's virtues, Indian women either disappear or are 'cast as the complete opposite of white women, as agents of the destruction of the moral and cultural health of the new community.' In the 1885 resistance, Métis and First Nations women were painted as 'active participants in violent and brutal acts against white soldiers' (Carter, 1997: xvi). After 1885, they were 'said to be accustomed to being bought and sold by their own elders and to be mistreated by their own men.' Depicting them as 'accustomed to many marital partners' cast doubt on the legitimacy of Euro-colonial male heirs. This was one of many cultural incentives promoting marriage within a Euro-colonial lineage. If such representations made Aboriginal women 'less,' they also made white women 'more' in these extreme constructions of difference.

Captivity of settler women by indigenous peoples is embedded in Euro-colonial accounts throughout the world (Carter, 1997: 28). North American portrayals of white female captives fall generally into three types or tropes corresponding with historical periods – the colonial survivor, the revolutionary-era Amazon, and the frail flower of western expansionism, typified in the accounts of the two Theresas. Captivity and femininity had a different meaning for Aboriginal women. Calf Old Woman, a Blackfoot girl captured by Gros Ventres, stabbed her captor with his knife, scalped him, cut off his right arm, stole his gun and horse, and evaded pursuit. Having taken the trophies of the warrior, she was given a seat in Blackfoot council (Carter, 1997: 27).

Euro-colonial anxieties about racial purity centred on childhood by the latter decades of the nineteenth century. In 1889, the correspondent of *Graphic* (London, England) Frederick Villiers saw a girl 'with not a drop of Indian blood in her veins' among the Alberta Blackfoot. The *Macleod Gazette* called on the Canadian government for her rescue from 'the horrible fate that is surely in store for her ... even if it brings every Indian in the North-west Territories about their ears' (Carter, 1997: 139). The New York *World* sent agents to rescue this 'flaxen-haired captive,' 'The Waif of the Plains.' 'The Supposed Captive White Girl Turns Out to Be a Half-Breed' – she was 'Papoose after All,' 'Her Mother a Squaw,' as 1890 headlines in the *World* blared (Carter, 1997: 40). A 'Canadian white girl' supposedly captured by Chief Sitting Bull was claimed by the Turton family of Manitoba in 1892. They had lost an eight-year-old girl to the bush and convinced North Dakota officials that Anatanwin, a fifteen-year old Lakota-speaking child, was 'our Gertie' dyed with walnut and tall for her years (Carter, 1997: 149–57). U.S. press opined that, white or Indian, the girl is 'a thousandfold better off in a good American [sic] home' than with her original family.

Images of otherness intensified in the post-1870 settlement of the prairie west. Their legacy is seen in streets of Canada, as elder Jeannette Armstrong (1996) observes (above). Armstrong centres on the destruction of the family-clan system, the basic unit of social order in First Nations, as leading to 'severe and irreversible effects on Aboriginal women' (ix). Aboriginal women struggled to survive 'under the onslaught of a people steeped in a tradition of hostile cultural supremacy.' Emma LaRocque (1996: 11) writes, 'Racism and sexism found in the colonial process have served to dramatically undermine the place and value of women in Aboriginal cultures, leaving us vulnerable both within and outside our communities ... subject to violence in both white and Native societies [and] to patriarchal policies that have dispossessed us of our inherited rights, lands, identities, and families.' Widespread acceptance of subordination to men, dependence on men and male systems, and physical, psychological, and social isolation contribute to intimate violence (Canadian Panel, 1993). These factors are heightened for many Aboriginal women.

British Humanitarianism and Canadian Solutions

Cultural images shape and justify social policy. Governments used notions of cultural debasement to justify genocidal Indian wars, policies of massive removal of Indian bands, army slaughter of buffalo, toleration of the Indian-hater frontiersman with his trespasses and random executions, policies of non-interference ignored where Indian lands could be bought cheap, and economic exploitation by government agents. The image of a once-great race falling into disarray and helplessly vanishing when confronted by a superior race received a scientific spin from nineteenth-century social Darwinism and its theories of cultural contest and survival.

In the Royal Proclamation of 1763, George III instructed colonial governors to maintain a protective, hands-off policy vis-à-vis First Nations. All dealings with the Indian were to be mediated by the Crown. Alienation of title was to be effected solely by treaty, with title then vesting in the Crown. The proclamation was vitiated for much of British North America by the American War of Independence and the creation of the United States. The U.S. constitution was strongly influenced by the work of rights theorist John Locke, who argued, among other things, that ownership results from the expenditure of labour to produce or improve goods or land. The inference for an expanding nation is that land not used or improved or visibly owned by another person could be claimed for minimal or no compensation by those who proposed to use or improve it. U.S. courts relied on this view to justify breaches of treaty and international law in support of 'manifest destiny.' Results included massive displacement of Indian Nations, war, and genocide. Hitler cited manifest destiny to justify his policies of *Lebensraum* and genocide of the racially and genetically 'unfit.' British-Canadian colonial governments, pushed by humanitarian demands yet faced with the enticements of nation-building, wished to avoid such extremes.

For the colonies of the Canadas and the Atlantic provinces, and the vast lands under the Hudson's Bay Company charter in northwestern North America, the proclamation of 1763 in theory remained law. It did not, however, deter European efforts to alienate land and convert Indians to Christianity outside as well as within government regimes (Bagot, 1845). In 1830, the British secretary of state for war and the colonies writes that 'the course which has hitherto been taken in dealing with these people, has had reference to the advantages which might be derived from their friendship in times of war, rather than to any settled purpose of gradually reclaiming them from a state of barbarism, and of introducing amongst them the industrious and peaceful habits of civilised life.' As the Bagot Report observes, the proclamation was in danger of vitiation in British North America by the predation of 'rapacious' white traders, squatters, and land buyers. Something had to be done for – and about – the Indian.

British North American Indian policy was very different from U.S. policy in the nineteenth century. With the termination of the slave trade in the empire, the attentions of influential British reformers turned to the welfare of its indigenous peoples. The equation of Aboriginal peoples with childhood and dependence is reflected in two massive reports, the *Report from His Majesty's Commission for Inquiring into the Administration and Practical Operation of the Poor Laws* (1834) and the House of Commons *Report of the Select Committee on Aborigines* (1837). The select committee was to investigate 'Native Inhabitants of Countries where British Settlements are made ... to promote the spread of civilization among them,' while the Commission on the Poor Laws was concerned with the social outcast closer to home. Both reports recommend the appointment of overseers or protectors, training programs aimed at low-level employment, and the assimilation of respective target groups – the impoverished and the Aboriginal – into the larger society. Both reports present childhood as central to assimilation, stressing education, 'civilization,' and the bringing into Christianity of the child pauper or the Aborigine. 'True civilization and Christianity are inseparable: the former has never been found, but as a fruit of the latter,' the select committee writes. The London-based Church Missionary Society joined with the Aborigines Protection Society to pressure the British government for humanitarian treatment of indigenous peoples and solicited reports from all corners of the empire. Among the small but select membership of the Aborigines Protection Society were de Toqueville, the French observer of democracy in America, and J. Egerton Ryerson, Methodist minister, educational reformer, and proponent of industrial schooling for Aboriginal children in mid-nineteenth century Canada West (Ontario).

In 1842, Governor General Sir Charles Bagot commissioned an inquiry into the use of the British Parliament's annual grant for 'the *benefit* of the *Indians* in this Province,' the affairs of resident and visiting Indians, and the conduct of the Indian Department. The commissioners tabled their report on Indian affairs with the Legislative Assembly of the United Province of Canada on 20 March 1845 (Bagot, 1845). Praising the humanitarianism of the British government, the commissioners stress schooling, Christianization, protective sequestration, and 'gradual civilization.' They take a highly negative view of marital alliances between Aboriginal and non-Aboriginal people and of their 'half-breed' offspring. The Indian should be kept pure and apart, his strengths and learning powers enhanced by a civilizing but protective segregation, his vacated ancestral lands fairly compensated for the use of settlement. Civilized Indian men should marry only civilized Indian women, and several examples of such unions are offered.

The Bagot inquiry did not extend beyond Canada's North-West frontier. 'The scattered tribes who derive a precarious and scanty subsistence from hunting and fishing over the prairies and wilds which occupy the extensive region between the Canadian frontiers, the Northern Ocean, and the shores of the Pacific ... are essentially under the influence and control of the Hudson-Bay Company,' states the *Seventh Annual Report of the Aborigines' Protection Society* (1844). 'Of the vast depository of information on Indian affairs of which that Company is possessed, little or nothing has transpired; and your Committee has received no information regarding the steps which it was the avowed intention of the Governor to take, for the benefit of the Indians ... [In Indian resettlement and agriculture] there exists considerable scope for improvement.' From the seeds contained in these reports would grow the reserve system and the residential school.

Indian governance fell to the new dominion government of Canada under the British North America Act of 1867. Canadian Confederation and the push to open the North-West to European settlement with the end of Hudson's Bay Company rule in 1869–70 impelled quicker solutions to 'the Indian problem' in the prairies than were required in long-settled eastern and 'central' Canada. European immigration, which would transform the prairie economy and fulfil the expansionist Canadian dream, required an unobstructed geographical and cultural space. At the same time, a system had to be designed to protect First Nations peoples from the anticipated cultural assault, meet immediate needs of First Nations for food in a time of general famine, and prepare them for the coming change. Treaties would legally secure lands for settlement. Seven 'numbered Treaties' were hastily concluded with Plains First Nations between 1871 and 1877, from Red River, Manitoba, to Bow River, Alberta; some were initiated by First Nations facing the demise of the buffalo, seeking a new economy, and desiring education for their children in white ways (J.R. Miller, 1989; 1996). Reserves were established, schooling was promised, and government annuities and equipment for small-scale agriculture were to prepare the registered Indian for the new economy.

These disciplinary regimes were designed to 'civilize' the Indian. The deviance of Indianness from the Euro-colonial norm would be corrected by surveillance and the tutoring of desire (McGillivray, 1997a, c). This required erasure of traditional forms of government and of cultural practices that interfered with assimilation. It centred on two systems – the reserve and the residential school. Images generated by Rousseau of the noble savage and the pure child fused in this reordering of Aboriginality. The Indian adult now became a ward of the dominion, infantilized and protected – a child of an ignoble nature who would perhaps mature into British-Canadian citizenship. The Indian child was the target of a more aggressive process of civilization. The result of these efforts is the institutionalized racism that has ghettoized Aboriginal people both on and off reserve (Dosman, 1972; York, 1990; Buckley, 1992; Fleras and Elliott, 1992; Frank, 1992; Armitage, 1995; McGillivray, 1997).

Reserves in the newly opened North-West were seen as neither treaty entitlements nor cultural preserves but as temporary retreats until assimilation occurred (J.R. Miller, 1989). 'The great aim of our civilization,' orated Sir John A. Macdonald in 1887, 'has been to do away with the tribal system and assimilate the Indian people in all respects with the inhabitants of the Dominion, as speedily as they are fit for the change' (Miller, 1989: 189). By the early twentieth century, resistance and the successful marginalization of the Plains Indians caused a shift in Indian Affairs policy. 'The government and the churches have abandoned, to a large extent, previous policies which attempted to "Canadianise" the Indians,' writes Indian Affairs Superintendent of Education Duncan Campbell Scott in 1909. 'Through a process of vocational, and to a smaller extent academic training, they are now attempting to make good Indians, rather than poor mixtures of Indians and whites. While the idea is still Christian citizenship, the government now hopes to move towards this end by continuing to segregate the Indian population, in large measure from the white races' (Bull, 1991). Scott, a career civil servant whose poetry celebrated 'the weird and waning race' of the Indian, carried nineteenth-century segregation and civilization policies well into the twentieth century (Titley, 1986).

Assimilation remained a dominion federal goal until the defeat of the White Paper of 1968 proposing abolition of the Indian Act and the reserve system drafted by Indian Affairs Minister Jean Chrétien. 'We have set the Indians apart as a race,' Prime Minister Trudeau argued. 'We've set them apart in our laws. We've set them apart in the way governments deal with them. They're not citizens of the provinces as the rest of us are. They are wards of the federal government ... It's inconceivable, I think, that in a given society one section of society has a treaty with the other section of society. We must be equal under the law'

(Bowles et al., 1972: 71–2). First Nations leaders condemned the proposal as a breach of treaty and a denial of federal responsibility for First Nations.

Tutorials in Civilization: Women and the Reserve System

Treaty terms reflect the tripartite nineteenth-century strategy of 'civilization' – Christianization, agriculture, and education. The reserve and the Indian Act were, for adults, the tutorial equivalent of the residential school. The Indians would be isolated for their own protection from the baser elements of Euro-colonial society. Subject to the gaze of the Indian agent, they would be restrained from practices considered harmful, such as traditional ceremonies and dances, travel, and use of alcohol, and their children would be educated, forcibly if necessary, in the new ways. Traditional systems of government would be replaced by a municipal system of elected chief and council, who would govern the internal affairs of the reserve. Enfranchisement – the right to vote and become a full citizen in return for relinquishment of Indian status and entitlements – would be available. As the Indian commissioner of the day observes, it was the 'policy of destroying the tribal or communist system and every effort made to implant a spirit of individual responsibility instead' (J.R. Miller, 1989: 191).

Introduced and expanded in the Indian Acts of 1869 and 1876 and entrenched in the 1880 Act, the reserve system was to replace systems based on lineage, kinship, and 'tribal or communist' relations. It would teach civic responsibility by introducing elections and granting band councils taxation and by-law powers. The Indian Department could unilaterally create bands, bypassing tribal alliances. The Indian Affairs *Annual Report* for 1897 described the policy as 'gradually to do away with the hereditary and introduce an elective system, so making (as far as circumstances permit) these chiefs and councillors occupy the position in a band which a municipal council does in a white community' (Indian Affairs, 1983). Women could neither vote nor stand for election in their bands until the Indian Act was amended in 1951 and, unless enfranchised at the cost of Indian status, could not participate politically elsewhere.

In her study of First Nations women during the early years of the reserve in the prairie west, Sarah Carter (1996) surveys images of reserve life in anthropological studies. Goldfrank's 1945 study of the Alberta Blood Indians draws on images left by European explorers of Plains women as 'slaves and drudges, who were bought and sold like chattels, stood in absolute awe of their husbands, and suffered many indignities.' Goldfrank concludes that 'women as a class have benefited from reserve life for the white man's law now protects their property and person' (cited in Carter, 1996: 51). This portrayal resonates with the Indian Affairs image of reserve life for women. Relieved of the rigours of a nomadic life and the role of 'servile, degraded beast of burden,' women would become disciplined, modest, and cleanly. Carter describes a second school of thought, exemplified in Clark Wissler's study of the Montana Oglala between 1902 and 1905. Reservations deprive men of traditional economical and political roles but leave women's roles untouched. Men become drones and women work. Later writers cited by Carter conclude that this change in traditional gender roles attests to Plains women's adaptability and ingenuity, but the disparity in roles creates dissonance between men and women. In this view, reserves do not enhance women's opportunities and legal status but rather diminish their status and power through an imposed system of patriarchy and altered means of production, which increases the dependence of women on men.

Indian Affairs used the legacy of centuries of negative images of Aboriginal women to justify the restructuring of the domestic economy on reserve. The manipulation of such images persisted in its discourses well into the 1930s. High rates of infant mortality and tuberculosis epidemics on Plains reserves, for example, it attributed to slovenly housekeeping, poor mothering and nursing skills and a wilful clinging to 'old ways' (Carter, 1996: 55). This strategy got the department 'off the hook' for inadequate living conditions provided for reserves. Carter (1996: 72) concludes that comparative and more nuanced studies are needed 'to combat the negative images and distorted assumptions that regrettably persist and limit our understanding of the past, which has been impoverished by a failure to recognize and include the part played by Aboriginal women.'

Policies of involuntary enfranchisement discriminated against women. The Indian Act of 1869 'presumed women to be dependent on, and the property of, their husbands. The act denied status to women who married non-Indian men and granted status to non-Aboriginal women marrying Indian men' (Carter, 1996: 53). In the evolution of the act, 'discrimination on the basis of sex and marital status had become law,' and bilateral or matrilineal lines of kinship and descent shifted to patriarchal lineage (Weaver, 1993: 94). Treating Aboriginal women equally with other Canadian women in terms of marital status and child custody in the nineteenth century meant that Aboriginal women lost status (Manitoba, 1991a: 479; Isaac and Maloughney, 1992).

Later gains for women and children – the vote for women, criminalization of abuse, and more nuanced approaches to family support and child protection – did not touch the dominion/federal enclave of the reserve. If nineteenth-century values thought beneficial for women and children were embedded in the reserve system and Indian Act provisions, this structure also froze out later innovations benefiting women and children. Bill C-31, in effect 28 July 1985, offered re-registration to women and children who had lost status through out-marriage. Bands received control over residency. Women and children might regain Indian status but be denied band membership, reserve access, residency, and housing. The act still discriminates against women returnees in terms of the future eligibility of their children for band membership (RCAP, 1996b; Isaac and Maloughney, 1992). Perceived as being 'less Indian,' 'Bill C-31 Indians' face discrimination by First Nations. Returnees are scapegoated for community problems, and those attempting to return have been litigated against by bands and subjected to exclusionary membership codes (RCAP, 1996b; Weaver, 1993). Discrimination against returnees and children 'repatriated' after apprehension by child welfare authorities is most severe in the prairies and parts of the Atlantic region (Weaver, 1993: 127). Resentment is in part based on a perceived attitude of superiority of these 'new' Indians and their erroneous expectations of reserve life. It also derives from the dearth of housing on reserves. Indian Affairs policy makes separate provision for building houses for Bill C-31 Indians, while lifelong residents must wait their turn, under a separate funding category.

Colonial policy focused on instilling Anglo-Canadian citizenship by eliminating Indianness. Aboriginal peoples were to be induced 'as speedily as they are fit for the change' into Euro-colonial ways and beliefs. The reserve system and the Indian Act overlay a complex and functional kinship structure. The new governance promoted individualism over 'tribal or communist' systems, created petty fiefdoms in place of tribes and nations, and embodied a Victorian patriarchy that erased women from the new band politics (McGillivray, 1997c). The removal of children for schooling denied motherhood and children's contributions to the economic and social life of their families and communities. In the nineteenth-century focus on childhood as the central site of citizenship, Indian childhood would be the target of the post-Confederation policy of 'aggressive civilization' in the Canadian west.

Civilizing the Indian Child: Industrial Schooling and Child Protection

The newly opened North-West needed a speedier form of assimilation than the uncertain system of civilization through mission education and unmediated Euro-colonial contact described in the Bagot Report of 1845. Despite the failure of European assimilation of Aboriginal children and the success of Aboriginal assimilation of Euro-colonial children, nineteenth-century Indian policy went forward with plans for large-scale assimilation through residential schooling, with the lessons of earlier centuries forgotten. In his *Report on Industrial Schools for Indians and Half-Breeds* (1879) to Indian Affairs, Nicholas Davin writes, 'There is now barely time to inaugurate a system of education by means of which the native populations of the North-West shall be gradually prepared to meet the necessities of the not distant future; to welcome and facilitate, it may be hoped, the settlement of the country; and to render its government easy and not expensive.'

The civilization of the Indian would begin in childhood, on a grander scale than the mission day schools and unsuccessful boarding schools of eastern Canada. The first stage, now past, was education by the missions, Davin writes. The second stage is the care of a mother 'who keeps children educated in white and Indian ways.' This mother is exemplified in the 'Five Civilized Nations' of the United States and, in Canada, in the Métis of the Red River. Where no civilizing mother is available, a third stage is necessary – the industrial boarding school for children, which Davin recommends for the civilization of First Nations in the North-West.

Nicholas Davin, Irish immigrant, barrister, Conservative candidate, and later founder of the Regina *Leader* and eye-witness reporter on the trial of Louis Riel, was dispatched by Indian Affairs to the United States in 1879 to report on a new model for assimilation – 'aggressive civilization' through the Indian industrial school. In Davin's vision, the 'Half-breed,' as proven cultural mediator and provider of a civilized home, is central to civilizing the Indian. Day schools for the Five Civilized Nations 'carry no disadvantage, because the child's home is a civilized home.' This, it was explained to Davin, is the real meaning of 'Civilized Nation.' Davin writes, 'From 1869 vigorous efforts in an educational direction were put forward. But day-school did not work because the influence of the wigwam was stronger than the influence of the school. Industrial Boarding Schools were therefore established, and these are now numerous and will soon be universal' for U.S. First Nations.

Yet there was little proof of a significant 'civilizing' effect in the scant ten years of 'vigorous efforts' in the United States. Industrial schools for Indian children were established in Canada West in the 1850s, but their failure was such that Davin, although he visited the schools, does not mention them in his report. Even so, he recommended 'industrial or boarding schools' for First Nations in the Canadian North-West, to be jointly managed and financed by the dominion government and one or another religious denomination. Davin, an agnostic, kept an open mind on the question of religion as a civilizing force but displays in his cautious arguments around the subject an acute awareness of its 'civilizing' role. The schools would be supported by child labour and might soon become self-supporting, as children practised new skills that returned monetary benefits to the schools. They would be far from the newly established reserves. 'The children must be kept constantly within the circle of civilized conditions. Msgr. Taché in his work, "Sketch of the North-West of America" – points out that the influence of civilized women has issued in superior characteristics in one portion of the native population.' This 'portion' consisted of the Métis and 'Half-breeds' of the Red River. Schooling, in Davin's view, should never have been included in the treaties, as it would give tribal leaders the idea that they had a say in education. The government, he notes, must provide education for all children.

The setting up of the early residential schools reflected collaboration with First Nations, but parents objected almost from the start to Christianization, devaluation of language and culture, corporal punishment, prohibitions on parental visits, head-shaving, and other practices (J.R. Miller, 1996). First Nations in the prairie west were most affected by residential schools, where attendance between 1920 and 1960 approached 100 per cent (Armitage, 1995). The effect on children and their families has been profound (Gresko, 1979; Manitoba, 1991; Bull, 1991; Cariboo, 1991; Ing, 1991; J.R. Miller, 1991; Grant, 1996; RCAP, 1996b). The psychological aftermath or 'residential school syndrome' includes inability to express feeling, a sense of inferiority, apathy, confusion of values, unwillingness to work, culture shock, 'anti-religion' attitudes, and creation of unskilled and unapproachable parents (Grant, 1996). The policy of taking children as young as three years of age into the schools reflects Davin's conclusion: 'If anything is to be done with the Indian, we must catch him very young.'

Replacing the natural mother with the 'civilizing mother' of state schooling achieved part of the aim – to interfere in Aboriginal acculturation and transmit some Euro-colonial skills and values. It failed in central ways. The curriculum did not fulfil its promise of fitting children for a changing cultural and economic landscape. Children were trained in low-skill, low-level occupations and given minimal academic instruction. Davin's recommendation of incorporating Métis and 'Half-breeds' into the system as teachers and pupils, to act as cultural intermediaries, was not followed (J.R. Miller, 1996). Corporal punishment was the norm, sometimes resulting in severe injury and always in student hostility. Sexual abuse was widespread. Abuse was not an uncommon experience in non-Aboriginal institutions of the day, but 'being Indian' increased the risk. Devaluation of childhood and culture and the attraction of staff members' ready access to children exacerbated physical and sexual violence in Indian residential schools. Most centrally, children were denied the contact with parents and siblings that instils parenting skills in the next generation. Practices of cultural devaluation began to abate after 1909. Enrolment declined severely after the Second World War, when the Indian Act was amended to permit Indian children to enrol in public schools, part of anthropologist Diamond Jenness's plan for the 'Liquidation of Canada's Indian Problems within 25 Years' (Haig-Brown, 1988). Residential schooling was phased out in the 1960s.

The schools graduated the majority of twentieth-century First Nations political leaders, contributed to the pan-Indian movement by bringing together children of different First Nations cultures, and taught basic farming and housewifery skills. Some graduates retain fond memories of the schools. The legacy of the schools, however, continues to play a strong role in intimate violence. 'The boarding school is where the alienation began. Children were placed there, plucked out of their homes. The bond between parents and children was fragmented severely – some lost forever,' Janet Ross told the Aboriginal Justice Inquiry, or AJI (Manitoba, 1991: 515). 'The boarding schools taught us violence. Violence was emphasized through physical, corporal punishment, strapping, beatings, bruising and control. We learned to understand that this was power and control.' Residential schooling stands as a powerful symbol of cultural and personal devaluation. 'One school principal in Brandon used to call us God's children three times on Sundays at the three services and the rest of the week call us dirty little Indians. No one ever told us they loved us. We were mere numbers,' William Clarence Thomas, Superintendent of the Peguis School Board in Manitoba, told the Kimelman Inquiry (Kimelman, 1985). 'Strapping, beatings, hair cut to baldness, being tethered to the flag pole, half day school with unqualified tutors, and slave labour the other half ... .' 'Residential schools taught self-hate. That is child abuse,' Grand Chief Dave Courchene told the judges heading the AJI (Manitoba, 1991: 478). 'Too many of our younger people got the message and passed it on. It is their younger generations that appear before you [in court].' Jeannette Armstrong (1996: x) terms residential schooling 'the single most devastating factor in the breakdown of our society. It is at the core of the damage, beyond all the other mechanisms cleverly fashioned to subjugate, assimilate, and annihilate'.

Canada apologized in 1997, and Indian Affairs established a healing fund of $350 million. By 1998, 1,200 former pupils had filed abuse-related lawsuits. Key First Nation, near Kamsack, Saskatchewan, is suing Canada and three Christian denominations for cultural destruction through residential schooling, alleging that schools promised in the 'numbered treaties' were to recognize Indian society and let it flourish but instead undermined elders' influence, prevented cultural transmission, and contributed to deplorable social conditions (*Toronto Star*, 23 June 1998).

By the close of the 1970s, First Nations had targeted two areas as central to self-determination (McGillivray, 1997c). Both centre on childhood. The first is control of education. Eighty-two per cent, or fifty of sixty-one Manitoba bands, now control an on-reserve school, ranging from kindergarten only, through elementary school, to kindergarten to grade 12. Seventy-eight per cent, or 19,000 of Manitoba First Nations children, attend a band-operated school. Funding for post-secondary education is entirely within Manitoba First Nations management. The second and more contested area is control of child protection. The assimilation begun by the residential school was continued by the child welfare system (Kimelman, 1985; RCAP, 1996a; McGillivray, 1997c). The brief of the Canadian Welfare Council and the Canadian Association of Social Workers to the joint parliamentary committee of 1947 on the Indian Act described inadequate living conditions and lack of social services for reserve children. The brief condemned residential schooling and noted that adoption 'is loosely conceived and executed and is totally devoid of the careful legal and social protection afforded to white children' (Canadian Welfare Council, 1947: 3). The Indian Act was amended so that provincial law, where not inconsistent with the Act, applied to Indians, signalling provincial provision of services to children and families on reserves. Provinces were reluctant to extend cost-intensive programs and continued to insist on federal responsibility. The Hawthorn Report of 1966 to Indian Affairs described conditions for Indian children as 'unsatisfactory to appalling' (1966: 327). The department signed a cost-sharing agreement with the provinces that same year.

The agreement made no provisions for maintaining culture and language or for employing Aboriginal child protection workers (McGillivray, 1997c). In Manitoba, as in other prairie provinces, patch-work service delivery left remote reserves with only life-or-death inter-vention. Overuse of the social work 'last resort' resulted in the apprehension of thousands of Manitoba Aboriginal children for place-ment in non-Aboriginal foster and adoptive homes throughout the 1960s and 1970s, explained as 'catch-up.' Hundreds of children were adopted out-of-province, many in the United States and western Europe, making agency follow-up, cultural and family reunification, and retention of legal entitlements virtually impossible. Extraprovincial adoption was continued in Manitoba long after its abandonment in Saskatchewan and Alberta. Children were apprehended who were not in danger, a result of cultural misunderstanding and inadequate training of social workers. Many endangered children received no help at all.

Preserving birth culture was not on the agency agenda of the day, nor did case planning consider the emotional damage done to children by the cutting of ethnic as well as family ties and the exposure of children to racism. Transracial adoption and fostering disrupted families, aggravated cultural destruction and exposed children to further abuse. While some adoptions were successful – most often where the birth cul-ture was respected – others were not. Some made news headlines. Two Manitoba adoptees, youths sexually assaulted by adoptive fathers in the United States, killed their abusers and served long prison terms. A Man-itoba woman bore two children in early adolescence to her adoptive father in Holland. She had kept a small photograph of home and remembered a song. She managed to return to her reserve but was too ill to pursue her lawsuit against Manitoba Child and Family Services. A contested adoption by the first Manitoba child and family services agency set up under First Nations management was decided in the Supreme Court of Canada in 1984. The court ruled in *A.N.R.* v. *L.J.W.* that Métis culture was virtually identical to the child's Ojibwa birth cul-ture. Although the word 'race' appears often, the court took a seemingly race-neutral stance, focusing instead on motherhood. 'It's just two women and a little girl, and one of them doesn't know her. It's as simple as that; all the rest of it is extra and of no consequence.' Ignoring ethnic-ity can have severe consequences in the formation of identity. The child around whom the case revolved became, at age fifteen, the first Manitoba child to have her picture and name published, with that of her young boyfriend, as a danger to the public under a rarely used provision of the Young Offenders Act, RSC 1985, c. Y-1, as amended, for her part in a rural 'house-jacking.'

The 1985 report *No Quiet Place* (Kimelman, 1985) condemned wholesale seizure of Aboriginal children, failure to seek culturally appropriate placement, failure to provide adequate follow-up, and deeply inadequate record-keeping as cultural genocide. 'The miracle is that there were not more children lost in this system run by so many well-intentioned people. The road to hell was paved with good intentions and the child welfare system was the paving contractor.' Beginning in the early 1980s, tripartite agreements between Canada, Manitoba, and alliances of Manitoba bands ('Tribal Councils') created Canada's only province-wide child and family services system run by First Nations. Lack of expertise, apathy, and political interference plagued the new agencies and left many children in dangerous situations or placed them at greater risk in unproven foster and adoptive homes (Giesbrecht, 1992; McGillivray, 1997c). Many of these problems are now resolved, but political interference, jurisdictional challenges with the province, agency turf wars, and abuse in foster homes continue. Although out-marriage resulted in enfranchisement under earlier Indian Act provisions, out-group adoption did not. The Supreme Court of Canada ruled in *Natural Parents v. Superintendent of Child Welfare* [1976] 2 SCR 751 that provincial law cannot encroach on Indian identity and entitlement. Confidentiality of adoption bars the state from informing a child of his or her Indian status, and, as there is no duty placed on adoptive parents to do so, adoptees are virtually enfranchised (McGillivray, 1986). But transracial adoption cannot erase differences in physical appearance or the racism that may follow, nor does it abolish the cultural connectedness of older children who remember their first families. Repatriation into reserve culture has not solved identity crises in adoptees, who share the scapegoating, rejection, and lack of cultural 'fit' facing returnees under Bill C-31.

In the last analysis, the assimilation of Aboriginal childhood through residential schooling and adoption has remained the one-way street described by Benjamin Franklin and his contemporaries. The Indian reified in Euro-colonial images has masked the diversity of Aboriginal cultures and the centrality of culture and ethnicity in defining the self. These images influenced state policies, agencies' practices, and judicial decision-making and created resistance. But 'race' does not equal ethnicity, and cultural stereotyping cuts many different ways.

Métissage: An Alternative Vision

An alternative vision, one of mutual cultural enrichment and respect, though not itself altogether free of racism, tension and choice, became briefly visible in the nineteenth century in the children of the fur trade. They were offspring of Hudson's Bay Company employees and traders and their country wives, married à la façon du pays – meaning according to the customs of the country rather than of the church (Smandych and McGillivray, 1998a). Their children are the Métis and Half-breeds of the Red River so admired by Nicholas Davin. In 1870, 'mixed breeds' numbered 10,000, comprising 80 per cent of the Red River (now Winnipeg) population (Payment, 1996). In the early years of Manitoba, Diane Payment (1996) writes, 'Métissage was viewed positively as part of the dual Métis Canadien heritage.' In her study of Métis women at Batoche between 1870 and 1920, she presents the oral histories of eighteen women elders born between 1886 and 1910, letters and journals of Métis women, and Métis accounts of the events of 1885. Her research informs Heritage Canada's interpretive signs at Métis historic sites. 'Fur traders, missionaries, and politicians had increasingly isolated the Métis from their AmerIndian counterparts, [and they were now] to live in settlements, abandon their traditional beliefs in favour of Christianity, and adopt British institutions. The racism, bigotry, and sexism of the Victorian era persuaded many Métis to declare "on n'est pas des sauvages" [one is not a savage] or deny their grandmothers' origins and to assert their French-Canadian "male" heritage' (Payment, 1996: 20). Women remained suspended between two worlds.

Payment summarizes early relations of Plains Aboriginal women with men as 'essentially egalitarian.' Their role in the hunt 'was as significant and as necessary as men's.' The restructuring of the economy in the fur trade 'placed women in a subservient and inferior productive role,' and European attitudes and behaviour 'slowly but effectively eroded the AmerIndian woman's position.' When the Métis settlement at Red River began to form around 1805, women of First Nations descent 'were entering a world where Christian marriages, social and economic dependence, and racial prejudice would soon dominate.' The experience of 'Half-breed' women of anglophone descent and Métis women of francophone descent differed. Anglophone women were more readily acculturated to what was becoming in Manitoba a predominantly British society, with its related distinctions between the higher-class and usually anglophone families of traders and factors and the lower-class and often francophone hunters, trappers, and freighters. Even so, the blending of cultures was not disparaged as it was by the Bagot Commission of 1845 but was often viewed, as Riel saw it, as mutual enrichment. The church in particular was an agent of both women's oppression and their protection. L'abbé Provencher of St Boniface commented on 'the cruelty and moral depravity of many French-Canadian voyageurs who abused their wives.' He failed to convince men to abandon marriage *à la façon du pays* for a church ceremony and notes that they 'liked the freedom of "turning off" (leaving) their wives.' Provencher saw the sphere of Métis women as domestic and their role as 'agents of civilisation and Christianisation.' So did his successor, Msgr Taché, quoted in the Davin Report, above.

By 1870, the year of the Métis Red River resistance and the negotiation of Manitoba's entry into Confederation, an ambivalent image of Métis women had emerged in St Boniface. Métis women were more educated than their Indian or mixed-marriage anglophone counterparts and acculturated to the Canadian francophone Catholic tradition. Displacement by Anglo-Ontarians, and by Roman Catholics from Quebec who disparaged such marriages, in the 1870s led to a decade of out-migration of hundreds of Métis families from the Manitoba parishes of St Boniface, St Norbert, and St François-Xavier to the South Saskatchewan River in search of economic opportunity, secure cultural identity, and freedom. Five hundred families settled at Batoche, Saskatchewan. Family groups centred on lines of female kinship. The first generation of mothers had participated in the establishment of the Métis nation at Red River in the 1830s and 1840s. Their children took part in the first resistance in 1869–79 and the second at Batoche in 1885. Payment documents the suffering of women and children as a result of the conflict, women's role in rebuilding the community, and women's labour, social, and religious life – above all their 'determination and resiliency.'

The assumption that pre-agricultural hunter-gatherer societies are fully egalitarian underlies some studies of women's place in these societies. This assumption is in part based on economics. The plants and small game gathered by women and children provided more than half the nutritional requirements of such groups, on a steady basis. Male hunting parties supplied the remainder. Their heroic and sporadic spoils were celebrated with feasting, with the division of the hunt an indicator of tribal standing. Classically based on studies of the African !Kung San – at the time of these studies one of the few pre-agricultural societies still existing – this egalitarianism is arguably a contrast with agricultural economies, which enable the laying up of wealth and thus enhancement of male–male competition, polygyny, multiple offspring, and patriarchal control, rather than a factual representation of current visions of untrammelled equality between men and women in all spheres of life. The egalitarian division of labour supposed in hunter-gatherer economies did not address, for example, the contributions of women and children to the hunt, significant in nineteenth-century buffalo economies and central to the fur trade. Nor were Plains Indians necessarily pre-agricultural. Archaeological evidence at Lockport, Manitoba, discloses agricultural and fishing economies existing from 2,000 years ago to recent times, closely related to the Mandan culture in tools, crops, and mound-building. Trade between agricultural, maritime, and hunter-gatherer economies was well established at the forks of the Red and Assiniboine rivers for at least as long. We know very little about how pre-contact agriculture and trade informed gender roles and status in First Nations of northern North America. Generally, First Nations societies were based on clan and lineage rather than on marriage, and on a gender-based division of labour that permitted greater autonomy to women and children than did the Euro-colonial father-headed family. Nancy Shoemaker's (1995) discussion of anthropological perceptions of gender roles shows that little can be concluded about gender roles and women's status in First Nations and how readily the bias of researchers informs such studies. We do know a little more about how colonialism affected these structures.

Cultural Devaluation and Spirit Murder

Colonialism and Indian policy eroded shared value systems and the spirituality and myth systems that create social, spatial, and familial cohesion. The overarching structure of legends, spiritual teachings, and mythic traditions – depicting relationships, clashes, and the achievement of harmony among humans and between humans, animals, and spirits – is the spiritual matrix and community ethos that provides the context of dispute resolution. Emile Durkheim writes, 'Modern societies can be stable only through respect for justice. But even in societies based on individual differentiation there persists the equivalent of the collective consciousness of societies dominated by mechanical solidarity. There must be sentiments, beliefs, and values common to all. If these common values are weakened, if the sphere of these common beliefs is seriously reduced, then the society is threatened with disintegration' (cited in Aron, 1967: 26).

Residential schooling provides 'a striking example of the interrelationships between racism, sexism, and violence' (Canadian Panel, 1993: 10). The forcible removal of the children of one culture for placement in another, through residential schooling and the child welfare system, constituted cultural genocide as defined in the Geneva Convention on the Punishment of the Crime of Genocide (1948). Cultural genocide also underlay the destruction of indigenous political and social structures under the tutelary regime of reserve governance, which infantilized adults as dominion/federal wards and further devalued women. The destruction of the communal spirit through bureaucratic policies and of the individual spirit through intimate violence has been termed 'spirit murder' (Canadian Panel, 1993; Grant, 1996). In addition to the kinds of violence experienced by all groups of women and children, Aboriginal women and children are also subject to 'spiritual abuse' or 'spirit murder,' defined as 'degrading a woman's [or child's] spiritual beliefs or withholding or limiting the means for her to practice her spirituality' (Canadian Panel, 1993: 21). 'Spiritual abuse erodes or destroys an individual's cultural or religious beliefs through ridicule and punishment' (Canadian Panel, 1993: 10).

Spirit murder may occur in connection with broader cultural devaluation, as a tactic of humiliation by an abusive partner or parent, or through the abuse of trust and position of authority by one holding a position of spiritual power. Members of the clergy, elders, band council members, tribal police, and medicine men may exploit their positions to legitimize intimate violence, enhance access to victims, silence complaints, and prolong victim contact. The Aboriginal Circle advised the Canadian Panel on Violence against Women that there is 'good medicine' and 'bad medicine' in Aboriginal communities (Canadian Panel, 1993: 181). Lists of sham or sexually abusive 'shamans' are routinely circulated between First Nations in Canada and the United States. The Family Violence Professional Education Task Force (1991) in Australia describes 'spiritual violence' as 'deeper than an individual's experience of betrayal: it involves the shame experienced when everyone in the community is aware of the violence, and when they too are implicated as victims of the violence. The victimization may be based on race, color or other forms of identification with that community, and it includes the abuse suffered from a history of genocide or persecution.'

The disjunction between ideology and practice is expressed in the words of a teacher blocked for years by chief and band council in her efforts to obtain protection for sexually abused children, 'Let them [Indian leaders] cry cultural genocide. They do that on a daily basis anyway' (McGillivray, 1997c: 165). Culture is an inadequate explanation for intimate violence, excusing too much, explaining too little, ignoring disjunctions, and hiding individual acts of cruelty behind a dangerous cultural relativism. As Emma LaRocque (1993: 76) curtly observes, 'Men assault: cultures do not.' Canadian historians, she suggests, have ignored the impact of colonization and the consequent sexism and racism in Aboriginal communities, instead explaining violence as the result of 'cultural differences' while distorting images of Aboriginal peoples and notions of culture. When a culture is undermined, its systems for controlling behaviour are weakened or lost. Aggression is directed at others within the same culture rather than at members of the culture responsible for devaluation. Aggression may be fostered by collective loss of memory (Monture-Angus, 1995) and by the collective loss of self-esteem characteristic of colonized, geoculturally isolated communities (RCAP, 1996b: 75). This situation is comparable to the 'collective trauma' experienced by earthquake victims resulting from 'injuries that act to damage the bonds attaching people to one another, to impair the prevailing sense of group cohesion' (Kai Erikson, quoted in RCAP, 1996b: 84).

The concept of spirit murder ties intimate violence to the collective and individual experience of cultural devaluation and to the destruction of belief systems and other institutions of community balancing. Yet 'culture' is not static. It is reinvented as each generation absorbs and responds to parental and community culture and, in a multicultural context, to external influences. The idea that culture is fixed at some historical point may invite a reassertion of cultural tradition that may be harmful to Aboriginal women and children, as LaRocque (1993) argues. Carol La Prairie (1994: ii) writes: 'The disproportionality of Aboriginal crime and victimization suggests the strength of the historical–contemporary link.' While we must relate intimate violence to its social and historical context, its practice is 'learned and normative,' the result of marginalization and 'altered relationships, diminished social controls, demographics and geography, and social and economic stratification.' The need for communities to stop blaming history, take responsibility for peaceful relations within their communities, devise solutions, denounce violence, and return equality to women was stressed by Aboriginal women appearing before the Royal Commission on Aboriginal Peoples (RCAP, 1993b).

3

The Experience of Intimate Violence

There was so many incidents – the things, the abuse that happened to me – I don't know which one to talk about.

Defining the Violence

Debates over definitions and causes characterize much of the literature on intimate violence. While community patterns and beliefs influence the definition of intimate violence as a problem, and control by abusers aims in part at blocking external evaluation of the conduct, intimate violence is ultimately self-defined. Yet the self is centrally the territory over which the other, as abuser, asserts control. Restricting victims' access to information, evaluation, and support ensures an abuser's continued access to the victim. 'If there is a single unifying concept to intimate violence, that concept is control' (McGillivray, 1994a: 242): 'Violence studies consistently suggest that the spectrum of violence, from emotional abuse (to stop women thinking), to hiding car keys and mis-setting alarm clocks (to stop women working), to preventing contact with family and friends (to stop women gaining perspective on the situation), to threats, assault and battery, stalking, child access and custody actions, child assault and murder are, in the end, about control. In the cycle of violence, making up is as much about control as beating up. Murder is the ultimate control move.'

Strategies of control focus on restricting the victim's access to friends, family, work, and community, destroying self-esteem, and thwarting attempts to get help or to leave. The abuser employs threats, beatings, humiliation, scapegoating, and blaming to induce compliance. He uses children to reinforce control of their mothers. He may use or threaten violence against children, threaten to prevent the mother from seeing them should she leave, and seek custody of them when she has left. '[A] father's unprecedented interest in his child after separation is a form of stalking, a continued assertion of the control which lies at the heart of battering' (McGillivray, 1994a: 238).

What causes intimate violence will always be subject to debate. The discourse has moved from individual pathology to broader ecological analyses of historical, societal, and behavioural factors. It is now accepted that there is no single cause of or explanation for the abuse of intimates. The aetiology of sexual abuse of children, for example, differs from that of wife-beating. There is some consensus on contributing factors. The *National Family Violence Abuse Study/Evaluation* (Dumont-Smith and Labelle, 1991) lists substance abuse, economic problems, and second- or third-generation abuse as factors. Isolation and marginalization based on race and geography are also contributing factors.

Easy hypotheses offered in the literature on domestic violence for violence against women and children do not explain phenomena that cross cultures and time. Most common are patriarchy (cited without analysis of distinct barriers between private and public spheres inherent in Anglo-Canadian law and social systems, or of anthropological typologies), colonialism (without examination of culture-specific policy and interaction between cultures), and racism (in the absence of the roots of ethnic differentiation or the psychology of othering in forming self-identity). Although explanations may fall broadly into these three categories, such violence may vary in forms of expression (for example, female genital mutilation in some cultures), rate, intensity, state response and public support, toleration or acknowledgment. We cannot say ultimately why women and children are targets of intimate violence.

In Canada, only some of the multiple forms of intimate violence as defined in the literature – physical, sexual, emotional (including spiritual and cultural degradation), and financial – are offences under criminal law. This is another complicating factor for victims. Political response and the public imagination most strongly identify with repeated physical assaults, sexual abuse of children, debilitating physical injury, or sexual violation. The criminal justice system does not address the emotional violence and threats of physical harm embedded in seemingly trivial acts of humiliation. 'Stalking' provisions introduced in 1993 into section 264 of the Criminal Code, RSC 1985, c. C-46 as amended, recognize the deadly threat that may be inherent in everyday acts (see chapter 4). Patterns of emotional or psychological torture may be so common – or so idiosyncratic – that the meaning of words and acts is known only to the victim. The conduct may be trivialized by others, making it difficult for the victim to get help. She may blame herself for being weak and 'overreacting.' Emotional or psychological abuse includes threats of harm to the victim, to loved ones, and to pets or property; threats of suicide; degradation; terrorization; attacks on personality, on attitudes, and on beliefs or spirituality; and controlling activities (Sinclair cited in McLeod, 1987: 15). Sexual assault and sexual degradation are aspects of intimate violence rarely explored in the literature. There is growing evidence to suggest that Aboriginal women, eight in ten of whom have been victims of sexual assault, are most likely to be assaulted by Aboriginal men; over one-third of Aboriginal men in federal prisons are sex offenders (McIvor and Nahanee, 1998). No figures are available for provincial jails.

The Respondents

With the guidance of a steering committee composed of directors of Winnipeg agencies and programs for Aboriginal women surviving partner violence, we designed and carried out a qualitative interview-style study in 1995 (see Appendix). We selected respondents with the help of support workers who managed case files and counselled clients. Respondents were to have experienced violence within the five years preceding the study, so that we could assess responses of the justice system against a background of consistent criminal justice policy. For their protection we sought to exclude women with very recent experiences of violence or who were still involved with abusive partners. In the course of the interviews, four respondents disclosed recent incidents of violence by current partners. None believed herself to be in danger. One planned to stay, as her partner was in counselling; a second intended to leave (*I don't believe he's going to change*); and a third wanted to leave but had financial problems. The fourth was involved with her incarcerated abuser, who was still controlling her from provincial jail by telephone at the time of the study.

The number of abusive relationships that respondents had experienced in adolescence or adulthood ranged from one to five. All respondents had permanently left or escaped at least one relationship because of violence. Nineteen women were either casually dating or not involved with anyone. Three were in relationships with non-abusive partners. Eight were being stalked, harassed, and threatened by former partners. Two had been assaulted by former partners more than five years before, but incidents of violence by recent partners, directed at children in their care, had brought them into contact with the agency and justice system. Two relationships were terminated by the death of the abuser: one died from substance abuse, and the other was *knifed to death* by the respondent. Five respondents reported a disability, in three cases caused by abuse – partial deafness, dislocation of joints, injury resulting from a *bad fall*.

Twenty-three of the twenty-six women participating in the study are status Indian, one of whom identified herself as *Bill C-31*, meaning that she had recovered her Indian status sometime after 1985, and another as an *urban Indian,* based on the source of her social assistance funding. All twenty-three identified themselves with a band and Nation. Three women said that they were Métis, two of whom were also affiliated with a band and Nation. Eighteen spoke or understood an Aboriginal language – six spoke Cree, nine spoke Ojibwa, and three understood Ojibwa. The cultural identity of the abuser was not a criterion of selection, but the matter is of interest, as the study deals with the diversion of Aboriginal offenders. Eighteen women had been involved in at least one abusive relationship with an Aboriginal partner, and two also had had at least one abusive relationship with a non-Aboriginal partner. Seven did not specify the abusers' cultural background.

Ages of respondents ranged from twenty-one to fifty-one years. Education and income varied: six had completed grades seven to nine, seventeen had completed grades nine to eleven, one had some post-secondary education, and one had a university degree. Five were enrolled in adult education or training programs at the time of the interview. Eighteen reported before-tax annual household incomes of under $10,000. Of this group, fourteen were on social assistance, three were students, and one was employed part time. Three of the remaining eight respondents reported an income of between $10,000 and $14,999, three of between $15,000 and $20,000, and two of over $20,000.

Twenty-five respondents have children, twenty-three with children under the age of eighteen and two with care or guardianship of grandchildren. Nine had all their children living with them, nine had one or more of their children in the custody of, or living with, a relative, and three had one or more children in the care of Child and Family Services. One child of twelve was staying at a children's shelter. Another child was in a treatment home. One respondent did not say where her child was. A respondent with legal custody of her child is banned from her community by the band council resolution. The child lives on reserve with the father. There is a legal duty to report a child in need of protection. This duty, which fell to anyone involved in interviewing or administering the study, was disclosed in the consent form. Two respondents reported children in need of protection. With the willing participation of these respondents, the research team informed provincial child-protection authorities, as required by Manitoba law and the ethical parameters of the study.

Violence in Childhood

Connections between intimate violence in adulthood and that experienced in childhood, whether it be experienced or only witnessed, are well established. One dimension usually omitted in the study of wife-battering generally and in indigenous communities in particular is childhood experiences. If we are to explain the heightened rate of intimate violence in Aboriginal communities in terms of intergenerational patterns of violence, violence as learned behaviour, and the normalization and internalization of violence, then the investigation of childhood is central to understanding partner violence.

Rather than confining respondents to a 'violence checklist' approach that imposed the agency definitions and categories, we asked open-ended questions, permitting respondents to name their own experiences. We framed our investigation of childhood violence in two cautiously worded and open-ended questions.

Q: I would now like to talk to you about your childhood – what growing up was like for you. Can you tell me about your family when you were a child?

Q: As a child, do you remember seeing or hearing violence or abuse around you?

Only one respondent, an older woman, reported a childhood that was happy and free of violence: *I was raised in a good and loving home. I didn't have any abuse. My parents loved me so much. I was the second youngest and I didn't ever see anyone harmed. We lived on a farm and I just feel it was a good life, where we were raised up.* Her abuse began in adolescence with a violent boyfriend after her parents died. *And that's where I lost the love I had.* A second respondent did not refer directly to childhood abuse but spoke about having had suicidal feelings in childhood and adolescence. All but these respondents admitted to experiencing and witnessing as children the abuse of others.

The transcripts reveal that talking about childhood was, for most respondents, more difficult than discussing their abuse as adults. The minimal responses and hesitations made it clear that their childhood still causes them a great deal of pain. Many seemed to be searching for protection and healing of their childhood selves and struggling to understand what had happened. We used probing questions to encourage disclosure.

Q: Did you have a happy childhood?
A: *I guess you could say yes.*
Q: Can you tell me more about that, what it was like?
A: *I don't know.*

When asked if she remembered seeing or hearing violence around her as a child, this respondent described how her father *beat up* her mother. This recalled her own frequent whipping by her father.

Q: Are there any other experiences as a child that you would consider abuse?
A: *I think so ... I always get whipped. Belt, my dad uses his belt, I get a lot of bruises on my back.*

The belt whippings and other physical abuse by her father lasted from the age of 'eight or nine' until she was twelve. At the same age, 'eight or nine,' her father made her responsible for preventing him from beating her mother.

I saw my mom being beaten up by my dad and I couldn't look at them any more. So I just went up over to them and pulled my dad's arm, like this, really hard, and said 'Don't do this to my mom.' And he looked at me and then he stopped ... My mom was crying and bleeding ... My dad says, 'You are my favourite daughter. Next time you see me beat up your mom, stop me.' So that's what I have been doing. But now my dad's okay.

The child traded her own body for that of her mother as target of her father's wrath. Belt whippings were inflicted for visiting friends or coming home late. Abusers gave similar rationales to their adult victims.

Twelve respondents reported witnessing violence against their mothers.

My father was never abusive with the kids, that I know of. He was very abusive to my mom.

I felt scared, just like I wanted the pain as I seen for her. I wanted it to go away. I was afraid for my mother.

One respondent witnessed her father's attempt to slit her mother's throat; police intervened: *Well, when I was five, my dad tried to kill my mom ... Mom died when I was fourteen.* Another, also at the age of five, witnessed her mother's murder by her father:

I heard my biological father coming into the house and rampaging. Then I got up and I noticed the rifle was gone. I heard people yelling ... I snuck out and hid behind a tree. It was so clear that night. I can see my mom standing there. And my dad. My mom kept telling my dad, 'Don't do that ..., we've got our children to think about.' And I could hear my father saying, 'You just want this man.' And he was going insane, talking insanity. He was enraged, like an animal. Finally, I saw my biological father taking his position and then he pulled that trigger and my mom went down.

The majority of respondents experienced more than one type of abuse in childhood from more than one person. Nineteen women reported physical abuse, seventeen sexual abuse, and fourteen emotional or psychological abuse, neglect, and abandonment. Most identified the relationship of the abuser to the respondent. Mothers were physical and/or emotional abusers in eleven cases. Fathers or stepfathers were sexual, physical, and/or emotional abusers in eight cases. Foster parents were physical or sexual abusers in ten cases. Uncles were sexual abusers in seven cases, and an aunt was a sexual abuser in one case. Brothers were sexual abusers in three cases and physical abusers in one case. A sister was a physical abuser in one case.

I still remember being thrown around by my mother, like for instance, on the bed, pushed against the wall. She'd pull my ears, and I would see her abuse my sisters, but not my brother because he was just a baby.

My mom did a lot of hitting ... It seemed like a day didn't go by that I didn't get hit.

I don't know too much about my family history but I know for a fact when I was turning eleven or twelve my mom always abused me ... I wish there was something that could have been done for her. Those days we didn't have CFS [Child and Family Services].

My mom and stepdad would sometimes physically abuse me, but then my uncles and cousins would sexually abuse me, or people from parties and stuff.

It was very lonely ... A lot of neglect and sexual abuse and physical, no stability, very dysfunctional family.

[My brother] raped me all night, sexually raped me all night, and beat me all night ... I forget some parts of the abuse because I kept passing out from all the pain.

I was raped by my brother at fifteen.

We were abandoned when we were kids. We were neglected. A lot of times there was hardly any food in the house. I had to look after my two youngest sisters ... My mother did the abusing ... physical and emotional abuse.

I know that there were times when I was a kid I wanted to commit suicide ... from being neglected.

Yes, the whole family was abusive towards me, my brothers, my sisters, and even the friends that I grew up with, they were abusive.

I grew up on the reserve. When I was a child I seen a lot of alcohol, alcohol-destroyed families. There was a lot of violence and there was a lot of abuse going on. A lot of kids were hurt.

There was so many incidents – the things, the abuse that happened to me – I don't know which one to talk about.

To be perfectly honest, it would be easier to go over what didn't happen ... I did not only get abused by my family, I got abused by my neighbours, too. There is just too many incidents to mention them all.

Respondents identified alcohol as a precursor of abuse in many incidents of childhood violence, but by no means in all, suggesting that while it may be a contributing factor, it is neither necessary nor sufficient as a causal factor – it does not by itself cause abuse, nor is it always a factor in abuse. It has been a quick and inadequate excuse for intimate violence. We did not put the question, 'Were drugs or alcohol a factor in the violence?' We anticipated that the respondents would volunteer this information if they felt that it was part of the pattern of abuse.

My dad was [a minister] and didn't drink. My parents didn't drink ... but ... my dad and my mom psychologically abused us.

Everything was kind of hard when we were growing up, especially living on the reserve ... There was a lot of drinking, lots of fights and we were never allowed out from the room until they had finished drinking. And it could be like a day or two.

I was forced to drink and smoke. I was threatened if I didn't want to do these things. After a while, I just went ahead and did them things without being told.

As I was growing up, there used to be a lot of drinking around, people fighting. First they'd look happy. Then after they got drunk they'd start changing their attitudes. I used to go hide under the bed or in closets.

Unlike women, children are not expected to leave abusive situations. When they do, and they often do, they are routinely returned, or denounced as street kids, child 'hookers,' and similar 'unworthy' victims. Parental custody is foundational to legal relations between parent and state, to be disturbed only on the finding by an agency or court of severe parental failure – sexual or physical abuse or its risk, neglect, abandonment, or failure to provide the necessities of life. Child protection agencies have been granted wide powers of search and seizure, but children may not be believed when they attempt to report abuse or escape it. Parental control over children's thoughts, acts, and interpretation of events is profound. It is axiomatic that this control is for children's protection and benefit. Where it is not, children have even greater difficulty defining their condition and escaping than women.

The social status of the abuser contributed to the silencing of these child victims. One woman did not think that anyone would believe her if she reported her parents' physical abuse because her father was a minister. Her strategy was to turn to criminal activity to force the state to intervene.

I was doing B-and-Es [break-and-enters]. I did that so they'd take me away because my dad was a very influential man. He was a minister. He worked with social services, chiefs and all that. And they said this kid could turn out bad. I thought they would never believe me.

Six women attended residential or 'boarding' schools, and two spoke of physical abuse and humiliation sustained there:

Yes, in the boarding school there was a lot of abuse from staff and the principal. [I was] hit for wetting the bed in the boarding school and foster home.

I was strapped in front of the girls because I was accused of stealing fifty dollars, which I didn't do. I had bruises on my bum. And to teach me a lesson, what the nun [did], she made me scrub the stairway with a toothbrush, making sure that all the marks were off the stairs. I find the nuns were also very verbally abusive. I ran away from school, too, about four times. I learned how to become streetwise at an early age.

Others were abused in foster placements:

I remember one of the first incidents, when I moved to the very first foster home. We were given our first meal and I remember sitting with tin plates on the floor, away from the family table. Everybody else was at the table except my brother, my sister, and I ... That's one of the first times I remember being segregated, or ostracized, or made perfectly aware that I'm different, or that I wasn't equal.

When gas was spilled in my face in one foster home ... they wouldn't take me for medical attention.

If I could take Child and Family Services to court for the abuse that I suffered because of the homes that they put me in, I'd win.

A single abuser can damage generations of family members, who may be frustrated in their attempts to obtain effective intervention:

My dad could die tomorrow and I wouldn't give a damn because I tried to charge him for molestation on myself and my oldest son ... I'm a little frustrated because I know there's no less than ten to fifteen of my nieces and nephews that are around him at all times and he is doing it to them everyday ... There is nothing I can do about it. I tried once, but they said no one would testify.

On her wedding day, this respondent, with *the women who stood up for me* (her bridesmaids), went to the farm to get her oldest boy. Her father had his hands *anywhere and everywhere* on her and her friends. During dinner he sat at the head of the table with her young nephew naked on his lap and *played with him – literally – the whole damn time we were there.*

The boy's mother – her maid of honour – made a four-page police report, but police said that they did not have 'enough' evidence to lay charges. The rest of her family resists intervention. She was herself investigated for the sexual assault of her son. Her sisters would not testify to their own sexual abuse because *they had put it behind them already.*

Nine respondents became involved in violent intimate relationships in their teenage years. Here the line between child abuse and adult abuse is blurred. Respondents themselves decided whether the abuse occurred in childhood or adulthood. For some, there was no clear demarcation.

It never really did end. It was always there. If it wasn't from one particular member of that family I was living with, it was somebody else, and if it wasn't them it was from the school. Like, the people we knew around the community, they were always willing to dump on us.
Q: So you experienced it from everywhere when you were growing up?
A: *Uh huh. Even from the church members.*

When I first experienced abuse [in a dating relationship] I was fifteen. At the time I didn't realize there was such a thing as help for me ... I didn't realize it was an abusive relationship because I was young and I didn't understand what was happening to me.

Probably when I was thirteen ... My stepmother kicked my father out of the house so we had nowhere to stay in the city ... so I ended up staying with this guy I was seeing, and that is how I got involved in drinking and that, and that is how the abuse started.

When I was a teenager, I turned to going with a guy and that's where I found the abuse, and my parents were gone ... The man turned around to be a wild animal and he put me in hospitals. It started when I was fourteen. He got so jealous of my old boyfriends ... he pushed me down the stairs. I got bruises on my head and my arms. But I never learned my lesson ... It's always 'I'm sorry, I'm sorry.' Twelve years he's been saying that. Even when I stayed with him when I was fifteen, at his mother's, he would not let me sleep. All night he'd talk about my old boyfriends ... He'd tease me, like it's how he does things. What he did, he tried to hurt me down there ... And he would fool around. Like, when I was about four months pregnant [at sixteen], he gave me VD. In my second pregnancy, he gave me another VD, and he would cry, cry, 'I'm sorry, it'll never happen again.'

One respondent was impregnated by her father when she was thirteen and had to carry the child to birth. Maternity ends childhood. Forced maternity is an ultimate abuse of a child's body and spirit, rights and status. Childhood experiences of violence merged into violent teen-age relationships, and violence became a hallmark of adult relation-ships. *One abuse from when you're growing up, and you get into another one.*

Violence in Adulthood

The respondents' collective experience of violence in adult relationships included all forms of abuse – physical, sexual, emotional, verbal, and financial. Self-definition of abuse is complicated by the victim's denial of it, and by her unwillingness to identify herself as a 'victim.' The ready categorization of the violence by many respondents may reflect a newly learned awareness brought about by counselling. All but one had been involved in abuse counselling by the time of their interviews. Eight women reported sexual assaults by intimate partners. Two were sexu-ally assaulted by outsiders – one by an agency worker and another by a stranger. The latter respondent was subsequently beaten by her partner in retaliation for the sexual assault, for which he blamed her:

I was walking home and I got strangled to the point where I blacked out. The guy was trying to take my pants off, and he had my pants off. All I remember was falling to the ground when his hands were around my neck. I think when I fell he thought I was dead and he just left me ... I was too scared to wait around so I just took off, I went to go find my boyfriend. When I did find him, he just beat the hell out of me because he thought the bruises and scratches on my neck were hickeys.

Intimate violence in an adult relationship was a painful reminder of childhood abuse:

[A counsellor] made a pass at me in my own home when the guy was being my friend. I minimized it for a while. I thought it was no big deal because he did not hurt me ... Hurt-ing meant getting raped or beat up. But he really hurt me emotionally. What he really did – he took me back to my childhood state of being victimized.

Respondents were pushed, punched, slapped, choked, hit with objects, had their hair pulled out, and were attacked or threatened with guns and knives. One abuser slapped the respondent with her own hands. The physical violence was frequent and severe:

It started off very slow, like a slap here or a slap there, name calling. From then on, I should have got out, but I didn't realize at the time, you know? I was trying to change him to somebody he was not ... It started getting worse and worse ... He knew I would always take him back ... I try not to remember, I don't want to remember I guess.

Well, the worst one was the first relationship. I was probably abused every day, beaten up, slapped, kicked around, thrown down the stairs, dragged around by the hair ... I guess one day I finally got fed up with that and started hitting him back, and I ended up stabbing him.

One time ... my common-law broke my shoulder. I was so drunk at the time, in the evening he done that, I went to sleep. I woke up in the morning and I couldn't get out of my bed. Just when I was waking up, he was leaving out the door and I found I couldn't even sit up. I begged him, 'Don't leave me. I can't move.' He didn't even care ... .

He beat me three to four times a day. I constantly had black eyes, thick lips, bruises to the body, dislocated shoulder, and [he] kicked out my partial teeth, always ripping my hair out. He never let me out of his sight.

He sexually assaulted me, broke my nose, knocked my teeth out. He hit me on the head so hard my ear drum was damaged.

Many respondents used the term *fighting* in depicting physical abuse, an expression rarely used by women who are not Aboriginal. They used the term to describe incidents in which a respondent argued, fought back, or otherwise felt herself to be a participant, even if an unequal one, in the altercation. A woman who was physically abused by her mother in childhood said *she still fights me.* No one used the term where the contest was overwhelmingly unequal:

He took me for granted and times would physically fight me ... He fought my children one time in front of me.

He started throwing me around outside and stuff ... My sister-in-law, her son, said 'They're fighting outside.' Like I'm really going to be fighting this six-foot guy, eh? ... He had my jacket and he was throwing me around on the ground, and he kept saying how he was going to bash my face in so no one would look at me – all these kinds of things.

He was very violent to the point where he would put scars on my body. He would kick me in the face or knock me out. He would just fight – whatever happens when abuse happens.

It may be that the term *fighting* serves a normalizing function by placing intimate violence on a par with more accepted male–male violence. It may give women a sense of strength, of being able to survive. Certainly, it masks the power differential inherent in intimate violence.

Substance abuse, as noted above, had been part of the lives of most respondents, witnessed in childhood or thrust on children at an early age, experienced in relationships with partners, a way of coping. Intoxication by drugs or alcohol was a precipitating factor in some but not all incidents of abuse.

The only time he used to abuse me was when he came home drunk. That was every Friday.

I guess when he was on medication, like those pain killers with codeine, he would get very abusive then.

He was verbally abusive, he sexually assaulted me, physically as well. Every time he drank, I feel I was his punching bag.

The only time he never used to abuse me was when he was not drinking.

I had a lot of abuse from my last boyfriend, whom I was living with common law, and he had knifed me in the neck, and he went to jail for this ... I could say drinking was involved again, on both of our parts ... The abuse started when my partner was usually very intoxicated.

Well, I was drinking with this guy. And one time we were drinking, I didn't want to have nothing, no sex with him, and he raped me, he ripped my clothes apart, off.

Intoxication was not a factor in other instances:

He wasn't doing drugs or any alcohol. He was in AA.

When he was stoned he wouldn't touch me.

I guess I got physical abuse when he was drunk and at times when he wasn't.

He was very, very violent, sober or drunk.

Some respondents used alcohol to mask the pain of the assaults: *I used to drink so I wouldn't feel it when he started hitting me.*

Respondents showed awareness of the dynamics of intimate violence and of the cycle of violence. This has been described as a three-phase cycle – mounting tension, culminating in assault, followed by a 'honeymoon' phase, where the abusive partner showers the woman with affection, care, apologies, promises of reform, gifts, and flowers (Walker, 1984). Many women describe a period in which they experience no 'honeymoon' behaviour but rather a cessation of the abuse – a period of calm, giving temporary relief. Rarely were relationships in this study described as following a cycle. Violence exploded out of nowhere, and tension was constant:

It started off very slow, like a slap here, a slap there, name calling ... It started getting worse and worse as time escalated.

I now remember for the first week or two when I started going out with him he would hold me and tell me that he would protect me and would never do anything to hurt me ... When he first started hitting me around, it happened so suddenly and so violently I wasn't even aware of what was going on until I seen blood all over the place, like all over the walls, all over the floor, all over his face, all over my face.

From the time he got up till the time he went to bed – basically, you walked on eggshells – you never know when he was going to blow ...

He never said, he never made any excuses, he never talked about it, why he did it. It just happens, even when you don't expect it. He'd just fly off the handle.

With [relationship] number one, seldom, but number two would be every three or four months when we drank. And number three, the abuse started three months after, for every day, for a good nine or ten months.

A victim who has learned to recognize and negotiate whatever cycle or trigger of abuse her partner offers may herself trigger the violence to 'get it over with' and choose a time when she can heal herself privately, often when her children will be away. Always, she 'asked for it':

When he would hit me he would say that was because I started arguing with him, and that was the cycle of abuse, and there were times when I did argue with him as I could not stand the tension and wanted to get it over with, so that I really believed him when he said it was my fault that I had asked for it.

All respondents experienced emotional abuse in an adult relationship.

Its impact was long-lasting and memories were detailed. They reported name-calling, humiliation, victim-blaming, cultural devaluation, and spiritual abuse:

[My] second relationship was with the two youngest children's father. He was physically, emotionally, and sexually abusive to me. [He] manipulated me using culture, as he was a medicine man.

He threw a night table at me ... At the time, I remember, he made sure I was naked first. And that's one of the things that did bother me – that he wanted me helpless, he wanted me more helpless. And I felt sorry for him for that.

It was years he was hitting me but ... it was the name calling that lasted the longest. And for me the hardest part was the name calling. He would call me down in my own language [Ojibwa]. He would just sit me down on the bed and call me down for hours without stopping. He would only stop to take a shot of beer or something. He could go for three or four hours. He called me every angry name you can think of ...

He used to blame me for getting him mad, for things that didn't go his way, or even if things didn't work out the way he wanted them to, he blamed me.

Yeah, he used to say, right from the beginning when I was very naïve about violence, I deserved it ... or 'You made me angry' or 'You made me do this.'

He'd just say, 'This is what you want, this is what you want.' Sometimes I don't understand why. And I always treat him nice. It's like, whatever he says, I do – put his socks on, cook him something, give him clean clothes, cut his hair. It's always do this, do that.

One night, ... he kept me up all night, which was a regular night [of violence] for us for many, many years. I had lost a lot of weight and I was burnt right out. He says, 'You're not even worth touching. You're not even worth raping.' He went upstairs and I went up quietly.

Respondents believed and internalized their partners' excuses for the violence. It was their fault, they deserved it, and it proved their partners' love:

I believe them [the excuses], and then he started blaming me, and then I started blaming myself.

I blame myself, like maybe I'm such a bitch, like that's why I get beaten up. Or, it's my fault, if I hadn't said this, it wouldn't have happened. Like, I blame myself a lot ... I feel like, one time I feel like committing suicide, in my last one, relationship, when he would hit me ... When the first guy abused me a long time, when I was in my late teens, I felt like he loved me, that's why he did it, because, like, that's all I knew. My dad hit me, and he hits me because he loves me, that's what I thought.

A consistent theme of abusive partners was fear of infidelity, possessiveness, and sexual jealousy – old boyfriends, current imagined relationships with other men, future relationships (Daly and Wilson, 1988).

He said, 'You're too attractive, I don't like men looking at you.' And he accused me of flirting with men. That was his excuse all the time. And the other one, he accused me of seeing someone else.

He'd find a reason to get upset and accuse me of old boyfriends and later, after ten to twelve years or so, then he started accusing me of new boyfriends, like I was having affairs.

He used to speak of his ungodly past and he would say, 'You women are all alike, nothing but sluts.'

He used to tell me what to wear, and sometimes what he would pick out for me to wear was a little bit too provocative, and then when I didn't want to wear the clothes that he had picked out for me, he made me wear them. He'd beat me up, pull my hair or something, slap me, and then I would wear them. As time progressed, he used to beat me up saying that I dressed like a whore. And meanwhile it was him who wanted me to dress this way.

Sometimes he would just throw me out ... I would go to my friend's place and just sleep there. He'd think that I'd been with another guy and get mad again ... When we're inside the truck, he'd accuse me. He drove out in the truck, really far ... and then he'd say, 'So, this is true' and 'I know what you're doing' [with other guys]. I'd just sit there. I'd get mad, I'd get scared sometimes.

Some were abused only in private – *not in public, my parents' place, or in front of his friends or my friends.* Other respondents reported public humiliation – an ultimate show of confidence and successful control by an abuser. Isolation and financial control were also reported. These tactics developed gradually. All were effective in maintaining control by destroying the victim's self-esteem and preventing complaint or escape.

For about five months it was pretty good. It was really nice. And he did a lot of things for me that nobody had ever done, like cleaning my house and buying lots of groceries. He was generous with his money at the beginning. Then he started isolating me ... It was pretty gradual ... He became really demanding in the way he wanted sex ... What he did was intimidate me.

I wouldn't go anywhere. I was too ashamed ... At Safeway, he'd have his tantrums and walk out and I would stand there like a fool, because he had the money. It was really embarrassing, in public places, you know? ... He started using the kids. It was nothing for him to give them a hundred bucks. When it came to me, I had to account for every cent, what bill did I pay or what did I buy, or did I use it on gas and stuff like that. He'd always be afraid, I guess, that I would try to save money to run away.

He won't even let me go out and visit my friends ... Sometimes I have made an excuse to go get my friends to visit ... and he would say 'If I don't see you in half an hour to an hour, I'll get mad.'

He was abusive. He practically controlled my life. Sometimes I felt like I was a prisoner in my own home. He chased everybody away that I got to know. He didn't want anybody to come and see me, or for me to make friends. He didn't even want my family around.

What he would do is make me lay with him, and wouldn't let me leave.

There were times when I was scared to be alone. I felt – well, I believed – that he would be the only man I could ever get and all those things he said about me were true.

Death threats were frequent and detailed.

Mental abuse. He would hold me with his arm around me and pretend he had a gun, pretending it went off on my head. I couldn't get away from him no matter what.

He always threatened me ... He had a gun and could just blow me away. That's what he always used, the mental stuff, he could blow me away or hire someone to do it ... It was awful, so unbearable.

I was threatened. I was threatened by him, to kill me, and that he would beat me up.

Respondents were asked whether their partners had ever directly harmed their children. 'Lessons' taught to respondents were also taught to their children:

[He] didn't really have to hit anyone to hurt them. He had a really mean mouth, he really does. I guess the odd time he did whack the kids too ... He whacked [them] to please his mom ... She was always encouraging him to hit the kids.

He was a very abusive man, the four years I lived with him. He abused the girls emotionally and physically. This was happening every day, this abuse.

My son was playing with an elastic and then he hit my ex-husband's cheek ... He told him, 'Take your shirt off.' So my son takes his shirt off ... and he [shot] the elastic bands on his chest area. It was about three feet away from him ... My boy was scared, and I know he was, but I couldn't say anything. If I try and stop him, he would say, 'Don't stop me. I'm trying to teach him a lesson.' And then he had bruises right on his chest from those elastic bands ... One time [when the child objected to his own Hallowe'en costume], [my ex-husband] took the broom, and I could hear my boy screaming. It was dark inside my boy's room ... I turned on the light and I see [he] got bruises on his face and a big lump on his forehead and he had a black eye and a lump on the head ... He didn't let him go to school for two weeks so no one could see the bruises.

I knew there was no turning back when he hit my oldest boy with a butcher knife. My son came into the kitchen to ask me a question and he just swung ... Lucky he was not cut because he would have been cut bad.

Well, the first [abusive partner] almost did. It missed her by an inch when he threw an axe. He missed me and it bounced right off the wall ... She was only a year and a half.

A year ago I found out my thirteen-year-old was [sexually] abused by their father – and my five-year-old daughter [was too].

Children witnessing their mother's assault was a source of pain and humiliation to respondents, proof of powerlessness, failure as wife and mother, and in itself a form of child abuse (Rabin, 1995):

I yelled for someone until my little girl woke up. I think she was about six. And I had to get her to help me get dressed so I could go to the hospital. So she did ... I knew all the time, she shouldn't be seeing this ... During those times of violence with my ex I often wished I were dead ... But my children need me.

My brother. He beat me to a pulp. He made my children sit on the bed, at the edge of the bed all night. My oldest daughter was only about four or five years old at the time. She told me that I had passed out from his beating ... He kept telling them all night he was the devil. He would get up off the couch and come towards me and jump in the air. And stomp on my face over and over. My daughter said that blood gushed from my mouth and nose each time he did this ... This is the brother that used to abuse me as a child.

He'd always belittle me in front of the kids and always talk about me like I wasn't even there. I just wanted it to end. Three months from then I took an overdose.

At one time, my son was in the hospital [for attempting suicide] because he seen me getting abused when he was just a baby.

Lonnie Athens asserts that the intensity and emotional impact of witnessing violence against someone close to you can be more destructive than experiencing it yourself (1989). Where the witness to the violence is a child unable to oppose the abuse, it begins the process of brutalization and violent coaching that may lead to a transgenerational cycle of intimate violence and to offending outside the family setting. Athens drew his subjects from incarcerated men who were legally designated dangerous offenders. Respondents worried about the effect on their children of violence against them. Partners used children to manipulate fears of leaving and to assert control after the mother left. They abused children directly, contributing to respondents' feelings of helplessness and guilt. This was seen as a form of abuse of the mother:

[The abuse is] still there. And now he uses my kids to get to me, even worse now than ever. That's an awful way [to be] abused – your ex-partner using your kids.

I was always afraid to leave him because he used the kids quite a bit – that he was going to take them away from me and I would never see them – and that he would kill me before I would divorce him.

Respondents were aware and afraid of the impact of their abuse on their children even where the children were not in direct danger. The abuse of another may impel action even if one's own abuse does not, and violence towards a child was for many respondents a precipitating factor in their leaving the relationship.

Getting Out

The question most often asked about a woman living with a violent partner is, 'Why doesn't she just leave?' If she does not, the assumption is that she likes it. If she returns violence with violence, she may be accused of precipitating, deserving, or wanting the violence. Self-defence analyses are problematic, in particular where the probability of immediate death or serious bodily harm is not apparent to an onlooker. This question inspired the leading Canadian case on self-defence in a battering relationship – R. v. Lavallee (1990), 76 C.R. (3d) 329 (Supreme Court of Canada). Lyn Lavallee shot her common-law husband in the back of the head as he was leaving the room. He had put the gun in her hand and told her to 'do it' or she would be dead in the morning. The court ruled that expert evidence is admissible to explain the state of mind of a battered woman and the impact of the abuse on her ability to leave. Lavallee's belief that death was imminent could be seen as reasonable – a requirement of the law of self-defence – only when the dynamics of intimate violence are understood. Prior acts of violence and future threats of deadly violence provide grounds for the immediate apprehension of death or serious bodily harm in such a relationship. Further, there is no legal duty to retreat from one's own home. While few courts have acquitted defendants, following Lavallee (Shaffer, 1997), intimate violence does have a mitigating effect. Manslaughter may be the charge, rather than murder, and the sentence may be shorter as a result of the battery and control.

The focus on 'why she stays' transforms a social problem into an individual problem and places the onus on the victim (Jones, 1994). The victim who has not been helped is for that reason unworthy of help. In self-defence cases, the worthiness of victims continues to be a problem for the courts (Merry, 1997; Shaffer, 1997). The simplistic dichotomy of the worthy victim who is feminine, docile, and sweet and the unworthy victim who is street-tough and mean-mouthed has yet to give way to a more nuanced understanding. The infamous sentencing 'discount' given in 1993 in Ontario to Karla Homolka, an apparently worthy victim, on the basis of Paul Bernardo's violence towards her, lost public support when the extent of her role in the murders of two schoolgirls and the sexual assault of a third became known at Paul Bernardo's trial (McGillivray, 1998a). Sympathy for Homolka was, however, less a factor in the plea bargaining than the need to convict her more dangerous partner. Factors keeping women such women as Lavallee and Homolka in abusive relationships are complex and multi-layered. Although *Lavallee* seems correct in both analysis and result, 'the battered woman syndrome defence' raises wider concerns. It pathologizes an individual caught in a complex of societal problems – social and family expectations, cultural beliefs about marriage and family, personal loyalties, financial disadvantage, lack of moral support, misogyny, sexism, and racism – and avoids the need to confront the basic conditions of intimate violence. Alternatively, it excuses the morally blameworthy, denies women's capacity to choose, or glosses over women's capacity for evil, contributing further to women's inequality. On a practical level, it sets too high a threshold in the law of self-defence for the 'ordinary' battered woman to meet; see the judgment of Justice L'Heureux-Dubé in *R. v. Malott* [1998] SCR 123. But the immediate condition of those caught in the web of intimate violence necessarily remains a focus of judicial, police, and agency attention, whatever the social dimensions of domestic assault.

Factors affecting the decision to leave or to seek help include the complex of controls exercised by abusers, societal pressure and women's cultural training to 'see things through' and keep the family together, the affection or love that women may have for their partners, hopes that the abuse that they may see as temporary will end, fear of losing their children, fear of being alone, lack of money and other resources, and conflicting personal, family, religious, and ethnic loyalties. Low self-esteem resulting from abuse further complicates the situation, robbing women of courage and self-motivation. *I was just chicken to leave, I guess. It was easier just to stay, you know, than to go through all the work.* Leaving is not the simple choice that it is popularly presumed to be.

More chilling is the fact that victims know from past experience that the abuse will not end when they leave. They may want to defer that threatened, major, and possibly fatal beating that will follow any discussion of leaving or any attempt to leave. That the violence will worsen after women have left is statistically borne out. Data collected by the federal Department of Justice between 1974 and 1992 show that a married woman in Canada is nine times more likely to be killed by her husband than by a stranger (Wilson and Daly, 1994). For each man killed by his co-residing wife in Canada, almost four (3.8) women are killed by their co-residing husband. The ratio jumps to 10.1 women killed after they have left the relationship as compared with every husband killed by an ex-wife. Separation increases the risk of a woman being killed by her husband by six times. In 1991, 270 women were murdered (Canadian Panel, 1993: 10). Two hundred and ten of the 225 women in cases solved were killed by men, over half (125) by intimate partners. Murder is of course the tip of the iceberg. Criminal harassment, physical and sexual assault, and other forms of violence may increase with the fact or even threat of separation. Martha Mahoney (cited in Jones, 1994) describes 'separation assault' as 'the attack on the woman's body and volition in which her partner seeks to prevent her from leaving, retaliate for the separation, or force her to return. It aims at overbearing her will as to where and with whom she will live, and coercing her in order to enforce connection in a relationship ... an attempt to gain, retain, or regain power in a relationship.' Provisions in the Criminal Code about criminal harassment and protection orders (see chapter 4) are a direct legal recognition of separation assault.

We did not ask the question 'Why didn't you leave?' We instead asked respondents whether and how the relationship ended. If it had not ended, we put the question: 'Do you intend to stay in the relationship?' Four women were involved with abusive men at the time of the study. All but one had left between one and four abusive relationships. Responses show that women were concerned about their children – the effects of the violence, leaving them behind. Respondents frequently cited the effect of abuse on children as a reason for leaving. Abuse recalled childhood experiences of violence, the need for nurturing, fears of being alone, and fear for children's safety and socialization:

Because I would like to break the cycle of violence, because my children deserve better. I wouldn't want them to go through what I went through. I don't want the cycle repeated and passed onto them.

I couldn't live like that any more and plus it was really affecting my kids.

I went into [a Winnipeg shelter] in September because I wanted to protect my children. I tried to stop the visitation rights right away but ... I had a hard time because I couldn't get a restraining order because he lived in a different province and he still had visitation rights. And I was afraid that he could still come and take my kids.

The biggest thing for me in leaving my last relationship was the realization that I had my own feeling. I used to get lonely when he was gone, and I always connected it with him, but being apart from him I came to realize that I was lonely anyways sometimes, even when I was with him. That is what helped me to know that all the feelings I had weren't only tied to my partner, that I come with my own feelings and things to deal with. He would always ask me if I was lonely and I would say, 'Yes, it was so lonely,' and he would always say it was for him. But I realize with time that I was just lonely in general, just missing a lot of the nurturing that I didn't get and things like that. And that is what helped me decide to stay away, and live by myself and look after myself and my kids.

It was safety, too, for my children. It hurt me to see them crying when they used to see me with black eyes ... I don't want them to see me like that for the rest of their lives.

I was tired of being abused, tired of having my children seeing me being abused.

One respondent told her partner to leave after he injured a child in her care:

I was going to sort out my laundry. All of a sudden a voice screaming – my grandson. I ran to him, and [my partner] was holding him, throwing him to the floor. I grabbed my grandson, and I was going to put him down on the floor, and he wouldn't put his leg down. I felt his leg and I felt the bone coming out so sharp from his leg ... I freeze – like I'm the one – I see the baby going through that pain, I got that pain too ... I told him, 'You better pack your stuff. I can't take it. I can't be around you.'

A month later, her partner reported himself to Child and Family Services in hopes that the child would be apprehended and she would then take him back:

The next morning he phoned me and he said, 'I think the Child and Family Services are going to come and see you. ... I reported what I did' ... I said, 'No matter what happens ... if I lose him, I will never want you back.' The next day the Child and Family Services phoned me and said to bring [the child] to the office ... I just started to cry. That time I wanted to die. Going to die sober, if I lost that boy. I was crying all day, and I just knew I was going to jump in the river when they came to pick him up – because I know I can't swim – just going to jump off that bridge.

She did not jump off the bridge, remained sober, told her husband that he could never return, and gained custody of the child and later his siblings.

Most respondents simply could not take the physical punishment and fear of death any longer. Leaving was less about one particular incident that triggered a decision to get out than about the accumulation of violence:

[I] just had enough, sick and tired of that, can't take it any more.

I was getting tired of being hit around and pushed around.

I was getting tired of that. I was tired of being abused. Seems I've been abused all of my life.

[Relationship] number one, I just got tired of the abuse, the running around, being taken for granted. Same with number two. Number three, I knew if I stayed in the relationship I'd be dead. So I had to figure out a way to leave.

I finally came to the realization that this time he nearly did kill me. I still remember him saying that he was going to kill me ...

If he keeps it up, one of these days he's going to kill me.

One relationship ended with homicide:

I never left the relationship, actually. It ended in a tragic way. I killed my husband in self-defence.

The court did not find self-defence, despite legally compelling circumstances:

We got into an argument. It got out of hand. Pretty soon we were fighting and fighting ... I tried to get away from that argument, but he followed me into the living room, his step-brother behind him, encouraging him to beat the shit out of me. And then I went into the kitchen, opened the drawer, got a knife. And he was standing about seven feet away from me, his step-brother still behind him, still encouraging him to come after me. And he did. He grabbed both my hands, the wrists. And we were fighting. I don't remember stabbing him four times. I don't even know where. The last thing I remember was stabbing him on his abdomen. I didn't pull the knife out. He pulled away. He ran downstairs where the bedrooms were, and that's where he died.

The respondent served a jail term of seven months for manslaughter.

Coping, Intervention, and Support

Despite the remorseless litany of violence, manipulation, and pain expressed in this chapter, women and children were not passive victims. A variety of coping strategies and survival tactics appear throughout these recitations of violence. The children who were locked in a room for two days until a drinking party ended, or who resisted alcohol and ciga-rettes, hid under the bed, committed 'break and enters' to draw official attention, ran away from residential school, and became 'street smart'; the women who 'fought' their partners relied on their children for help, protected their children as well as they could, and precipitated violence at times when they could deal better with it; the children and women who asked for family help, however unsuccessfully. All demonstrate coping skills.

Coping is defined as constructive action taken to avoid or control dis-tress, as active adaptations to difficult situations – here, experiences of abuse (Liz Kelly, 1988: 160). How a victim defines her experience, the context within which it occurs, and the resources available to her shape her coping strategies. *Coping*, as we use the term here, means any way of dealing with violence short of full involvement with the justice system and child protection. Calling the police (chapter 4) is an important cop-ing strategy. As children growing up on reserve, where services ranged from minimal to non-existent, respondents experienced many barriers. *Back then, you were seen and not heard.* Respondents were acutely aware of the liabilities and vulnerabilities of childhood:

I remember we used to have big beds, and I remember always sleeping against the wall so my father or anybody wouldn't bother me ... I was safe because I slept against the wall.

Well, I ran away from home when I was twelve.

At the age of fourteen, I ran away from home because I got tired of being abused by my mother.

I just asked, when I was fourteen years old, I asked to be put in a foster home.

No, it didn't end until I was sixteen. I guess that is finally when I got angry with my mother, what she was doing to us, abusing us. That was the last time she ever hit me, because I hit her back when she hit me. It was just a reaction, quick reaction. And after that she left me alone. I never asked [for help]. I didn't understand what was going on.

Coping strategies change in adulthood:

I guess I was trying to arrange for my own safety. I asked my neighbour if she would call the police if I banged on the wall three times. I lived in a row house so I started – like I was losing it and wasn't in control of anything – I would bang on the wall, and she would call if I was not able to do it myself.

Well, with my first partner, whenever he used to fight me he used to pull me by the hair. He used to punch me while he was dragging me by the hair. I know this is surprising, but it felt kind of embarrassing to me – but I got to the point where I started getting really short haircuts. Because I always liked long hair, but after a few years of getting dragged around by the hair, I just had it cut really short, and kept it that way. But that did not stop the violence.

Self-harm, while not meeting the definition of coping as 'constructive' behaviour, was frequent. Some respondents attempted suicide in adolescence or adulthood. Some reported blocking pain with alcohol and releasing tension through grim humour and slashing – cutting one's arms with a razor blade or piece of glass. Even less a matter of conscious strategy, but still forms of coping, are the self-protective mechanisms of denial, memory repression, and eating disorders. Treatment for anorexia for one respondent brought to the fore suppressed memories of sexual abuse in early childhood.

I started finding out that there are self-help groups and support groups, and so I agreed to come to several of them. I think it started actually when I was about sixteen, fifteen or sixteen, when I realized that there is something wrong with me ... I wasn't healthy in my way of thinking. I mentioned to a couple of my workers that I think I should see somebody ... I just hinted around at it [..]. And that is why I ended up in the hospital when I was sixteen because I had no idea I had anorexia.

When I was a teen ... the only way I could cope with the whole thing was by drinking.

It just went from one bad incident to the next. It was going to a point where we began joking about it. I would be passed out at a party, and I would wake up and find out he had gone home. My friends would say, 'It's time to get up and go home for your daily beating.' We began joking about things like that.

I used to see my dad and his common-law always fighting when they would drink. That is where I got slashing of arms, from my dad's wife. She used to do that.

Respondents varied in their awareness of the need for help and in the help available to them. Some did not think that they required help, defining their condition by the condition of others around them. Others wanted help but could not find it. Some were able to gain access to the justice system. Children growing up on reserve and women who lived in or married into a reserve community often face a near-fatal lack of resources and denial by kin and community. The abuser's social position and manipulation of the system controlled not only self-definition and help-seeking but also the victim's access to resources through his political control in a closed environment:

I sought help from many people I thought were my friends, but because he was a medicine man many people felt they couldn't assist me, because of my husband's position. Many thought I was lying because of what was happening to me.

That's what kind of bothered me when I was younger. My older sister knew [I had been sexually abused] and all she did – I was made to feel so bad – I told the priest I had sex. It was really sad. I didn't realize back then that I was a victim. I don't know, making a child feel so bad.

Nobody wanted to be involved. They knew how crazy [he] was, he was capable of anything ... Like, we have a CFS agency, and they won't even touch him because they know him. He knows the policies and stuff like that. He knows his way around. He's very knowledgeable in that sense. He does consulting for a living, so he's very good with his mouth.

There is a notable variety in the response of service providers on reserve to intimate violence. This situation derives from the therapeutic model of social services, which centres on family unification, and the focus of tribal council agencies on maintaining ethnic and community connections (McGillivray, 1997c). *On the reserve, all they do is talk about couples, like, those [social] workers there ... Strange. Except they do want married couples to stay together, no matter what, like that. It seems that they don't care how much, they don't care if, there is an abuse there. They take the woman out of the house for a while and take her to another home for at least a couple of days and put them back to the spouse. That's what they did when I got really beaten up one time.* Isolation and lack of services were the reality for others. *When he took me back home to his place [on a reserve] up north, I felt trapped. I had nobody to talk to, and I felt really alone. I felt I was in jail. I felt I couldn't escape.* Delays in response by the service system (and by the justice system – chapter 4) may escalate the violence where the abuser knows that an outside authority has been contacted. Delay also gives him time to convince the victim to forgive and forget the violence. *The social workers that I had in rural Manitoba weren't aware of what was going on. By the time they did come around and check up on us [children], we were buttered up so much, you know, it was like water off a duck's back. The violence and the experiences we went through, we completely forgot all about them by the time the social worker came around.*

Getting help is tangled with self-definition and decisions about leaving the relationship. Ambivalence surrounds every level of decision-making. Getting out might depend on the help of friends and the random kindness of strangers, while 'the system' might come later. Respondents' memories of leaving were detailed:

After a while he left [and] I went down to the basement where we stayed, and all my furniture was there and all my clothes. I had beautiful clothes. And I packed two bags, took all my children's ID and my ID, and I snuck out the basement door, a little door, I walked away ... I hitchhiked ... and he dropped me off at [the] shelter.

I called my friend and told her I was getting tired of this. Can't take it any more. He went for a ride, so I left that Tuesday night. It was still daylight, and I went through the bushes to make sure he doesn't see me ... and I asked my friend, 'Come and pick me up with a boat,' and she did, on the other side of the lake. She was waiting over there, and she took me home, and I spent the night over there. I was hiding from him. And that was the morning I was wondering what to do. I wanted to go back because I wanted to get my kids ... I called the crisis line here in Winnipeg ... Somebody answered the phone, and I told her I need help and I can't go home and I need my kids ... They told me to try and get hold of my kids.

The child protection agency told me, 'We are not going to take him away for good, we are just going to take him for a few days.' ... I have to go to a women's shelter 'cause ... mentally sick inside. I need to talk to somebody, I need help. So I go to a women's shelter, and from there they protected me.

Although the availability and helpfulness of agencies varied, respondents spoke positively about the agencies with which they were associated at the time of the study. These included shelters, counselling services, treatment centres for substance abuse, healing centres, and crisis telephone lines:

I'm satisfied, like I said. I really like that place where they just like open the door for me to go a new way of life ... They got me a lawyer so I could go for guardianship.

From the experience, I'm learning that it is not my fault. I used to believe that I was the only one on the face of this earth that was getting abused and nobody understood. But coming to [a second-stage housing facility] really, really helped me. And that I am not alone.

I've been in [a shelter] for group [therapy], and I've been in the shelter. And that's when I found out about how to get restraining orders. And I was finding out ways of how to escape from my partner. There's [a social services and counselling agency], somebody referred me here, too.

I don't think I'd change anything [with] support services as an adult, because I think they're all doing a great job. I wish there was a kids' hotline back in the sixties.

Respondents would not change a thing about their present support services but strongly criticized other services. One respondent reported that a Child and Family Services (CFS) worker gave her address to her abusive partner. Another was put on hold on a suicide hotline. One woman experienced racism in a medical clinic. Another was sent from one clinic and hospital to another with a badly injured child, and no doctor reported the injury to CFS. One was still angry about the lack of response by CFS to her counselling needs:

I was seeing a doctor at [a] clinic. He was my doctor. I felt that I was being discriminated and racially treated in that clinic because I would be the first one there, the last one out every time. You know, they told me to come at nine, and I would not get in until five after twelve.

I asked the worker to help me to protect my children because the visitation rights weren't stopped. She suggested, 'Go to a shelter,' so that's what I did ... She didn't provide any kind of services for me. I felt like I was being victimized by her. I felt like she was just judging me ... I don't know what she read on a piece of paper. I felt like she just judged us when she read that paper. I don't think a worker should do that to a family that's in crisis.

I took [the child] to the walk-in clinic and the doctor sent us to [an X-ray clinic]. We went back to the doctor with the X-ray. And right away when I seen that X-ray, I ran out and cried ... The baby had to suffer so long. We took him to [hospital], and we waited and waited. A nurse came to us and said, 'Why did you bring him here? This is not Children's [Hospital]; you have to take him to Children's ... ' They never reported it to Child and Family Services. They just didn't do nothing about it.

Well, this last relationship, about a year ago, I phoned Child and Family Services – well, we both did, me and him – saying we need help, because he was abusing me and we were fighting a lot, and we don't like it, like fighting in front of the children ... Then Child and Family Services said, 'OK, we'll contact you in a couple of days with numbers where you can go for help.' They never did. They never phoned us.

We asked respondents if they and their children felt safe after the relationship ended. Careful precautions were taken – protected housing, alarms, escape plans, protection orders, moving – but many respondents still did not feel safe.

Probably not, but while I'm living at [second-stage safe housing] he knows he can't come here. That's why he hates this place. I don't think I am. I still watch my back and whatever.

I have a protection plan in case I have to get out of the house. I know what to do to get away if the place is unsafe to be at.

I would say yes. I moved six hundred miles to make sure of it.

Oh yeah, [the child] is safe. We are. The place where I am living, I put a security system in there. I'm paying over a thousand dollars. And when we sleep we put the alarm on.

Yeah, now, because I moved three times this year already, just to try to have [my children] in a place where he might not find out where I live.

Well, I kind of figure he's still trying to control me by using my daughter, so I don't know if that's a form of abuse right there. But as far as physical [abuse], I left him.

I don't really know. I can't really say for sure. I wish I could say I am safe, but with the games that [my ex-partner] plays with me, I will probably not feel safe for a very long time. He uses his past, he uses his history of violence, he has used it to keep me in check by saying things like, 'If I ever got mad again I don't know what I'd do.' In fact, one time when I was going to leave him he said, 'If I ever get mad again I don't know how many people I am going to kill this time.' It really scared me, like it scared me so much I went back to him.

Respondents needed support and protection after leaving and required assurance that services would continue to be available to ensure their healing and safety. Often the only available source of help on reserve is the police. Calling police invokes the criminal justice system. In the next chapter, we explore criminal justice policy in the prosecution of intimate violence and discuss respondents' experiences in the justice system.

4

The Criminal Justice System

What I've seen or experienced myself, it's sure in hell not for the victim. It's for the abuser ... As far as I'm concerned, I haven't seen any justice.

Intimate Violence and Law Reform

Experiences of respondents took place in a changing environment of law and policy reform. Historically in Canadian society as elsewhere, the exercise of power within and over the domestic sphere, and the social power to define abuse of domestic powers as criminal or marital offences, was a male prerogative. With a brief exception at the close of the last century (Doggett, 1993), intimate violence was not viewed as a public problem or as a matter for criminal justice intervention until the 1960s. Its very domesticity rendered it invisible to the public gaze. Law was itself a large part of the problem. Intimate violence has been commonplace, tolerated, encouraged, and at times legalized as a necessary part of the husband's domestic role.

The Roman law doctrine of *pater familias* placed the father as legal and spiritual head of the household. Christian doctrine influenced by Roman law held that man and wife are one and that that one is the man. These influenced the common law doctrine of *coverture*. *Coverture* subjected married women to the quasi-juridical power of the husband and unmarried women and children to that of the father. Women unless widowed were the wards of men. The requirement of domicile, an aspect of *coverture*, for example, meant that women who left an abusive relationship could be kidnapped and imprisoned in the husband's home. The 'moderate correction' of wives through physical assault and domestic imprisonment was recognized in early English law as a civil power of husbands, and the correction of children as a natural power of fathers (Doggett, 1993). Although the doctrine of moderate correction was not intended to excuse severe assault and bodily harm, criminal prosecution was rare, and courts were lenient. One infamous English judge, lampooned in political cartoons of the day as 'Judge Thumb,' ruled that wife-beating was acceptable so long as the stick used did not exceed the thickness of a man's thumb. Wife-beaters were, however, subject to a variety of informal community controls such as the *charivari* – a serenade with pots and pans to expose the abuser to public shame. Only widowed women had control over their person and property. Legal, social, and economic barriers to escape were reflected in and compounded by the difficulties in obtaining divorce.

A series of reforms to Canadian divorce law from the nineteenth century onward culminated in the no-fault provisions of the federal Divorce Act of 1968. The power of moderate correction of wives was clearly gone from English law by the 1880s (Doggett, 1993), although it remains a justification for the assault of children in Canada's Criminal Code (see below). Intimate violence was taken up as a cause by the nineteenth-century women's suffrage movement and by family reformers of both genders in turn-of-the-century Canada (Chunn, 1992; Ursel, 1992). Vigorous campaigns took place in the last decades of the nineteenth century for the criminalization of wife-beating. Children's Aid Societies were formed, and new legislation granted the societies the power to apprehend beaten and neglected children. Sexual abuse and exploitation of children were addressed by new legislation amid public panic over the 'white slave trade' in which young women were supposedly kidnapped for prostitution. These discourses lost momentum in the early twentieth century, because of the extension of the vote to women, the recognition of women as legal persons and the professionalization of social work and its adoption of a family-oriented therapeutic approach that made women responsible for family health and morale. The world wars and the Depression created sympathy for men, who were not to be blamed if they took out some of their frustration on women and children (cf. Gordon, 1988, McGillivray, 1992). Wife-beating and sexual abuse of children faded from the public, agency, and criminal justice agendas. Sociology texts relegated wife-beating to occasional incidents among the lower classes, and sexual abuse of the young was almost exclusively a medical concern. When child abuse and wife-beating returned to the public agenda in the 1960s and 1970s, propelled by feminist consciousness-raising circles and the shared experiences of women, barriers to prosecution remained.

Subsection 4(3) of the Canada Evidence Act, RSC 1985, c. C-5 as amended, preserves the privilege in common law afforded to spouses. Spouses cannot be compelled to testify against each other, except in cases involving a variety of offences against children. This legal principle is a spin-off of *coverture* – if husband and wife are one and that one is the husband, then he is in effect testifying against himself, and no accused is required to take the stand. A common law exception in English civil law made a spouse a competent witness against a spouse whose acts endangered her life, liberty, or health. This was extended to criminal law in the English case *Hoskyn v. Metro Police Commissioner* of 1978. The dissenting judge would make a spouse compellable to testify, as well as competent. The Ontario Court of Appeal adopted the dissent in *R. v. Czipps* (1979), 12 SCR (3d) 193, and is followed by Canadian courts. The Canada Evidence Act was amended in 1982 to make a spouse a compellable witness in sexual assault where she is the victim, but not in physical assault, where *Czipps* is still followed. Women who refuse to testify or misrepresent the assault during testimony are subject to charges of perjury or contempt of court. They are not in fact charged, for reasons of judicial policy, as that would mean punishing the complainant by fine or jail while letting the alleged offender go free (McGillivray, 1987). Making women competent and compellable witnesses against a spouse in intimate violence cases has removed some of the last vestiges of *coverture* in the law.

Coverture was also reflected in pre-1982 immunity in Canada to charges of marital rape. The Criminal Code defined rape as the unconsented-to penile penetration of the vagina of a woman who is not the wife of the assailant, whether or not 'seed' is emitted. This was replaced in 1982 by gender-neutral, three-tiered provisions for sexual assault, found in sections 271, 272, and 273, which mirror the legal structure of physical assault. The requirement of penetration was dropped, and rules governing belief in consent and the meaning of consent were tightened (section 273). Men are no longer immune to charges of raping their wives.

The protection from sexual assault extended to children under earlier law centred on the protection of the chastity of young girls, with clear lines drawn around age and previously chaste character. The victim's consent was no defence. The laws were for this reason referred to as 'statutory rape.' Bill C-15 introduced a range of reforms into the Criminal Code, coming into force in 1988 (McGillivray, 1990). These included more subtle age-based provisions for consent, a gender-neutral tier of age-related offences (sexual interference, section 151; invitation to sexual touching, section 152; and sexual exploitation, section 153), and provision for a child victim of sexual assault to give evidence behind a screen or on closed-circuit television, shielding the child from the accused but rendering her visible to the court and the accused (subsection 486[2]). The child may give evidence-in-chief – the account of the events – by way of videotape made within a reasonable time after disclosure of the abuse (subsection 715[1]). However, the child must be present in court to testify that the videotaped account is true and to undergo cross-examination by the defence. Rules in the Canada Evidence Act and the common law governing children's testimony were also reformed, permitting child victims to testify on a promise of telling the truth rather than having to meet oath requirements based on Christian doctrine (section 16[1]).

While these reforms have an important place in the prosecution of intimate violence, section 43 of the Criminal Code preserves the power of moderate correction of children in a form substantively unchanged from early Roman and common law origins (McGillivray, 1993, 1997b). The section states: 'Correction of child by force – Every school teacher, parent or person standing in the place of a parent is justified in using force by way of correction toward a pupil or child, as the case may be, who is under his care, if the force does not exceed what is reasonable under the circumstances.' This poses central problems for child victims of physical violence. The presumption of corrective motive, the impossibility of defining excessive force, and conflicting social values have a chilling effect on complaint, charging, and prosecution. Physical assault against children continues to present more difficulty for the legal system than assault of wives, and prosecution remains rare unless the case involves severe injury or unusual modes of correction. Sex offences involving children are more readily viewed as wrongs by the public and the criminal justice system, but, despite the 1988 reform surrounding sexual assault of children (above) and stepped-up rates of reporting and prosecution (Clarke and Hepworth, 1994), child victims continue to suffer systemic prejudice. According to Winnipeg prosecutors and child protection workers, children under the age of ten or twelve rarely testify. Perceptions of the weaknesses of child witnesses – lying, fantasizing, mis-remembering, communication problems – and a desire to spare the child from testifying often result in major reductions to charge and sentence (McGillivray, 1990, 1998b). This situation in turn distorts the extent and severity of intimate violence against children.

The 1993 enactment of Criminal Code provisions for criminal harassment (section 264) provides another protection to victims of intimate violence. Behaviour that appears innocent may constitute criminal behaviour where a victim is followed, spied on, contacted against her will, and otherwise stalked or harassed. Such conduct often but not always involves a former partner. A discussion paper from the federal Department of Justice covering both stalking and corporal punishment of children was shelved and legislation on criminal harassment speedily enacted when two Winnipeg-area women were murdered early in 1993 by male stalkers. The men imagined a reciprocal romantic interest – a condition called erotomania (Manitoba Law Reform Commission, 1997) and achieved 'possession' of the women by killing them. Data collected by Statistics Canada (1996) show that one third of the 4,446 stalking incidents reported in 1995 involved a spouse or former spouse. The actual number of such cases is estimated at about 10,000 per year, suggesting that over 3,000 Canadian women are stalked by former partners each year.

Other charges laid in cases of intimate violence include culpable homicide – murder, manslaughter, and infanticide – all levels and degrees of physical assault (except the 'reasonable' assault of children), incest, uttering threats of death or serious bodily harm, threatening with or using a firearm or other weapon, break-and-enter, unlawful confinement, abduction, fraud, theft, arson, robbery, wilful damage, breaching the peace, and breaching a recognizance, protection, or probation order. While the Criminal Code is silent on some forms of intimate violence, many forms can be prosecuted under laws that have been available for centuries. Emotional abuse, for example, is reflected in a variety of criminal charges – uttering threats of death or serious bodily harm, threatening with a weapon, pointing a firearm, unlawful confinement, and, since 1993 in Canada, criminal harassment. But charges of any kind were rarely laid in domestic violence (McGillivray, 1988). The problem lay at the first level of engagement with the criminal process – with the police. Police refused to lay charges on the spot, and the complainant had to swear charges formally at the police station by noon the following day. Police perceived the victim's continued contact with the abuser as implying consent (below) and often experienced women's reluctance to carry charges forward, having them dropped the next day or 'forgetting' on the witness stand.

Whatever the variable legality of wife-beating under the common law, the greatest hurdle for women for centuries has not been law's edict but its enforcement. We should place Monture-Okanee's observation that

'Aboriginal women do not share with Canadian women the history of legally sanctioned violence against women' (1992) also must be seen in this shadowy context of enforcement. First Nations may have valued autonomy to the extent of not intervening in intra-adult male–female violence, but most Nations, if not all, did provide for open divorce by women. In English and Euro-colonial law, as in First Nations dispute resolution, dealing with intimate violence has been largely a matter of self-help and private regulation. This arrangement was to change with the introduction of vigorous policing and prosecution policies in the early 1980s.

'No-drop': Responding to Domestic Violence

The first wave of feminism in the second half of the nineteenth century placed intimate violence on the public agenda. In the second wave of feminism in the 1960s and 1970s, there was again an intensive campaign to recognize intimate violence as criminal behaviour. The feminist methodology of consciousness-raising led to the 'rediscovery' of wife-beating and sexual abuse of children. Feminist groups lobbied for change to correct historic inequities in criminal justice responses to assault of wives, including the practice of requiring women to lay charges themselves. All provinces adopted 'no-drop' charging and prosecution policies in the early 1980s (McGillivray, 1987).

Manitoba's 'no-drop' policies, instituted in 1983 by Attorney General Roland Penner, directed police officers to lay charges in all cases of domestic assault and the crown to prosecute all cases vigorously. Charging was no longer the complainant's responsibility, nor would charges be dropped at her behest. Wife assault continued to be trivialized and troubled by prevailing myths; victims' fears and ambivalence encouraged police in requiring victims to pursue complaints actively; and the repetitive nature of such assault lent the appearance of consent. If she doesn't like it, why doesn't she leave? (McGillivray, 1987). There was some legal truth behind this rather bizarre interpretation of consent. In the case of R. v. Jobidon [1991] 2 SCR involving a brief fist fight between two men, in which one died, the Supreme Court of Canada set policy-based limits to consent to assault. The court observed that genuine consent has traditionally been a defence to almost all forms of criminal activity. One can consent to sexual activity, for example, or to invasive surgery. 'Fisticuffs,' the court ruled, can never be consensual, as they serve no social good. The case law surveyed in Jobidon to some extent explains police response to recurrent domestic assaults as consensual fisticuffs.

Manitoba's Pedlar Report (Pedlar, 1991) confirmed that the 1983 policies had been unevenly applied. The report identified gaps in policing, prosecution, legal and paralegal services, judicial response, corrections, firearms regulation, medical response, economic support for women and education of personnel. Province-wide consultations disclosed the need to increase the availability and improve the enforcement of protection orders, central to victims' safety and protection. Without information backup and police and judicial enforcement, the order is literally just a piece of paper – law-as-legislation and not law-as-practice (Smart, 1989). A second need identified by the Pedlar Report is the routine use of 'victim impact' statements in sentencing (Pedlar, 1991). In 1986, trial projects on the use of these statements in sentencing took place in six Canadian cities, Winnipeg among them. Victims of a range of criminal offences were asked to submit impact statements, and the results were surveyed. Victims of offences involving intimate violence were not included. Although 81 per cent of participants supported the use of such impact statements, they are rarely if ever used in Manitoba courts. This began to change in the autumn of 1998, as a result of recommendations in the Lavoie Inquiry Report (Schulman, 1997, below). Such statements help bring before the court the victim's own perceptions of the injury done and assist judges where a plea bargain has vitiated the facts (cf. McGillivray, 1998b). In the absence of information to the contrary, courts often assume that a victim has not suffered damage even where the conduct is extreme. The Criminal Code has since 1985 provided for the admission of victim impact statements, and amendments in 1995 require the courts to consider statements 'describing the harm done to, or loss suffered by, the victim arising from the commission of the offence' in disposition and sentencing (section 722).

In September 1990, Manitoba's Family Violence Court began operation (Ursel, 1991). The court hears all cases at the provincial court level involving intimate violence from charge to sentence, the first domestic violence court in North America to do so. Sensitivity to the dynamics of intimate violence and coordination of victim services are goals of the court. Special prosecutors handle cases. The move to special senior prosecutors changed the professional culture of 'domestics' as lowly cases that would not enhance one's career (Ursel, 1998b). Prosecutors involved in these cases blamed ambivalent victims as obstacles to their winning cases. Designating cases of domestic violence as of high priority and using trained prosecutors changed the culture and diminished blaming of victims. Judges were to apply for permission to sit on the court but this requirement has since been dropped – all provincial court judges are rotated through the court, a move criticized in the report of the Lavoie Inquiry (Schulman, 1997). A primary goal of the new court was to ease the backlog of cases resulting from the stepped-up prosecution of spousal assault.

Prior to the 1982 changes in the law of sexual assault, offences against children under eighteen made up 43 per cent of cases reported to police in Winnipeg (Clarke and Hepworth, 1994: 121). The figure rose to 67 per cent after 1983. While the assailant is known to the child in the vast majority of cases, many do not qualify as 'family' for the purposes of the Family Violence Court. Sexual assault and sex offences against children are the most frequently charged offences involving young victims. Yet the court hears only a minority of child sexual assault cases. Sexual assault is a hybrid offence, which gives the crown the choice of proceeding summarily, for less serious acts, or by way of indictment. An indicted accused can and usually does choose trial in the non-specialized Court of Queen's Bench.

In 1993, the Winnipeg Police Service introduced detailed guidelines on family violence for cases involving spouses, children, and the elderly. The guidelines removed police discretion and transferred this to the crown, generating higher arrest rates (Ursel, 1998). A separate guideline was prepared on child assault and section 43 of the Criminal Code, the defence of 'reasonable correction of a child by force [assault].' The guidelines reflect the uncertainty of section 43 and made no appreciable difference in charging rates. Criticism of the response of Manitoba's justice system to violence against women continued. In 1995 alone, these included the COVAW Policy Statement, the Spousal Abuse Tracking Project Report, and the NDP Caucus Task Force Report on Violence against Women. In 1996, the minister responsible for the status of women instituted a 'protected names' procedure to prevent those under judicial non-contact orders from tracking victims through the land titles computer database, and databases for protective orders have been established. These measures have not plugged gaps in the system. Perhaps the most serious remain at the level of prosecution and case overload. When 'no-drop' policies were introduced in 1983, 629 spousal assault arrests were made (Ursel, 1998b). By 1989, the number had risen to 1,137. In 1990–1, the first year of operation of the Family Violence Court, 1,444 charges were laid. In 1993–4, when all charging discretion was shifted from police to prosecutors, 3,387 charges were laid. In 1994, for example, the crown failed to subpoena a Winnipeg woman as witness, with the result that all charges against her husband were dismissed and his harassment of her continues (*Winnipeg Free Press*, 29 May 1994). Rhonda Lavoie was abducted and murdered in 1995 by her estranged husband, who committed suicide. He had previously staged to the last detail the manner of her death – abduction and carbon monoxide poisoning in the family car. Police had missed or misread the import of this and other significant elements of her abuse, and failed to intervene effectively. Lavoie was granted bail on charges resulting from this first abduction because of incomplete information about the seriousness of the assaults and their pattern of escalation.

The Lavoie murder-suicide precipitated an inquiry begun in 1996 to review failures in police, prosecutorial, and judicial response to the victim's complaints of violence and harassment (Schulman, 1997). A police officer testifying at the inquiry referred to 'modest shortcomings' in Winnipeg police response to cases of domestic violence – failure to follow police protocol, 'bargaining out' charges of criminal harassment, incomplete information in police computers, insufficient specialized policing, inadequate follow-up, and failure to flag cases in which the offender has a history of intimate abuse (*Winnipeg Free Press*, 7 March 1996).

Aboriginal Women in the Justice System

Criminal justice reform over the past two decades to improve the justice system's response to intimate violence is in effect a movement towards criminalization. In discourses on First Nations self-government, the direction is the other way – bypassing the criminal justice system in favour of local policing, circle sentencing, diversion, and ultimately a separate justice system. Aboriginal women subjected to intimate violence are caught between competing discourses. Such reports as *Battered But Not Beaten* (McLeod, 1987), *Changing the Landscape* (Canadian Panel, 1993), and the documents from the Aboriginal Justice Inquiry (Manitoba, 1991) suggest that Aboriginal women reject the Anglo-Canadian justice system and favour mediation and alternative measures. Women in this study responded differently.

Enforcement of the provincial 'zero tolerance' policy is all but nonexistent on Manitoba reserves (NDP Manitoba, 1995). An officer on one reserve locked the office door and refused to open it; a child was passed through the window to call for his help in a domestic violence episode (*Winnipeg Free Press*, 17 Dec., 1995). On another Manitoba reserve, the trick was to throw a rock through the police station window to get help in domestic assaults. On yet another reserve, according to a resident, a known abuser was appointed band constable by chief and council to ensure that he avoided charges of domestic assault. In a 1995 case in a northern Manitoba town, the court acquitted a man charged with assaulting his wife and daughter. Sick of her mother's years of abuse, the daughter had intervened in an assault, was injured, and pressed charges. On the witness stand her mother denied the assault. The daughter's testimony on both assaults was disregarded. The court stated that it would not stand in the way of the father's appointment as band constable.

In the second interview given to participants in this study, attention focused on respondents' experiences with the criminal justice system. We asked women about their impressions of the purpose of the justice system, their experiences of calling the police and police responses, the enforcement of protection orders, the prosecution of abusers, going to court, legal services, and sentencing. We then asked them for their views on diversion and alternative measures. The interview began with an open-ended question:

Q: First of all, I would like to ask you about your experiences with the justice system – who you talked to, who helped you, how you feel about that experience. First, I would like you to tell me what you think the justice system is for.

Of the twenty-five women who participated in the second interview, fourteen saw the purpose of the justice system as protecting victims:

To help – supposed to help – people who have been victimized.

To keep you safe.

To maintain the safety of the majority of people.

For protection.

To protect people, to protect your rights.

Five saw the purpose as punishment.

To have offenders put away.

To pay them back.

To pay for their crimes through jail, community service, or to be accountable for their actions, to bring justice to people who need it.

Putting drunks in jail and helping other people.

The emphasis on the protective function of the justice system was consistent throughout. Even so, some saw the system as unfair, favouring the rights of the accused over those of the victim, or were cynical about whether the justice system in fact protects victims.

I feel that the justice system is more geared to protecting the accused, not the victim.

I didn't really like the justice system, it wasn't fair. I didn't think it was fair. My ex-husband got away with a lot of things.

What I've seen or experienced myself, it's sure in hell not for the victim. It's for the abuser or criminal ... As far as I'm concerned, I haven't seen any justice.

It just seems when you have no money you have no rights.

Recent studies have identified a history of abuse in female offenders and in Aboriginal female offenders in particular (Shaw, 1990; Comack, 1996). Ellen Adelburg writes, 'Aboriginal women who end up in prison grew up in prison, though the prisons they grew up in are not the ones to which they are sentenced under law ... All too often we are the victims of long-term and systemic violence' (Adelburg, 1993). Fourteen of twenty-six respondents had been charged with at least one offence. Four respondents were charged as juveniles with minor offences such as shoplifting and vagrancy. As adults, four were charged with common assault (one received a conditional discharge), and three with theft. One was charged with assault causing bodily harm (acquitted), one with robbery (convicted), one with child neglect (convicted, two years' probation), and one with manslaughter (convicted, seven months). Other convictions included public mischief, destruction of property (driving over a tree), breaching a court order, impaired driving, driving without a licence, vandalism, and forgery. The fact that they had experienced the criminal justice process from both sides – as accused and as complainants against abusive partners – lends further weight to their observations of the system, its purpose, and its functioning. They had the most to say about policing.

Calling the Police

Respondents' involvement with the justice system ranged from calling the police, with no further contact, to testifying at trial. The experiences of women at all levels of the justice process, including occasions when they did *not* contact the police, provide us with valuable insights. At some point in their lives, all respondents contacted police, but there were also many times when they did not. Although they spoke of *deciding* not to call the police, they were in many instances prevented from calling. *There was only me and him, and I couldn't get out of the house.* Almost all respondents reported that a neighbour, friend, or relative had contacted police without her knowledge at least once. The most frequent reason for calling police was *fear* for her safety and that of her children and, for one respondent, fear that she would kill her partner.

I was really afraid that he would get really out of hand, worse than the last time.

The reasons I contacted the police was because he was abusing me, he was hitting me, accusing me. And he was scaring the girls.

I wanted him to pay for hurting me.

I wanted him out of my home.

What made me call the police was my fear, my fear of losing it, and I had it in me sometimes to physically harm him or kill him. I also feared for my life because he did threaten to kill me.

Some called the police frequently but became discouraged by the response.

I was calling so often, my common law and his family were beginning to call me '911' just to make fun of me.

I've always called the police. As a matter of fact, one time when I called the police, the staff sergeant was upset with me. He says, 'I'm getting pretty upset with you, you're always phoning, calling here, you're getting to be a bloody nuisance ... I should charge you for harassing, phoning here all the time.'

Because they always seemed like they were getting disgusted with you, because it is repeated over and over again, being abused and then charge him, and then it would happen again, being abused and then I would charge him. Pretty soon it seemed like even the police or whoever got tired of it and didn't take it seriously any more.

There was a lot of times I did not call them because I thought it was no use to call them ... There was always the way they were playing. One policeman would talk to me really nice, and the other policeman would talk to my partner really nice, then they would switch over ...

Sometimes they took my partner away, and they dropped him off at his favourite bar more often than not ... It got to the point where he was calling [the police] his taxi, because a number of times he was dropped off at the bar during or after one of our disputes.

I called the police quite a few times. I'd say about ten times in total in the four years I was with this person. That's including the times when I would call them and they wouldn't show up because they probably looked on their computer and said 'Oh, it's her again' [and] there were times he would make me phone them back and say we didn't need them to come.

Some gave up. *You know, I really felt like, what's the use? They never did anything. [My ex-partner] knows how to talk his way out of anything, so what was the use?*

Fear was also the reason many women did not contact the police – fear of accelerating the violence, that children would be taken away unless it was obvious who was the dangerous parent, that a partner would go to jail, of being alone.

I was terrified that he might be worse than before.

He threatened me a lot of times. He told me that the cops were his friends, and he would easily get information from the cops where I was and where I would be.

Most of the time, I didn't want to call the police because I was scared of what this person was capable of, because of his threats to kill or his threats to commit suicide right in front of me and the kids.

One thing was fear of the person, mostly fear of the person.

I was scared the police would get CFS involved. [I called] when he really did actually break bones ... because I knew for sure the police would charge him and take him away. It was like I was always sitting on a fence. I didn't know if I should or shouldn't.

I didn't want the police there. I was most scared they would take my kids away.

I guess – more or less protecting him from the charges of drugs, possession of narcotics.

I didn't want him to go to jail.

Also the threat of him telling me he was going to leave me ... I didn't want to be alone.

Fear of police response, of how police might react to her as a victim, was a strong deterrent.

[A] lot of times I feel, like, ashamed and I always feel guilty and embarrassed.

I just didn't want nobody to get involved ... I was embarrassed.

I guess because I felt that if I wasn't hit enough or something and the police may get mad if they don't see marks on me and stuff.

The criminal justice system is the primary recourse of victims of violence, but 'all too frequently victims have been exposed to risks of further violence as a result of their efforts to obtain protection from the justice system' (Busch and Robertson, 1994). This risk came not only from the abusive partner but also from police inaction, prejudice, racism, and victim-blaming.

Respondents were asked what they hoped or expected would happen when the police arrived. Many answered *charge him*, but the most common response was *I was really hoping that they would take him away.* Once initial contact was made with the police, there was a wide discrepancy between the expected response and what actually took place. Some women reported that the police arrived soon after the call had been made. Others had a longer wait:

They didn't come right away. I waited all night for them. Morning came, I was really tired ...

They came very late. You don't know what could happen in the meantime while they were coming.

Sometimes it would take them an hour to get there, more than an hour. That's why I never feel like – sometimes I didn't feel like – phoning them, because it takes them a long time ... That time he assaulted me ... the caretaker phoned ... It took them two hours to get there. [My partner asked the police] 'Who called you?' ... He says, 'You had the call two hours ago.' And I guess he was saying to them something like 'How come it took you guys so long? ... I could've killed her already by the time you guys got here.'

This last incident triggered the respondent's decision to leave. According to Manitoba policy, it was her partner who should have been removed.

Police response in remote areas was less than adequate compared to that in urban centres. Policing services for reserves are provided by contract. Some reserves lack a consistent police presence. Difficulties may be compounded for women on reserves where a band maintains its own police force and on small reserves, where everyone knows everyone's business and takes sides. Children are particularly vulnerable to the public shaming that may result.

I never bothered to charge him because I thought he'd be taken care of in one way or another. It had a lot to do with my kids, especially my oldest one, because she has to live in the community and it's such a small place. I guess that's why I never bothered, because I thought of her feelings. In court there, everyone else listens, the whole community.

It wasn't until an hour later they got dispatched from Winnipeg or something. I don't even know where. I was so upset, crying on the phone, and they say, 'What would you like us to do?' I says, 'I want him removed from the premises.' And they said, 'Who lives there beside you?' I said, 'His whole friggin family.' And they said there's nothing they could do. I was disappointed in that one.

[The band constables] took me to the nursing station. They made me stay there for a while. My head had bumps all over it, and my forehead too. My chin was bruised. And they asked me to press charges, those Native cops. And I said, 'no,' and told them I didn't want any trouble – kind of scary and I don't want him to go to jail ... Maybe if the RCMP was there – you know how it is on the reserve ... Chief and councillors are helping him because he works for them.

In this case, the band constable contacted the RCMP, and charges were laid. Despite a longstanding history of abuse, and severe injuries inflicted on the respondent in the presence of her young children, this offender received only a three-month sentence. He was still stalking the respondent at the time of the study.

Where respondents were involved in abusive relationships on the reserve, the victim rather than the abuser faced community disapproval and the possibility of permanent banishment from the reserve. In order to save themselves, some had to leave the community without one or all of their children.

The bottom line is, they don't understand how you can leave your kids with someone like that if he is abusive. So many moms have had to leave their families ... Yet the cops and law, whatever, they don't – I don't know what the difference is, living in the city or a community.

How can you leave with your kids when you're not allowed to, you know?

I first called the RCMP and they said, 'Go to [an Aboriginal child protection agency].' ... I went over and talked to them, the RCMP, and I told them, 'Can you help me? I need help, I need my kids. I'm trying to take my kid. Because if I go over there, my ex will be there and he won't ever let them go.' ... They said, 'We can't help you,' and I said, 'Why?' 'Because we're not on anybody's side.' They couldn't do anything. Then I called the [band] cops again, and they couldn't do anything too. I guess they're scared of the chief ... But the RCMP, they couldn't really do anything in that reserve [and they were told by chief and council], 'You have to tell us first if you want to come to our reserve.'

This respondent had to sneak to the airstrip to catch a flight arranged by a Winnipeg shelter and leave two of her children with her abusive partner, an employee of the band council. His relatives assaulted her when she tried to take the children from the reserve school. Police response in this case suggests that a side was in fact taken. Both parents have lawful custody of the child unless a court rules otherwise. Without such an order, no parent can deprive the other of custody. However, the Criminal Code since 1993 has protected a parent with lawful custody who takes, entices away, conceals, detains, receives, or harbours a child; he or she is not guilty of criminal abduction if such action 'was necessary to protect the young person from danger of imminent harm *or if the person charged with the offence was escaping from imminent harm*' (section 285, emphasis added). Policing in any event includes helping parents and agency workers to ensure children's safety, stop the violence, and obtain a judicial determination of custody. This respondent's lawyer later helped her obtain orders for sole custody and non-molestation and arranged for the RCMP to help get her two remaining children from the reserve.

Respondents characterized police responding to domestic calls variously as *too young, naïve, prejudiced,* and *macho,* and they reported racist responses. One did not contact police to report a rape because she feared being blamed for drinking and being Native. Police assumed that another respondent was a prostitute because her partner was Black. A third was told that she deserved the abuse – the police officer would do the same.

I thought the police wouldn't – like, I feel when you're drinking and especially when you're Native – they don't, I don't know, they don't really want to get involved with you. Like it's your fault. Like, I felt it was my fault, like I shouldn't have been drinking with him. So I didn't do nothing about it.

I was starting to not want to call them, because, I don't know, they made me feel like somehow it's my fault. Like, when I phoned the cops on my last boyfriend, they thought I was working for him [as a prostitute], maybe because he's Black. It's just like they're stereotyping. It's kind of sad.

There were a lot of times when I did call ... I don't think they believed me. Or else they would take one look at me and say – well, I got a lot of smart comments from them like – 'You probably deserved it, look how drunk you are.' 'If I had an old lady like you that was as mouthy, I would slap her around, too.' You know.

Some time after the new year [1995] I phoned the police, but the police didn't even press charges. They just took one look at me, you know, I was hysterical.

I went to the [Winnipeg] division, spoke to the sergeant there. Then he looked at me. I can feel prejudices. And he recommended that I go back to the apartment and wait for the officers to arrive at the location. I said, 'You're telling me to go back there when you know for a fact that I am in danger?'

This respondent was herself charged while attempting to lay charges against the abuser and was held in a cell in the Public Safety Building. Although she had been cooperative, police refused to let her have her epilepsy medication and she suffered a *grand mal* seizure. A police officer assumed that she was drunk.

Protection Orders

Courts issue protection orders under a variety of statutory provisions. Orders serve two central functions of justice – to bind the abuser to abstain from conduct specified in the order and to alert police to the danger that such a person may represent. Police bear primary responsibility for enforcement; but the burden of complaint is on the victim. Twelve respondents were being threatened or harassed by partners or former partners at the time of the study. All but four respondents had taken out a variety of protection orders or knew of no-contact orders issued by the courts as conditions of recognizance, bail, or probation. Applying for a protection order was as fraught with ambiguity for some respondents as calling police or insisting on charges:

I have applied for a restraining order about three times. And the first two times I cancelled because of the threats. At the same time, I was scared to lose him.

I didn't want the restraining order in the first place, but I was forced into it.

Twenty-four of twenty-six respondents had been stalked, threatened, and harassed after leaving an abusive partner. Protection orders did not protect them. An order was just a piece of paper that you had to show police or they would not believe you.

A restraining order is just like a piece of paper. You just grab it and throw it away.

That paper I signed – that non-molestation order, I keep it in my purse in case I bump into him in Winnipeg.

You have to have this restraining order with you twenty-four hours a day for it to work. I did not know that. They can easily be torn up. Your partner can just take it, grab it, and rip it, and it's your word against theirs.

With him, he used to say 'It's nothing but a piece of paper.'

He kind of took the paper and ripped it up.

It is really hard to use a non-molestation order or even a restraining order. Even though I know I have the law backing me up, it is still me that has to do the calling and deciding, and none of my partners have respected or obeyed these restraining orders.

I've got a restraining order right now against somebody here in Manitoba. I called 911 because he was smashing out my car window. And that was about two weeks ago. I still have not talked to the police on that 911 call ... They're just lucky I was not hurt because I would have charged them. I would have charged the police for non-response.

He was in my home when I called them, and now they were giving me heck for having allowed him in the house. So I just told them it was not for them to judge whether or not he was in my house or not, that it was their job to charge him for being there ... I don't know what happened with that. I haven't heard from them since. They said they were going to charge him for breaching the non-molestation order and that they would let me know when they caught him or arrested him. But I have not heard anything since that time.

Abusers knew how to circumvent the orders.

He came to my home, yes, to my home, but he stayed in the vehicle, so he couldn't breach his order as he didn't have any contact with me ... It was just like he was taunting me. And because he used to be a police officer himself, he knew the ins and outs of the system

He calls me up, even last weekend ... Then he gives his girlfriend the phone, she said. 'I'm going to get you, you're going to get it. See you in Winnipeg.' I keep on hanging up, and they keep on phoning, and then my auntie over there, the one that's in the wheelchair, she answered the phone again.

An abuser does not have to be a police officer to gain expertise in manipulating the system. Breaches of protection orders were commonplace.

Got a non-molestation order against him. He violated the order seven times. And I'm still waiting for my restraining order to come through.

Second restraining order I received, he wouldn't abide by it. He was still phoning me, harassing me, leaving threatening messages on the ... answering machine.

Abusers ignore or circumvent orders. Enforcement is lax. Where police lay charges for breaching a protection order, the penalty is usually subsumed into the penalty for the original charge, rendering prosecution for breach meaningless. *[In the last two months], he has breached the order seven times. The first four times he breached, the officer – one of the officers – gave me a phone call, informing me that the crown prosecutor would not proceed in this matter. I was very upset. Then the officer that did file me [took the complaint]* said, 'Our hands are tied. It's up to the crown.' ... The crown prosecutor should have followed through. Where prosecution goes forward, the result is often a meaningless penalty combined with inadequate penalties for the substantive charges. This is a major source of frustration for women who have worked their way through levels of increasing pain, fear, threats, manipulation, and the endless decisions to be made about the private and public regulation of their lives.

The Manitoba Prohibition Information Registry (PINS), maintained at the Provincial Court, was established in 1994. It records all protection and prohibition orders – peace bonds, restraining orders, orders of recognizance, probation orders, and non-molestation orders – issued by the Provincial Court and the Court of Queen's Bench. The database is accessible to Winnipeg police through the Canadian Police Information Centre (CPIC) computer system, which records convictions across Canada. As other police forces including the RCMP and band police obtain PINS information only through the Winnipeg Police Service, enforcement remains precarious for women in isolated communities. The Winnipeg Police Service companion database (PARCS) provides information on convictions in Manitoba. Neither database indicates whether charges are for domestic violence, and police must search both PINS and CPIC. Non-molestation orders under the Family Maintenance Act are not recorded on CPIC, the most accessible province-wide database. The report of the Lavoie Inquiry (Schulman, 1997) recommends flagging domestic violence-related offences and interfacing PINS with CPIC to track offenders and keep victims informed. The report also recommends that *ex parte* no-contact orders (orders granted without a hearing from the other side) be recorded on CPIC, to ensure that breaches can be prosecuted more effectively. With the advent of PINS computer access, protection orders will no longer be *just a piece of paper*.

Laying Charges, Dropping Charges, and Counter-Charging

Despite mandatory charging, charges were not laid in very recent cases. One respondent insisted that charges be laid for uttering death threats. Police refused. *Yeah, I was living in Winnipeg. I don't know why they didn't charge. When I think back, it's because mental abuse wasn't quite common, because they never saw me cut up, or anything marked on my body. Maybe they thought we were just arguing.* Where police applied the stepped-up mandatory charging policy, a frequent response of the women in this study was relief, both because charges were laid and because responsibility was deflected from the victim to the system itself. This shift dispelled some – but not all – of her fear of reprisal by the abuser for her engagement of the justice system.

When the police finally came forward and said they were – that they were going to charge him – I felt really relieved. Because a lot of the times when I did phone and they did come to my place, I always backed out of it ... I understood that the police were firm in their decision that they wouldn't drop the charges.

I feel that, yes, it's good to protect us again. You see, if they had this policy when this was happening to me, I would have charged him. I wouldn't have been afraid.

It wasn't very long after they had left my house, after they took all the information from me, that I phoned them back at the station, and asked them if I could drop the charges. They said, 'Well, we are sorry, we are going to proceed with the charges regardless of whether you want to or not.'

At that point I can't really remember whether I was feeling relieved or whether I was scared for my safety.

The importance of police presence and the laying of charges was clear for two respondents who reported that the abuse stopped as a result. *[He] ceased to [physically] abuse me altogether. He would raise his hand to me once in a while, but he never followed through with the body contact ... I think he knew that I would phone the police should he ever touch me again.* One respondent saw mandatory charging as a tool used by women to gain power in the relationship. *I think a lot of women use it just to scare their men, to have a little bit more control, power over them. I think it's just a using tool.* She is right, and this is surely the point. If women dangle the threat of criminal charges even if they are not in direct danger, then the policies are working as everyday prevention – the ideal use of such law. The essence of policing and prosecution, and of reforms to law, policy, and practice, is to equalize power where violence has created inequality and denied power and autonomy. Where women are prevented from leaving an abusive relationship, or have chosen for the time being not to leave, police protection and the threat of prosecution and exposure offer some protection.

The complexity of intimate violence was played out in a Winnipeg pilot project in 1993 that offered complainants an opportunity to petition the Winnipeg Family Violence Court to drop charges. Requests were heard at a special weekly sitting of the court. Although the overt intention was to empower women and respect victims' choices in the complex circumstances of intimate violence, it was expected that lawyers would advise their clients to plead guilty where complainants were ready and willing to proceed to trial. The goal was to increase the number of guilty pleas and decrease the court's caseload. However constituted, easy charge-dropping is dangerous to women (COVAW, 1995). Guilty pleas did not increase in number, and the project was dropped.

Jane Ursel describes 'testimony bargaining' as 'the most original and creative strategy' adopted by the Manitoba crown in recognizing victims' sensitivity (1998b: 77). A victim-witness who is reluctant to testify because she cannot afford the income lost if her abuser goes to jail is given choices by the crown prosecutor, based on her desired outcome. If she states that she does not want her husband to go to jail, but just wants an end to the violence, then the prosecutor will offer to drop charges leading to a jail term and recommend probation with treatment, in order to secure her testimony. 'If she agrees, the Crown notifies the defence that the witness will testify and, most often, the case is resolved through a guilty plea' (78). Ursel argues that, while conviction rates in the Winnipeg Family Violence Court may be lower, crown prosecutors do not view stays of proceedings resulting from victims' refusal to testify as a failure of 'zero tolerance' policy. Ursel sees 'testimony bargaining' as part of a longer-term lesson to the complainant, who will come to view the system as taking her complaint seriously because it has respected her wishes in the case at bar.

Despite the stepping-up and gap-filling of Manitoba policy in the five years preceding this study, six women reported that charges were dropped or stayed against partners. This statistic compares favourably with the reports of twenty-two respondents of charges being laid against at least one partner but falls considerably short of 'zero tolerance.' Four respondents told a crown attorney or Women's Advocacy worker that they would not testify. Charges were stayed as a result. Two were forced or cajoled by the abusers into dropping charges.

The following response illustrates the layered complexity of prosecution of intimate violence because of the abuser's power over the victim and the victim's ability to defeat prosecution policy:

Q: If there were charges, were they ever dropped?

A: *Yes, he always got around them somehow. With my help.*

Q: Can you tell me more about that?

A: *It's just a really sick cycle. I'd charge him, I'd leave him, he would ask me to come back to him. Then we would have to figure out a way to get these charges dropped so he wouldn't have to go to jail ... I would call the prosecutor and tell him that there was no way he was going to get me to testify against him. I had to go through the Women's Advocacy Program, and I had to talk to a woman there, and they had to tell the crown what I said. And what I said was that he was very apologetic and ... that was the very first time he had touched me ... Not enough evidence. And my partner made me drop them, too.*

One spoke of the long-term consequences of dropping charges: *I feel, obviously, all of this not charging him is not helping. I feel it is my duty for myself, for my kids, and his next possible girlfriend, that he understands that his behaviour is wrong and he has to pay for it.*

An unintended consequence of the 'zero tolerance' policy of 1990 was a steep increase in charges laid against *complainants* – in almost every case the female partners of male assailants. Police responding to a domestic violence call might be told, 'He punched me and threw me into the wall' and 'She slapped me.' If 'zero tolerance' is taken literally, both parties must be charged, despite extreme differences in the violence alleged. Counter-charges laid against four women in this study were all dropped.

I was charged under the zero-tolerance policy. My ex-husband counter-charged me ... [Charges] were dropped because I had a witness that was there at the time and denied I ever hit him.

I was very fortunate. There was a witness to verify that I had not hit my husband like he claimed. I think about the situation as being unfair because how many other women are being charged under the no-drop policy that have no witness to verify that they had not [hit him] and as a result they are being charged?

You both get charged even if you're defending yourself, apparently. It's not fair if you're defending yourself.

In the view of the last respondent, counter-charging discourages women from calling police. Another respondent jailed as a result of a counter-charge was afraid to involve police again. *I'm kind of scared to phone them any more. I'm scared to get thrown in jail again.*

Where cases involving counter-charges have gone to the Family Violence Court, the result might be the staying of charges against both complainants. Assault charges laid against complainants proved to be based on false accusations (as in the case of the respondents quoted above), a trivial act by the complainant (a retaliatory push or slap, smashing a plate), or a legitimate act of self-defence. The attorney general issued a 'counter-accusation charging directive' in 1994. The directive applies in cases in which a victim is alleged to have precipitated the violence or retaliated for the purpose of defence and self-protection. Police are now permitted to distinguish between serious and frivolous charges in making arrests and must seek Crown opinion before proceeding with counter-charges against a victim. This has alleviated the problem.

Going to Court

Respondents were asked about the courtroom experience and their legal representation – experience with family courts and civil lawyers; with criminal courts, prosecutors, and defence counsel; and with such advocacy services as the Manitoba Women's Advocacy Program. We asked general questions about the criminal process. A major concern of respondents was delay in processing cases, a concern reflected in the report of the Lavoie Inquiry (Schulman, 1997). Delay gives abusers a wide window of opportunity to manipulate complainants into dropping charges or 'forgetting' the abuse. It reinforces the abuser's belief in the 'rightness' of his conduct. It contributes to the victim's risk, fear, and ambiguity:

It takes too long for situations of abuse. I think eventually the woman loses sight of why she brought her old man to court ... He would sweet talk to me ... ask me, 'Would you drop the charges?' ... He had his chance to work on me.

They seem to be dragging it out for too long. That happened in October, and ... he appears in court [in July]. That's too long, I think.

I would just like to get, if they go to court, just get it over with instead of remanding each month, because they remand every two weeks ... because this is holding up your life too, if you don't know what's going to happen.

Expedite it, even faster. It's slow.

A lot more faster, and quicker to deal with these problems so they don't get backlogged.

The physical setting of the courtroom conveys messages about hierarchy. One respondent expected the courtroom to be set up like a sentencing circle or, at least, in a less hierarchical and adversarial way: *physically how it is set up – the way the judge sits higher up than anyone else and people are sitting on opposite sides of the room – it's just set up like a battle zone. I guess I was thinking in terms of a circle with everybody sitting around one table all together.*

Having come this far in the prosecution of their violent partners, respondents still felt torn and blameworthy. The courtroom experience was confusing, frightening, *traumatizing* in its exposure of personal problems, *alienating* in its impersonality. Respondents worried about how they would perform on the witness stand. One woman did not know that she would be called to testify. Another was surprised that she had not been called as witness, where a guilty plea was entered.

It was hard to be a witness, hard to be a witness against someone that you live with. Because you are so used to being blamed for everything, that you can sit in court knowing it is not your fault [but] you still feel like it is.

I find the court process is very, it is quite traumatizing, because it is hard to talk about your personal things in front of how many people are there ... I felt really, when I was going to court with regards to charging my ex-husband, I felt very alienated and just, like, I felt I was in the way. I felt I was just another number, another page.

I was afraid to [testify], to be in a court of law. Intimidated by that whole process, cross-examination. I'm scared of being confused at cross-examination.

I feel that I am being victimized again, victimized by the system. From past experience, you have to tell your story to the police and then once again if the individual pleads not guilty. Then he has to go to a preliminary hearing, and then next is the final trial. I feel that I'm continually being victimized. And you get emotionally drained out.

I felt scared because I didn't think I had to go to court ... I figured he was the only one who had to go to court. I didn't have to go, and my best friend didn't have to go. But we got subpoenaed to go to court, so we went. If my friend and I didn't show up, the charges would have been dropped.

The last case involving us, he pleaded guilty. And I can't understand that ... I didn't have to show up in court. I was subpoenaed but didn't even have to show up in court. And I was kind of relieved.

We asked, 'Would you like to see the victim have a "say" in sentencing?' All but two responded that they would – it would give them a greater sense of control and ensure a more appropriate sentence:

I would love to see the judges listen to the victims and really understand where the victim is coming from, to the point where they ask the victim what they feel would be a fair sentence, and take that into consideration before they do sentence a person ... Right now, the abuser is getting away with a slap on the wrist, and the victim is right back where they started from, even if they have left the person.

Yes, I think so, for instance, I would like to be in a meeting with somebody from the court alongside with my partner in the same room. Usually they don't do this. Then I could express my view or what I think should be done to him.

[I would be] providing them with a woman's point of view of being abused.

I would like to see only one change – that the time when my partner got charged – that I would appear in court so they could hear my side of the story, my version. But instead he just pleaded guilty and he got a sentence, and I wasn't there to see this.

That's about all I'd like to do, is just tell them, sentence them to a treatment program, or some program after that. But at the same time, if I'm charging him for assaulting me, I'm going to be very angry. And when I go to court, I might just say, 'Throw him in jail and forget about him.'

One respondent echoed the Pedlar Report (Pedlar, 1991) in recommending routine use of victim-impact statements in cases of intimate violence. Despite Manitoba's reluctance to use such statements, the Criminal Code now requires that the statements, if made, be submitted to the court.

'Going to court' centrally involves legal representation. Respondents had experience with crown counsel in the prosecution of partners, with defence lawyers where respondents had faced criminal charges, and with civil lawyers in divorce and child-custody determinations. Some found their lawyers helpful:

The lawyer that I have, I've known him on a personal level. He guided me through the whole process, and I feel confident with him because he specializes in abuse cases.

Well, my lawyer [in family court] is a woman ... She helped me a lot, like my good friend.

She helped me with my phone bill, and my non-molestation order, and I won child custody. But back on the reserve it's hard to get my kids.

One respondent's lawyer was able to intervene with the RCMP and arrange for her children to be returned to her from the reserve. However, the majority of respondents found their lawyers to be unaware of the dynamics of intimate violence. Some were rude or dismissive. One family lawyer breached the Law Society's Code of Professional Conduct in his failure to call key witnesses at a custody hearing.

Right away the lawyer will say, 'How many times did you get a beating?' When you say, 'I didn't,' they kind of look at you – like, what are you doing here? They don't realize the emotional or mental [abuse] is just as bad. Or being held in your bedroom for many hours ...

My lawyer [in family court] said he was surprised they allowed [my child] to live with me. Like, well, what kind of comfort is that from a lawyer, I'm thinking, you know? The first one was even worse, he didn't do shit for me.

Sometimes, from my own knowledge, the crown are not trained properly to defend the victims. This is what I felt, anyway, at that particular time when I went to court. I was looking at the crown to jump forward and say something to the defence counsel when he was tormenting me.

The only lawyer I ever found helpful was the [defence] lawyer that I had when I was getting charged with assault ... I find the other lawyers too impersonal, uncaring.

It just seems like, if you can afford a good lawyer, then you're going to get different results.

I feel that the crown should meet with the victims long before the trial, to actually get all the information, rather than meeting with them five or ten minutes just before the hearing. This is not acceptable at all. They are not using their professional ethics.

I wish that more lawyers would have a better understanding and compassion for the victims. Most victims, it's hard enough to talk about different things – abuse, especially sexual abuse – without having a lawyer that figures, 'Yeah, right' or trying to say 'What did you do to deserve it?' That's bullshit. If I ever had a lawyer telling me that, I'd tell him where to go, no hesitation at all. Lawyers are supposed to be there to help you, not to make you feel worse [about] the situation that you're trying to get out of for your own protection.

This last time I had a lawyer, I don't think he was working for me on my behalf. I believe he took my ex-husband's side, because my ex-husband wrote a letter stating that I was an unfit mother and I was very abusive. So my lawyer went and turned around and had me investigated because of what my ex-husband had stated. He had told me on several occasions that my ex-husband was innocent until proven guilty. My lawyer could have stopped the custody battle, and he could have stopped the visitation rights. I had talked to those two police who are taking care of this case, and they told me that my lawyer could have easily put them on the stand – and that social worker that my daughter disclosed to – to prove that he was being investigated because of the sexual abuse. I told the lawyer what the police had told me. And he didn't do that.

We asked respondents about support services used in the criminal process – translation services, social workers, Native court workers, and Women's Advocacy counsellors. None reported the availability of translators or Native court workers. One was assisted by a social worker from Winnipeg CFS. Respondents had the most to say about the Women's Advocacy Program of Manitoba's Department of Justice, established in 1986, which offers short-term counselling, victim-witness support, and referrals to other programs. Some were helped by the program.

They were very helpful, ... telling me what's going to happen to me and explaining it ... They helped me a lot.

They stood by me when I was going to court, to trials.

They're more supportive and understand, like, the fear of being in a courtroom.

Well, she was with me most of the time when I went to court, and they were preparing me for court because he was going to plead not guilty. They were very helpful.

The Women's Advocacy Program convinced one respondent to testify against her partner. Other respondents did not find the program helpful.

Not really. Their workload was too – there is too much workload ... I didn't get any assistance from them. My lawyer and the women at the shelter had already explained [the court process] to me. And they said they would be at the court date with me, but they never showed.

To some degree, some. I feel that the Women's Advocacy group is just a babysitting ser-

vice, you know. Once a woman goes through the courtroom, that's it. There's no long-term follow-up.

I didn't know who to see, who to talk to. When I tried to get help, they referred me to somebody else, and that person wasn't there for me, to explain what was going on. ... It is frustrating not knowing what is going on. I felt that there was no support while I was in court.

Respondents criticized 'zero tolerance' for doing too much, as in counter-charging, and for not doing enough, in its lack of clarity and uneven enforcement. Enforcement is particularly weak in Aboriginal communities (COVAW, 1995; Family Violence Professional Education Task Force, 1995; McIvor, n.d.). Such policies recognize that victims are under enormous pressure to recant, discount the injury suffered, or lie about its origins. The pressure comes from abusers, from psychological, cultural, economic, and family constraints, and, for many women in this study, from chiefs and band councils.

There can be no true 'zero' tolerance. No system, certainly not criminal justice, can be run without discretion. The policy is intended to balance power relations between victim and abuser by giving support to victims, deflecting blame on victims for invoking the criminal law's response onto police and prosecutors ('We have to lay charges in cases like this') and placing domestic violence where it belongs, on police and prosecutors' agenda. Confusingly, in enforcing long-denied prosecution of crimes against women (Doggett, 1993), these policies may in fact deny women's choice. Already disempowered by abuse, women are further disempowered when the justice system 'takes over' the criminal prosecution of a partner. Given the persistence of myths about battered women, such a move could return the situation to pre-1982 conditions. Further, many women do assert control over the criminal process by refusing to testify or claiming to have lied about the violence (McGillivray, 1987). Women who take the stand against a partner find, with other victims, that their interests are subordinated to broader justice goals, and their role is simply as witness for the crown. The more general pursuit of justice, not justice for the victim, is the professional responsibility of the crown attorney (Law Society of Manitoba, 1992). The victim is 'essentialized,' and her subjectivity is important only as it fits within the confines of the system. Her own voice, her experience, and her damage may be lost. Recent Criminal Code amendments with respect to victim impact statements, restitution and compensation, availability of protection orders, and recognition of intimate violence as a breach of trust and an aggravating factor in sentencing (discussed in chapter 5) are intended to improve the position of victims.

Respondents' cases steadily eroded as they progressed through complaint, charging, prosecution, plea bargaining or trial, and, particularly, sentence. What the judge hears may bear little resemblance to what happened. This slippage derives less from victims' ambivalence than from the system's response, which did not accord with justice policy and professional ethics. There is no formal requirement that prosecutors take victims into their confidence or embed their perspectives in prosecution and decision-making about plea bargaining and sentencing, although many do. Manitoba policy in cases of spousal assault prosecuted in the Winnipeg Family Violence Court would seem to require victims' input (Ursel, 1998b). For respondents, this did not happen. Case overload (and perhaps a self-protective professional callousness) makes this difficult. The justice system cannot be run without discretion, but its exercise should be guided by the facts of the case, the input of the victim, and the crown's enlightened understanding of the dynamics of intimate violence (Schulman, 1997).

Unless cases are thoroughly scrutinized and victims are counselled on the need to support the prosecution of the case, charge-dropping can become one more tool for abusers, reopening the potential for manipulation that no-drop policies were meant to prevent. *I don't feel [the no-drop policy] made a difference in my case.* Victim advocacy programs can restore some measure of balance for victims, but they are limited, as respondents observe, and may not be culturally sensitive. Although their experience of the justice system in general was problematic for many respondents, the police response was most visibly fraught with racism and misogyny, as was that of lawyers. Political interference also visibly affected police response on reserve. In the next chapter, we turn to diversion from the system and other reform issues.

5

Thinking about Reform

Everything that can be done. Workshops, resources, places to go. Talk to our kids. If you don't work on your issues, you end up finding the same partner anyway, whether you're male or female.

Should He Go to Jail? Punishment and Treatment

This project emerged from the question, 'Should Aboriginal men who assault their partners be diverted from the criminal justice system?' First Nations dispute resolution is non-adversarial, directed at restitution and community reintegration rather than punishment (Valencia-Weber and Zuni, 1995; Green, 1998). The circle, representing unity, holism, and equality, is both symbolic and procedural, balancing individual and collective interests in restoring harmony. For most transgressions, the offender's compensation of the victim as decided by the circle is the end of the matter. The formality of the criminal justice system, its separation from the community and community input, and its focus on the past and on establishing guilt stand in opposition to pre-colonial First Nations justice. Some First Nations in northern and northwestern cultures in the New World punished sex offenders by having women whip them (McIvor and Nahanee, 1998). Banishment leading to almost certain death in the wilderness was a last resort for serious interpersonal offences. Some Nations used the death penalty, distinguished from personal vendetta by community accord. Most offences were dealt with through restitution – making up to the victim and the family the equivalent to the damage done through gifts and labour – similar to damages under the common law. Sentencing options of the criminal justice system once included capital and corporal punishment and still include incarceration – remedies rarely used by indigenous justice systems. Compensation of victims, which is central to First Nations justice and was recently added to the Criminal Code, is not used in sentencing in cases of intimate violence. Despite the exposure of Manitoba's Aboriginal peoples to the Anglo-Canadian system of criminal justice for a century or more, its goals and processes may remain foreign or simply irrelevant to many. The Law Reform Commission of Canada observed (Canada 1991: 5): 'From the Aboriginal perspective, the criminal justice system is an alien one ... deeply insensitive to their traditions and values; many view it as unremittingly racist. Abuse of power and the distorted exercise of discretion are identified time and again as principle defects of the system. The commission viewed the establishment of Aboriginal justice systems as desirable.'

There have been numerous examinations of the massive over-representation of Aboriginal youth and adults in carceral facilities – prisons, young offenders institutions – and of children in state care (Canadian Bar Association, 1989; Manitoba, 1991a; Adelburg, 1993; La Prairie, 1994; Griffiths and Verdun-Jones, 1994; RCAP, 1996). Foucault's 'carceral archipelago,' stretching from family through state institutions such as the school and the orphanage to the prison system (Foucault, 1977) is for Aboriginal people more than metaphor. The system detailed by Foucault is the youth correctional facility of Mattray, whose disciplinary regime bears a striking resemblance to educational institutions for Aboriginal children and to the facilities for young offenders in which they are overwhelmingly represented today (McGillivray, 1997b, c). Six in ten young offenders in Manitoba's correctional facilities are Aboriginal. Studies of Aboriginal people in the justice system almost uniformly call for diversion and alternative measures. Some recommend working towards First Nations justice systems, an issue raising complex political and constitutional issues. Without strong representation of the interests of women and children in designing alternatives, it may be that little will change for them under such systems.

The over-representation of Aboriginal people in prisons and correctional centres, and the ineffectiveness of the penal system in promoting community reintegration, diminishing violence, and rehabilitating offenders, pose serious problems for criminal justice in Canada. A report commissioned by the Aboriginal Justice Inquiry, or AJI (Manitoba, 1991) listed the advantages of alternative measures from the point of view of the justice system – relief of court backlogs, decrease of waiting time for offenders, restitution for victims, and assurance of community support for offenders (Fossett, 1990: 17). The report expressed concern that diversion may become an impersonal layer of bureaucracy, jeopardize the presumption of innocence (the accused must admit guilt in order to be eligible), avoid open-forum justice, diminish police discretion, and lead to inequities in justice administration by de facto decision-making. While there are good answers in traditional criminal law theory to such concerns (Manitoba, 1991; RCAP, 1996; Green, 1998), large-scale diversion of Aboriginal offenders has not occurred, nor do most diversion programs accept those accused of violence against partners.

Ross Green (1998) identifies six models of diversion and alternative sentencing measures developed in First Nations in Saskatchewan and Manitoba. The measures enhance input from elders, community, offenders, and, usually, victims. Those who know and care about the offender and the victim – family and friends, community leaders, criminal justice personnel – can speak. Initiatives are small, localized, and dependent on accommodation by the system and support from the community. Judges have taken a leading role. All initiatives require the support of police, prosecutors, probation officers, and defence counsel. Case selection disfavours offenders whose victims are spouses or children. Most such programs do not divert offenders from court proceedings but deal only with sentencing. One exception is the Hollow Water project for ending sexual abuse of children and healing offenders who were themselves victims (see below). In its most recent phase, the offender is diverted from the justice system and dealt with in a community healing context. The victim receives separate support, and her autonomy and healing, whether or not she chooses to take part in the circle, are protected. Some communities hold sentencing circles in which all interested parties are present, with or without the judge. Others use sentencing committees – advisory groups of community members – which make recommendations to the court. The most common diversion model is the youth justice committee for offenders under the age of eighteen, accommodated in the Young Offenders Act RSC 1985, c. Y-1 as amended. Related strategies include healing lodges and the protocol on responses to family violence developed at Waywayseecappo Reserve in Manitoba (Green, 1998).

With the exception of Hollow Water, projects for diversion and alternative sentencing in reserve communities make no special accommodation for victims of intimate violence and leave open the potential for manipulation of the process by an offender with strong political connections. The diversion project developed for the Metro Toronto Aboriginal community, instituted in 1990, is based on a traditional model of peer justice (Aboriginal Legal Services, 1992; Spotton, 1998). Aboriginal court workers direct suitable candidates to the project. Prosecutors control the decision to stay charges and divert offenders (with their agreement) to the community council. Three members hear the matter and seek a reintegrative solution through counselling, restitution, community service, and treatment. If the accused does not follow the advice of the council, charges are not reinstated, but the person will not again receive this opportunity. The Toronto project does not accept cases of spousal violence but does take on some involving offences against children. The project aims at accountability and community reintegration. It runs at 65 per cent capacity and is inexpensive, with few formal needs apart from administration, cooperation of crown and defence counsel, and the involvement of the existing Native Courtworkers Program. While such initiatives are new and relatively rare, they promise to reduce the impact of the criminal law and the penal system on First Nations.

Diverting those who have violated intimate relations of trust raises a number of problems. A wrongful act committed by one in a situation of trust invites greater, not a lesser, penalty than a similar act committed against a stranger. The voice of the victim may be more obscure than it is in the existing system, as there is no prosecutor to represent her interests, however inadequately. At the root of the problem with mediation is the power imbalance created by intimate violence. Hillary Astor (1994: 150) argues that mediation – potentially part of any diversion program and characteristic of circle sentencing – is undesirable in intimate violence because 'violence creates an extreme power imbalance between the parties, because the parties do not have the capacity to mediate and because mediation does not provide for the needs of the person who has been the target of violence.'

In undertaking our study, we were asked to find out the views of Aboriginal women on diversion of abusive partners. Questions about the purpose and utility of jail, we hoped, would suggest how women might feel about diversion and sentencing alternatives. Respondents expressed overwhelming support for punishment. They also supported effective treatment programs. Twenty women thought that jail was a good way to deal with men who abuse their partners, and thirteen of the twenty stated that the men should get stiffer sentences. Inconsistencies in responses – eight respondents did not believe that jail did any good yet three of the eight wanted stiffer sentencing – illustrate the classic tension in criminal justice between punishment and rehabilitation. An abuser rarely comes into contact with the justice system for a first offence. *For the first thirty-five times I got beat up, I never contacted the police. I think it was about that many times, at least.* This is the average number of times a woman is assaulted before she reports the violence (McGillivray, 1987; Ontario Native Women's Association, 1989; House of Commons, 1991). The first time her case gets to court may be the first time she has laid charges. The absence of a related criminal record often results in a discharge or minimal sentence for the offender, even if there is a long history of assault.

Respondents told us about the prosecution of their partners. Their confusion about charging and conviction again points to serious communication problems between prosecutors and victims. Many respondents were not sure what happened with the charges in some cases. Twenty-two reported that at least one partner had been charged on one or more occasions with an offence related to the violence against them. Partners of nineteen women had been charged between 1990 and 1995. (The numbers do not 'add up,' as more than one partner of a respondent may have been charged with more than one offence.) Two respondents were under subpoena as witnesses for pending cases at the time of the interview. Fifteen reported that one or more of their abusers entered guilty pleas. Four reported that the offender was convicted on trial, and a fifth, that a partner was acquitted. Charges were dropped or stayed in the remainder of the cases.

One or more partners of nine respondents received a jail term of less than one year. One got six months for a reign of terror of repeated assaults, in which he broke the respondent's nose and eardrum and knocked out her teeth. *He's laughing now. He made a mockery out of the system.* Five sentences included probation orders, three of which mandated counselling. One offender was fined, and two were sentenced to community service. Partners of fifteen respondents received counselling orders, either as terms of a conditional discharge or in post-sentence probation orders. Partners of three were never charged. *Even to this day, I don't quite remember why he was never charged, even though I used to tell the police I wanted him charged.* Victims' ambiguity cannot explain these results.

All respondents said that sentencing was too lenient. One was grateful for the guilty plea, as it spared her children, all of whom were subpoenaed as witnesses, the trauma of testifying:

I did not feel [six months' probation and court-ordered counselling] was enough for what he put the kids and me through, but at the same time, I'm glad he pleaded guilty, because it saved the kids from testifying. Because they all had subpoenas. Unfortunately, four days later my youngest one attempted suicide, for just seeing [his father] at a distance.

Those guys got it so easy today, like some went to court and they gave him a fine option, so they know it's an easy way out ... They don't care.

He had to report to a probation officer every three months ... I thought they were extremely lenient given ... all the previous abuse.

Most cases you could have, they could half kill you and walk away with a slap on the wrist, basically. When they get out of jail, they're just going to turn around and come looking for you, whether they got a restraining order or not.

Yes, once he was [sentenced] but not sentenced to jail. He was just given 100 hours of community service work ... He didn't learn anything out of it.

On three counts of physical and emotional child abuse against the kids, he got six months' probation and ordered counselling. On one assault on myself he got nine months probation. It just don't make sense.

I think [his sentence] was too lenient, like he's only doing five months. He told me one time, he says, 'Oh, I've been in jail before. It's nothing.'

Plea bargaining was seen as one reason for lenient sentences. Sparing a victim of intimate violence the trauma of taking the stand can result in a sentencing discount, as does the guilty plea itself. The violence of the conduct may be minimized, particularly in the absence of victim input and impact statements from the victim, and a long and perhaps unreported history of violence may be ignored. In charge bargaining, facts central to sentence and protection of the victim may be lost with the dropped charges (McGillivray, 1998a; 1998b). Sentence is distorted because the facts presented to the judge are distorted. *What I would do is to promote a change to the crown policy so crimes of violence against the person would not be plea bargained down to a lesser charge ... and to provide the right to justice for victims without fear of ... prejudice, discrimination.*

Jail means punishment, and punishment means the possibility that the offender – and the community – will recognize the wrongfulness of the act. The symbolic function of jail as punishment or *payback*, as public denunciation of the conduct and as a lesson taught to the offender, was important to respondents.

I think they should get hard punishments.

I wanted him to get put in jail and for him to realize what he is doing is not right, and for him to get help.

I wish [the courts were] more severe in most cases as far as sentencing.

I know that he assaulted me, and [the fact that he went to jail shows that] he knows that he assaulted me too.

It's just like he thinks that he didn't do anything wrong. Because he told me, 'If I did anything wrong I'd be sitting in jail.'

He had to see what he was doing was wrong, that it was a criminal act.

They should send them, give them more time ... more time to go there and think about what they did wrong to other people.

I felt my ex-partner should have done more than seven to ten months for what he did to me. Because of that, it caused a great deal of fear in me. I don't think my children will forget what he did.

I feel bad ... Maybe I still loved him at the time. I realized I didn't want a broken family. Maybe that's why. I tried to hang onto my marriage.

It hurts me when I see a person like that [in jail], but he has to learn for what he done wrong.

I didn't want to see my partner go to jail. I only wanted him to admit he did something wrong in hitting me – not to say he was right because he got acquitted.

One respondent saw jail as just another easy way out. *Personally, I don't see jail helping very much. I have known men who see jail as a means of getting three meals a day.* But incarceration means more than punishment. It also provides a period of absolute safety for victims and gives them 'time out' to heal.

When he went to jail I was no longer scared or afraid because I knew where he was, and he couldn't do any harm to me, at least for a while.

For me, when my abuser was in jail, I felt safe. I'm sure I'm not the only one that feels like that.

I knew I wouldn't be getting a licking for a while again, and I could walk on the street without getting scared.

Well, it was different. I feel kind of relieved. And you know, I keep saying to myself, 'There you go, now I can get on with my life.' But after that, when I know he's out, I used to say to myself, 'Oh no, not again, why didn't they put him in there longer?' While he's in there ... I can get on with my life to try to make myself better first, before he even gets out.

They should really put their foot into this crime and ... not just put this person away for a couple of years. It has to end sooner or later. We need safety nowadays.

I feel safe and protected right now because he is in jail, for other matters. I don't know how long this feeling is going to last, because they can't lock him up forever. But I wish they would.

[I felt safe] because he was incarcerated, and it felt too good to know that he was not lurking around looking for me. Even though he was in another relationship, he was always trying to have a hold on me. He really wanted to dominate me. I felt that with him going to jail, I had inner peace in myself. I didn't have to be afraid anymore.

Respondents feared the offender's release.

I was afraid – because of him being involved in a gang – for the safety of my family and friends. He threatened my friends and family. It's hard. Because I've seen other girls go through it who are involved with the same gang. They kind of torment them ... I feared for the safety of my child. If he has contact with me when he gets out of jail then, yes, I'm seriously looking at getting a restraining order.

I'm always waiting for something to happen. I'm always constantly on the lookout for him or anyone that he knows that I know could hurt us, could hurt me and my kids.

Jail alone is not going to solve the problem. All respondents saw a strong need for effective treatment of offenders, and here they had much to say about the goals and importance of enforced treatment. They wanted treatment combined with or incorporated into a jail term, longer jail terms that would incorporate long-term treatment, and programs that forced abusers to confront their denial and deal with personal problems:

It didn't help him out when he was in jail. I used to think he'd smarten up, but he didn't. There was no counselling for him in there or anything like that. All he was thinking was getting out of there ... I thought he'd learn his lesson, but he didn't learn anything in there.

I don't think it helps them. It just happens again, even when they are in jail, after they come out of jail. We still go through the same thing, in jail, not in jail. I wonder what they learn in jail? Do they learn more abuse in there?

For me, I wouldn't want a guy or somebody just to go to jail and stay there. I would want that person to get some help and get some counselling done for himself in there. Because putting him in jail, you're not doing anything to them, you're just letting them rest, that's the way I feel, like you're just letting them stay there.

It's ineffective and expensive and they don't receive the counselling that they need, in the situation at jail. It makes them more resentful, not only at their spouse but at the whole judicial system ... It's dead time ...

They can put a person in jail, but I feel that they should be getting some kind of treatment and counselling in there.

He's got eight months and he's getting out in five. He should do eight months and some sort of treatment. When he gets out he's not even asked to go for treatment, just probation. Three years' supervised probation or something.

A person can go to jail and just do their time and walk out. And with the same intention they will repeat. I would feel that they would have to go through some rehabilitation program, anger management.

A lot of these guys that abuse their partners ... need help, and putting them in jail ain't helping them. I think that [treatment] would make them aware that it's not right for them to do that. A lot of them need ongoing therapy when they get out. I think that's what they should pressure more of these guys [to do].

I think I would like to see them make it mandatory to take something for rehabilitation. And that would be regardless of whether it's going to serve a purpose to them or not. At least they would become aware that it's not right for them to go around and abuse women, children or anybody, for that matter.

If you're going to put them in jail, you have to not just think about the physical aspects of helping the man or woman. I think they should have back-up support for them, in and out of jail after they are released. Make them take an AA counselling, anger management counselling, like not just a dinky little program, but a severe, hardcore, hit-hard-home program that will break through their denial.

I think this man I was involved with should be in a drug and alcohol treatment program for at least a year, not just for six weeks or eight weeks, the way they have it nowadays. I don't think that's enough time for a person to heal or change.

I don't know if Manitoba has a |lock-up| treatment centre for prisoners. They should build one, try to get one anyways. It gets the prisoners to better understand themselves, where they come from, why they abuse, why they commit crimes and all of that.

Maybe even a specific holding cell, or holding block, or have a jail that you can send all of the assault cases to this one centre. Have a program where they can deal with what's going on with them, or whatever is making them violent.

Regardless of how you look at it, the bottom |line| reality is the abusers have to deal with the issue, whether they're incarcerated or not ... I have learned there is no long-term program for the inmate, just short-term programs ... Once they are released, there's no long-term program for them.

I don't think |jail is| the place for them. They should be sent somewhere where they can learn that |violence| is not healthy. They really should get help in that way. We are really fortunate to have strong women to have places for us, like shelters. They should have these for men.

They should start some kind of men's groups, or men's homes or whatever, and let men know you don't have to be an abuser to be a man.

Yeah, I would like to see, again, more programs. I want to get to the root of why they abuse their women. Have they seen this when they were younger?

|They should get treatment to| learn how to handle the anger, and probably to learn

why they abuse. They probably don't even know themselves. There's a lot of insecurity.

One respondent suggested that the type of sentence – jail with treatment or mandatory treatment outside the penal system – should depend on *how they abuse*, on the severity and frequency of the violence. In her view, adult offending is closely related to abuse experienced in childhood, and therapy is central to preventing further offending. Another, in favour of effective treatment, saw treatment orders as just another way for an offender to avoid jail. *If they're asked to go for treatment – if they are asked and they don't really want to change – they'll just go there ... and just, you know – 'So what' – right? You're still out.*

The criminal justice system has addressed violence against women by law reform and mandatory prosecution policy. Notable gaps remain in judicial decision-making in intimate violence, as a study of decisions by the Manitoba Court of Appeal in cases arising out of the Winnipeg Family Violence Court discloses (Jensen, forthcoming; McGillivray 1998b). In two recent cases, the court cited the 'consent' and 'willing participation' of a twelve-year-old girl who was sexually assaulted and the 'instigation' of fellatio by a seven-year-old girl as mitigating factors reducing sentence. Physical assaults of women also received comparatively light sentences. The Manitoba Association of Women and the Law (1991) compares two 1989 Manitoba cases. In one, the accused assaulted his spouse with a spade, breaking the handle on her body; he received a suspended sentence. In the other, the accused abused a kitten and was sentenced to three months in jail. Suspended sentences, intermittent sentences, and alternative dispositions were common for intimate violence up to and including 1997 (Jensen, forthcoming). The domestic and relational context of intimate violence may lead courts to presume that the victim provoked the assault, and this mitigates sentence (Mahoney, 1992).

Protection and safety are central concerns of respondents, but treatment is also seen as key. Treatment can be accommodated within criminal justice through orders that mandate treatment and counselling and inmate programs. Stony Mountain Penitentiary offers inmates a Family Violence Program – optional treatment that recognizes Aboriginal cultural values and traditions (Proulx and Perrault, 1996). Least effective, from the viewpoint of respondents, are such alternative dispositions as community service orders. These sidestep the question of women's safety, and neither victim nor offender see them as 'real' punishment or as rehabilitation. A news article titled 'Justice System Failing Women' notes that 'critics of the justice system say tougher action by police and courts – not stricter legislation – is the key to preventing violent men from hurting former spouses' (*Winnipeg Free Press*, 16 Jan. 1996).

The law must be made to work, by police, prosecutors, and judges in bail and sentencing courts, in sentencing that reflects the seriousness of the conduct, in issuing orders that protect women and children, and in enforcing those orders. Respondents valued jail terms for reasons of punishment, denunciation, and their own personal safety. They saw jail as real and symbolic punishment, as a guarantee of some period of immediate safety. Treatment would ensure future safety for themselves or for other partners of their offender. Even so, they doubted the effectiveness of treatment without jail. *'So what,' right? You're still out.*

Diversion and Alternative Measures

It is difficult to frame a question about diversion (dropping charges or not charging in order to divert an offender to a program or disposition outside the criminal justice system) and alternative measures (where the disposition is decided and provided in a community context) without adding detailed explanations that would condition the response. We consulted Aboriginal women on how to approach this question and decided to proceed in four stages. The first two stages, dealing with jail and treatment, are reported above. Responses give part of the picture, in the stress on safety, punishment, and treatment. The question was then asked, 'Would it make a difference to you if those in the justice system were Aboriginal or non-Aboriginal?' Finally, we read a description of diversion and invited responses.

Fourteen respondents stated that it did not matter whether justice system personnel were Aboriginal or non-Aboriginal, as long as they *did their job*. Two added that it did not matter because they themselves were *not racist*. Ten thought that more Aboriginal people in the system would be a good idea; one did not know. The responses here constitute a layered discourse on otherness, equality, and accommodation.

I think it might help if they were Aboriginal, but it's not a matter of race. To me, it's about people doing right and wrong.

I feel that people are all equal, no matter what.

To me, it doesn't really matter if you're different Nations because the way I see things is

... some people are kind-hearted and some are violent. It won't matter as long as they have the same kind of justice, in the same way.

I think that there is enough situations already in society without adding to discrimination. I mean, if we're ever wanting to become equal, as we're always complaining about that we're not equal or being treated this way, treated that way, why do we want to go ahead and say exclusively, 'I want an Aboriginal person to help me?' I don't think that there should be ... something that is set out so definitely.

It doesn't matter what race they are.

There should be more Aboriginal people working in the justice system.

It might help if you had more Aboriginal people in the justice system. In some ways they would have a little more understanding of the Native culture and what the Natives have been through or the Métis have been through in the past.

I think it would make a difference. We have to deal with our own people. If they are not Aboriginal, they don't take it seriously. I sense prejudice coming from them. With police, they should have one Aboriginal and one non-Aboriginal.

They would understand more from where you were coming from. There wouldn't be a cultural barrier ... They could explain in Ojibwa – the proceedings – for those who don't understand English very well. It would be a fairer process.

Within the correctional institutions, provincial and federally, you are looking at anywhere from 70 per cent of the population are Aboriginal ... especially in the province of Manitoba.. In a city like Winnipeg, there is a great percentage of Aboriginal people.

I think Aboriginal people are a little too soft. Non-Aboriginal just gives you a sentence. Because I know, being on the reserve, a lot of people are going to court in Aboriginal court and everybody is getting off ... It's not like I want to throw everybody in jail. But it's just that Aboriginals are too soft on people.

I think they should have some Aboriginal ... When I walk into the courtroom, or whatever, sometimes you can just feel the prejudice. It's just like they're looking at you and saying, 'Well, another Indian woman got beaten up.'

Both. Because we are human beings. We are no different than others. Those white people got suffering, suffering like me ... In years back, I listened to a woman – I was having a really hard time, talking about the Skid Row – and this woman said, 'You don't have to be on the street to be a Skid Row. I was living in a million-dollar house,' she said. 'I was a Skid Row in there.' And even those people who are rich, they suffer. And they don't want to … ask for help. But nowadays I see young girls coming into the program, suffering. That's why I say, both ways.

We asked an open-ended question, 'Are there any other changes you would like to see in place to deal with men who abuse their partners?' Then the interviewer gave the following description of diversion:

Q: Some Aboriginal communities have tried counselling and healing as a way to deal with offenders, instead of going through the justice system. This is called 'diversion.' It involves police but not the courts. The offender must admit he is guilty before being diverted. Instead of having a criminal record and serving a jail term, the offender is given a sentence by a committee in the Aboriginal community, such as restitution, community service, wilderness camps, counselling, and healing. What are your views on this?

Respondents were concerned that diversion was *an easy way out* for offenders:

I see men as manipulating that system, as an easy way out. [In] the majority of communities it is usually relatives that sit on [the committee] anyway.

I think they should send them to jail instead of going through all that – behind bars for what they did to people, for what they did to partners. Because if they send them to something like that, camps or something like that, they're going to think, like, 'I can do it again,' because he's not behind bars for what he did to his partners. They're going to say, 'They're just going to send me to camp' or something like that.

It's too easy. It's too easy for them. Because most abusers don't realize what kind of pain they put their partners and kids through … I don't mind him being sentenced by Aboriginals, but it's just, like, that it's too easy for them. Restitution, or going to counselling, community service work – that's just too easy for them.

I think it's much too lenient.

Four respondents restated their view that jail was a good way to deal with abusers, especially if treatment could be included. Nineteen thought diversion worth a try but set out conditions that were to be met if it were to be acceptable to them. These included ensuring the safety of women and children, taking into account the nature and severity of the offence, the supervision, nature, and length of the disposition, deciding who should be present at the meeting or circle, and protection from the offender's manipulation of results:

It might work as long as there is good supervision where the person or victim didn't have to worry about being stalked or maybe even killed.

In some cases it might work ... It depends on how severe, or to what extent the violence or abuse is ... It depends on the type of abuse, whether it is sexual or what. It depends on the length of the program.

I think it is good, even though these offenders are harming people ... I think trying to help them would be a lot better than trying to get revenge on them or trying to do something to them worse. I don't think they are going to learn anything – they will just become very resentful or they will just keep doing what they are doing – if nobody is there to help them.

I guess it could be a good thing. But it could be a scary thing, too, depending on who's involved and whose family is there. It would have to be pretty open, of course.

Some of them have ... just about killed their partners. Those are the ones that should go in court. And struggle there, too. But those that are not doing bad – like not really hurting their partners – should go and ask for help. Maybe those are the ones that will get better soon. But the bad ones should go in court, and [the public can] see what is going on out there.

Well, it depends on what kind of person that it is. If it was a child molester, I think the whole world should know who that person is.

One respondent became enthusiastic about the idea:

I think it is an excellent way. It would probably work better than the [present] justice system ... It wouldn't spit out hardcore criminals the way institutions do. Someone goes in for a petty crime and come out hardcore, because, you know, that is the way jail is.

Others expressed cautious optimism:

Sounds like a good idea, but one that will take a lot of time. I think you can't deal with such a big problem in such a short time.

If they admit they are guilty, yes, I think this will work, but not all offenders are going to say that they are guilty, and if they do they don't mean it.

A lot of times, a lot of us [Aboriginal people] are forced to come into Winnipeg [for court] ... We're already community-oriented ... It would be nice if [a diversion program] was started like that – instead of just being dropped off in Winnipeg and just left there with all these new things like all the laws, courts and all this. It would probably feel more comfortable.

I guess I'm so used to seeing the white justice system. I'm finding that, in that way, it doesn't help ... Maybe if I see progress or something different happening, when they decide to use the Aboriginal culture, then my views will change.

That sounds like a good idea. We should do it our way. Maybe it could work if we all work together ... All I'm saying is, good luck. I hope it works.

Although opinions on diversion were mixed, giving no clear mandate on the question, the inclusion of elements of Aboriginal culture in justice measures was viewed positively.

Culture wouldn't be a problem. Usage of sweats, sweat lodges, pipe ceremonies, healing circles, vision quest, fasting would help them to see themselves as they truly are, not what they're disillusioning themselves to believe.

Very much ... because [Aboriginals] deal with holistics, not just one aspect of, not just physical, the way the white man does ... We are just a sick, spiritually sick, people who need to restore themselves.

I would like to see that happen, to get into [Aboriginal] culture. Because that's very important not to lose that culture. Because we're slowly losing that.

Some thought that diversion would work better in a large urban centre than on the reserve – that the process would be more closely scrutinized and that an urban setting would provide protective anonymity for the victim. Others thought that it might work in reserve communities, where people are known and the process is more familiar and comfortable. One saw problems either way. Others feared that diversion on reserve would be biased by prior knowledge of the victim and the offender, both to the detriment of the victim. One had experience with healing circles for sexual abuse of children (chapter 6) and was concerned that personal disclosures by abusers may be ridiculed:

It's different being in the city than being in the country. I know that when I lived in the country [on reserve], and was living in violence, the police were never called because nobody would do it or could do it out there. I think it would have a better chance to work here [in the city], because it's in full view of everyone.

When [I went to] court, it kind of gives me a different look – how the courts are dealt with in the white community. I think going to court on the reserve is kind of – well, everybody knows you, how you are, how you live. The people that sit on that jury box [sentencing committee] tend to judge you because they know you. From where I come, we have that kind of system. But living up on the reserve, people kind of judge you. And that was the main reason I didn't go to the reserve to be judged ... I would rather go to the white community court, where people don't know me.

It would be very hard ... It might work, and in some cases it might not work. When you are in a community, everybody is almost the same, and when you are living in the city you meet up with different kinds of people, and there is so much pressure coming from different directions.

Within our own community, people tried to start healing circles regarding child sexual abuse, and people from the community were invited. And some people were dealing with issues, and they brought it out in public. And one man that brought out [childhood sexual] abuse was ridiculed, and he was just laughed right out of the room by the other men.

Respondents' concerns about a fair hearing for the victim surfaced in chapters 3 and 4, in comments on abusers' manipulation of 'the system,' and in responses to questions about policing, control by band councils, and Aboriginal justice personnel. Concerns also arose in discussions of diversion. Respondents criticized the political setup on reserves both for inappropriate interference in reporting, policing, and prosecution and for failure to develop protective and proactive programs. *Right now I'm feeling angry towards the chief and council for not doing anything about what's going on, on the reserves, not trying to clean up their own community. The chief and council should organize some kind of a group, like a support group, for women on the reserves. There is a lot of kids being hurt, being neglected, abused, abandoned.* Alternatives to the criminal justice system will not be acceptable to victims of intimate violence unless diversion can do what jail is now seen as doing, however unsuccessfully – *punish*, visibly, actually, and symbolically, and *protect*, at least long enough for victims to begin to get their lives back on track. Alternatives will not be acceptable without reliable indication of successful treatment for abusers in programs that also guarantee victims' safety for the duration of treatment. Concerns about political interference, lack of fair hearing for the victim, and lack of protection resulted in a generally negative response to the diversion of cases of intimate violence.

Aboriginal Ganootamaage Justice Services of Winnipeg held its first healing circle, or 'community justice forum,' on 30 September 1998 (*Winnipeg Free Press*, 30 Sept. 1998). The case involved a man of twenty with no criminal record who shoplifted twenty dollars worth of hair products from a pharmacy. He was 'interrogated, cross-examined, psychoanalysed and lectured for ninety minutes' by the circle and told to apologize to the store, commit himself to weekly counselling and sweat lodge ceremonies, and perform volunteer service for three months. He would have been fined or discharged in the ordinary courts. Ganootamaage hopes to hear up to 300 cases per year. One purpose of the forum is to ensure that offenders reflect on their lives and on the harm to the victim. A council coordinator interviews participants and provides the forum with a synopsis of the assessment (*Winnipeg Free Press*, 29 Sept. 1998). Cases of spousal assault are not diverted, in accordance with justice policy in Manitoba and the findings of this study.

Changing the System

In chapter 2, we outlined a theory of intimate violence that seeks to account for the normalization of intimate violence in some Aboriginal communities. Cultural devaluation, we argued, is inherent in the protective marginalization and tutorials in civilization offered by the reserve system and the residential school. Proposed in the Bagot Report (1845), these systems became aggressively assimilationist with the opening of the prairie west and the totalization of the reserve structure under late-nineteenth-century dominion Indian policy. 'Aggressive civilization' – the normalization of Aboriginal children into an Anglo-Christian citizenship – was the overt aim of residential schooling for First Nations. *I believe that we have been brainwashed over the years by Christianity ... We need to reclaim our own culture, our own religion, own way of life, our own way of thinking ... It may have been different, but it wasn't any less than the European way of life we were led to believe for so long.* Women and their roles were progressively devalued in trade and mission contact and in Indian

Act provisions for elections, registration, and entitlement. Apprehending children for alternate 'mothering' by residential schools and child welfare agencies further devalued women. Men were legally infantilized as wards of the state and were made legal guardians of their wives in the Victorian patriarchy underlying the Indian Act. The status of Indian women was tied to that of their husbands. If their husbands were not registered Indians, they and their children lost Indian status. With the induction of new modes of governance, the intrusion of the Anglo-Canadian justice system, and the deliberate crushing of First Nations leadership following Riel's defeat at Batoche, traditional methods of dispute resolution and lines of authority further eroded. Ultimately, the greatest destruction was wrought by the devaluation or deliberate destruction of traditional spirituality and the myth systems linking ethos and governance.

Corporal punishment and the sexual and physical abuse characteristic of institutions for children plagued residential schools. Equally damaging was the denial of opportunities to learn parenting skills and the erosion of culture, tradition, and band and family ties. Images of otherness and relations of subjectivity became internalized and were expressed in and reinforced by sexual and physical violence, further disturbing balances of power between men and women, parents and children. Patterns of intergenerational violence emerged. Intimate violence, witnessed or experienced, became the norm for many Aboriginal families and communities. When the federal enclave of the reserve was opened to provincial agencies for child protection in the 1960s, Manitoba's Child and Family Services (CFS) apprehended thousands of children for placement in non-Aboriginal families and institutions. Over-intervention may have reflected increased rates of serious violence against children. It also reflected a misunderstanding of shared child care in tribe- or clan-based and extended-family communities. It certainly exacerbated the process of cultural genocide, increasing the apathy and despair of Aboriginal communities. *Oh yeah, that definitely would be a big part of it, for sure. It all comes down to who we are, bottom line. And if you don't have your culture, your roots, your background, that really plays a big part in our lives, I find anyway.*

Our analysis accords with the political discourses of Aboriginal peoples on the historical context of intimate violence – colonization and cultural devaluation, social and geographical marginalization, the experience of residential school, and the '60s scoop' of Aboriginal children by the child welfare system. In undertaking this research, we were asked to discover Aboriginal women's views on diverting men charged with spousal assault from the criminal justice system. We found that, despite their dissatisfaction with policing, legal representation, sentencing, lack of treatment, and other aspects of prosecution and the judicial process, they valued the criminal process for its public denunciation of intimate violence, while they saw jail as central to safety and the need for *payback*. Unless diversion could guarantee treatment and victims' safety, and be immune to manipulation by abusers, they would not support it. Our investigation of the experience of intimate violence in childhood, adolescence, and adulthood disclosed serious gaps in policing, service provision, and legal services for Aboriginal women, despite recent reform. Proposals for further reform emerge from responses reported in chapters 3 and 4. In this chapter, we explore these recommendations. We then turn to the emergent construct of intimate violence as a violation of human rights.

One of our respondents captures the essence of countless recommendations generated by hundreds of studies and academic discussions of intimate violence in Canada: *Everything that can be done. Workshops, resources, places to go. Talk to our kids. If you don't work on your issues, you end up finding the same partner anyway, whether you're male or female.* Respondents, as Aboriginal women expert in intimate violence, had many ideas about the nature and origins of violence, the relationships between childhood and adult violence, policing and justice, and improving the system's response.

The Nature of Intimate Violence

Women in this study collectively experienced, within relationships of trust and dependence, thousands of incidents of physical, sexual, and emotional assault inflicted by at least a hundred different perpetrators. This violence may not be unusual for women who stay in shelters or transition homes, from which more than half of our sample is drawn, or for women who have approached treatment programs for domestic violence, who form the remainder of the sample. It does reflect astounding rates, frequency, and severity of intimate violence and lends support to studies that point to the heightened risk and rate of abuse for Aboriginal women. All respondents have reserve connections, and almost all experienced intimate violence while living on reserve. Normalization of intimate violence was widely reported. Lack of comparable services on reserve and reserve policing and politics complicated the process of getting help and getting out. Leaving was far less the response to a single incident of extreme violence than the culmination of numerous incidents of violence, tiredness, anger over the constant breach of trust, worry about exposing children to more violence, and fear of being killed. Emotional abuse – public and private rituals of humiliation, spiritual abuse, threats, stalking – was for respondents the most damaging and least publicly recognized form of abuse, eroding their capacity for independent thought and action.

Women need support and protection during and after leaving a violent relationship. They need assurance that support is available, should they decide to leave. Most respondents had only praise for the agencies that assisted them at the time of the study but strongly criticized other services. Shelters and related services for reserve communities range from inadequate to non-existent. The provincial 'zero tolerance' response to spousal assault is vitiated by the absence of family and community support and, centrally, the support of agencies and police services. Winnipeg's shelters, safe housing, treatment programs, and counselling services for Aboriginal victims and abusers are not adequate to serve even urban communities, yet they serve most of Manitoba. A major reason for the urban migration of Aboriginal women is intimate violence. While men leave reserves for cities in search of economic opportunities, women most frequently leave because of abuse (LaRoque, 1993). On-reserve shelters are essential but risk exposing residents' identity, and are less easily hidden, giving abusers ready access. Urban resources remain a necessity for many women escaping from small, isolated rural communities. Culturally appropriate public education on the nature and damage of intimate violence, which does not target groups as inherently violent but rather addresses the basic right to be free of such violence, is needed. Improving service delivery in reserve and urban communities and ensuring continuity of help for women and children travelling between agencies and localities are essential to effective response.

Most important of all is women working together to improve conditions in their communities and lending strength and support to one another in ending the violence against themselves and their children. The Aboriginal Justice Inquiry (Manitoba, 1990) was of the view that women should never have to leave their reserves because of violence. Yet, without safety, support, and healing structures for women on reserve, and without strong community commitment to ending violence against women and children, women will continue to be driven away from their reserves.

Childhood and Violence

Although this is a study of violence against women, childhood emerges as a central issue. Respondents demonstrate the correlation between abuse in childhood and abuse by an adult partner. Their responses reflect the interconnectedness of intimate violence in all its forms. All but one respondent witnessed the abuse of others as they were growing up, including the abuse of their mothers. All but one reported abuse in childhood, most by more than one abuser and in more than one way – physical abuse (nineteen), neglect and emotional abuse (eleven), and sexual abuse (seventeen). Abusers were in almost every case close family members (siblings, aunts or uncles and parents), with mothers reported as primary abusers by eleven respondents. Some implicated *the whole damn community*. Four respondents reported institutional abuse – two in residential schools and two in foster homes. The social status and system manipulation of abusers silenced many young victims. Others were blamed or disbelieved. Lack of services for them complicated help-seeking. Such early experiences merged with violent teenaged relationships for nine respondents. Intimate violence was the norm in childhood and adulthood.

Respondents were in mourning for their lost childhoods, still seeking healing for their young selves. They found childhood experiences most difficult of all to discuss. Many were also mourning lost offspring in the care of others because of the impact on their children of their own abuse by a partner and the effect of abuse on their parenting abilities. Political manipulation by partners was also a factor in their inability to gain or enforce custody. Two respondents reported children in need of protection, left with an abusive partner despite his abuse of them. That respondents recognized the effects of childhood violence in the violence of their abusers is reflected in their discussion of treatment. Many indicated awareness of a continuum of violence in their own progression from childhood victimization to violence by boyfriends in adolescence and 'choice' of, and loyalty to, abusive partners. Their concern for children's direct safety and breaking the cycle of abuse for their children was deeply informed by their own experiences of intimate violence in childhood. This factor played a major role in their seeking help, leaving the relationship, and getting treatment. Children of all respondents with children (two did not have children) witnessed their mother's abuse and in eighteen cases were the direct targets of threats and violence by their mother's partner. Witnessing the abuse of a child and recognizing the impact on children of their own abuse impelled decisions to leave.

But fear of children being taken away by CFS was a deterrent to calling police, based on their own experiences with child protection. Respondents remained with abusive partners longer than they might otherwise have done because of their fear that they would be forced by the abuser or by CFS to leave their children behind. Threats against children were a major form of emotional abuse for children, and mothers. Abusers used children to control partners both before and after separation, using threats and sexual and physical assault; 'buying' approval with money and gifts; and illegally blocking the mother's access and custody. That 'zero tolerance' did not include children was regretted by women recalling their own childhood, but women trying to escape spousal violence deeply feared the apprehension of their children by 'the system.'

Ages of respondents ranged from twenty-one to fifty-one. Their experiences embrace several eras in provision of child and family services to reserve communities and changing policy about prosecution. System response to childhood violence is difficult to assess. Service delivery to reserve communities, aside from community nursing and contract policing, was virtually nil until the late 1960s. Children needing protection were moved to other reserve homes or institutions or sent to residential schools by the Indian agent. Child protection services in the 1960s and 1970s focused almost exclusively on apprehension and fostering or adoption rather than on family intervention and support. The age range of respondents suggests that all these regimes are reflected in responses. Yet in almost every case, children tried and failed to get protection. Manitoba Tribal Council CFS agencies began service in the 1980s, but growing pains led to poor placements and politically controlled decision-making that left many children in dangerous situations. This may have complicated help-seeking on behalf of their children by younger women in this study.

Violence in childhood has emerged in this study as a major factor in the abuse of Aboriginal women, both as a precursor to abuse as adults and as a factor in seeking help. The right of children to be free of sexual violence is confirmed in 1988 reforms to laws on sexual assault of children, but the defence of reasonable correction still stands in the Criminal Code. The defence provides no guidance to parents or the courts on what is 'reasonable.' It is a deep derogation of the right to legal protection from assault and other forms of cruel or unusual treatment or punishment (McGillivray, 1997b). No line has been drawn in five centuries of English and Canadian jurisprudence between reasonable corporal punishment of children and criminal assault. The lack of 'framing' circumstances typical of other Criminal Code defences, seen in self-defence and defence of property, invites judicial subjectivity. The defence has a chilling effect on intervention by police and agencies. Recent empirical evidence shows that corporal punishment makes children more aggressive, while correlations with adolescents' offending and intimate violence in adulthood have long been established (Straus, 1994). Decreasing intimate violence in adulthood is tied to decreasing the violence against children that contributes to it. Setting childhood apart – *seen but not heard* in law as well as in the legally privileged privacy of parenting – and then permitting parents to assault children at will creates a licence for abuse. For Aboriginal parents indoctrinated into corporal punishment by Christian doctrines of 'the rod' in residential schools that sought to erase 'being Indian' and invited further devaluation down the social scale, children became a legal target of violence, as in Euro-colonial society. In an odd reinvention of original culture, one elder nostalgically recalled the birch switch by his grandmother's kitchen door and mourned the demise of the rod as a 'lost' First Nations 'value.' Yet early observers of child-rearing by First Nations are unanimous in their observation of lack of corporal punishment.

Early and effective childhood intervention that is culturally sensitive and balances needs for protection with the need for cultural and family connections is central to breaking the intergenerational cycle of intimate violence. Children's bodies need protecting as much as their culture, and culture means little when it ignores or condones their injury. Concern for children is a major factor in women's deciding to leave an abusive relationship. Responses from agency, police, and shelter must follow accordingly. Children's crisis lines should be widely advertised and aimed at culturally distinct as well as mainstream groups. Public education programs should stress, in culturally appropriate ways, a community's responsibility for protecting the young. Healing for adult victims of intimate violence should include healing the effects of childhood violence and providing insight into connections between childhood and parenting. The aim is to free parents from the violence that they underwent in their own childhoods so that they can focus on their children rather than be driven by their own inchoate childhood experience of violence.

Better strategies and improved educational programs need to be developed for police, lawyers, and front-line protection workers to address the dynamics of intimate violence in childhood and the impact of spousal abuse on parenting. Distinguishing between dangerous and protective parents is at the cusp of child protection, and mothers assaulted by partners tend not to be seen as protective parents (Hooper, 1992). Given appropriate support, it is probable that they in fact are. In the reserve context, mothers need to be enabled by police and social workers to withstand political pressure and bypass the social status of the abuser. Women need support and reassurance in intervening on behalf of their children. Children need their own support systems that promise return to the home, if their mothers are protective. Police need better training in the requirements of sections 282 and 283 of the Criminal Code governing abduction of children.

In studies of violence against women, more attention needs to be given to violence in childhood and its differential impact on male and female children, and much more is needed in the special context of Aboriginal and First Nations communities (McIvor, 1998). While a 'bad' childhood does not excuse violence in adulthood, violence against children must be addressed for the sake of adults as well as children.

Responding to Intimate Violence

Childhood experience, geocultural isolation, and individual and systemic racism shaped and controlled the ability of respondents to define their situation, assess the need for help, and get help. 'Being Native' touched almost every aspect of their experiences with policing and social services and with the justice system. Isolation, inadequate services, community norms, kinship networks, and band politics silenced respondents' complaints. Respondents reported elaborate strategies of isolation used by abusers, which included public humiliation, threats, physical incapacitation, economic control, public harassment, blaming the respondent for her own abuse, and shaming her for her culture or for supposed infidelity. Intimate violence across the life-span had seemed a normal, inescapable part of everyday life. Some respondents came to believe that they deserved or caused their own mistreatment. This in turn fed back into their own perceptions that intimate violence is normal and that those who report it will be demonized by their communities. When they were able to define the behaviour as abuse and to see themselves as not responsible for that abuse and as worthy of help, they were better able to seek effective assistance. Even so, they were demonized.

Inadequate policing prolonged the abuse. Police racism had a chilling effect on decisions to call for help. Fear of police was based on how respondents believed police would see them in these extreme circumstances – a fear, for many, derived from experience. Policing was often contaminated by racism and stereotyping. Seeing themselves through the eyes of police – as responsible for the violence because of their inadequacies, as morally or culturally corrupt, as female and unworthy – reflected back to respondents the lessons of inferiority beaten into them by parents and partners. Victim-blaming, explicit in police comments and implicit in failures in police response, reinforced self-blame and feelings of worthlessness. How police respond is a central indicator to victims of how the justice system, strangers, even society as a whole will respond to their situation. The system spoke that message when police did not come, or came too late, or showed by words or attitudes that the respondent was a nuisance or even just 'Native,' or when she had engaged in 'fighting' or otherwise resisted the violence and so might be portrayed as an offender, or when she was intoxicated or ill or did not have broken bones or other convincing proof of her 'worthiness' as a victim, and when charges were only reluctantly laid and lamely prosecuted. When an abuser convinced his victim that the police were on his side, or that her children would be apprehended, or that he would go straight to jail and his suffering would be her fault, if his family controls her access to telephones, if police do not charge because of 'who' he is, then the system spoke in its silence. It is not difficult to see how the maleness of the abuser and his association with male political and police culture in the complex micro- and macro-politics of the reserve add a convincing element to claims of power over the justice system. These claims were verified in cases where the offender's status silenced complainants and, even more, where charges were not laid or were dropped at the behest of chief and council. Where police did respond appropriately and pressed charges, respondents were relieved, despite inner conflict and guilt.

Respondents recommended that police be better educated in the dynamics of intimate violence and in Aboriginal culture:

I think police and justice system should be more sensitive to women that are battered, know more about them, be more educated.

I feel that the officers were very young and naive, and I, you know, I just felt like I was violated, like they made me feel that I was responsible, like, for what happened.

I think that the judge and the police should try and be more understanding about the repeated abuse and why the woman goes back. For most of the time, the woman doesn't know why she ended up going back. There's a lot of reasons. And the police should be there to help you, not judge you.

[Personnel in the justice system need] more understanding and, once again, their learning the cycle of violence so that they can be more empathetic rather than cynical.

Even when I went to that police academy awareness [training session] – they don't give a hole about Natives, and I sat there and I couldn't believe how ignorant they were. I really don't know. Even with Aboriginal awareness, it's still going on.

Education of police must focus on the dynamics of intimate violence, the historical dimensions of violence, cultural awareness, the nature of emotional violence (and related Criminal Code provisions), the needs of victims, and response protocol and policy. Training of police and in particular band constables in response to domestic assault needs to be improved and steps taken to counter problems inherent in the private policing of closed Aboriginal communities. Police accountability both on and off reserve must be clarified and better strategies developed to reassure victims, recognize conflicting loyalties and cultural differences, and avoid aggravating the problem.

The track record for lawyers was not much better. This is perhaps more surprising in civil and family law, in which lawyers represent clients, than in criminal justice, which subordinates victims' needs to fair trial and public interests. Intimate violence has been identified as a major issue in criminal justice and public protection. Prosecutors who exclude victims from plea bargaining and sentencing input defeat the goal of public protection. Plea bargaining masks the severity, frequency, and impact of the violence, by suppressing its history. Charge bargaining may lead to the suppression of facts necessary to judicial assessment of the conduct and the risk of future violence. Stricter controls on plea bargaining and greater involvement of victims in the prosecution of the offender are necessary if prosecution is to be truly 'vigorous,' as required by 'zero tolerance.' Lawyers representing respondents in matters of divorce, child custody, maintenance and support, and civil protection orders fared both better and worse. Respondents were enthusiastic about those who helped them with these matters. They were angriest at those who belittled or denied their claims of abuse, refused to call witnesses on their behalf, or, in one case, had his client herself investigated by CFS.

Crown attorneys and the legal profession in general need to be better informed of the dynamics of intimate violence and its effect on victims. For example, victims may experience problems in credibility because of the effects of abuse and the complex relations of intimate violence. Ambivalence about leaving the abuser and about prosecuting him may be interpreted as lying or exaggeration. Disclosure may occur slowly over time, as victims come to trust their lawyers and disentangle for themselves the meaning of their experiences. Piecemeal disclosure may be interpreted as embroidering on the truth. Acts of violence that profoundly trouble victims may seem trivial to the uninformed and take on criminal dimensions only when understood in context. Lawyers need professional education and upgrading in the dynamics of intimate violence (Mills, 1996, 1997) and cross-cultural services and response. The Lavoie Inquiry (Schulman, 1997) echoes these concerns. As judges cannot be forced to take professional training, the training of lawyers assumes a larger dimension, as all judges begin as lawyers. Law schools and bar admission courses need to take responsibility for this education.

'Zero tolerance' is intended to restore equality to victims of intimate violence in the justice system. Mandatory charging, vigorous prosecution, and a central information base for protection orders shift responsibility from complainants to police and prosecutors. Women then cannot blame themselves or be blamed by abusers for pressing charges. But in many cases, charges were not laid, not prosecuted, or dropped. Countercharging rose steeply as a result of stepped-up policies and, perhaps, police resistance to mandatory charging policies. Protection orders remained *just a piece of paper*, despite accessible computer records, although this may change with increased access.

Respondents expressed relief about the policy but saw many problems in its enforcement. They recommended routine use of restraining orders and improved response to breaches, greater police presence and involvement in taking women and their children to a place of safety, and longer sentences to improve victims' safety:

Stick to zero tolerance ... Follow through on it to see why she called, why she is scared.

[The police] should escort that person who has been abused. They should escort her to some safe place where she can get help.

I believe all [abused] women should have a restraining order against their partner if they don't want their ex-partner to be around them any more. I think this is for safety ... A restraining order has to be something we have to have because there is that possibility that the partner could just kill you. With it I feel safer.

That's one of the things I would want to know ... if I'm going to find out if he's going to be released. I wish they'd let me know instead of me running into him somewhere, you know?

Send them to jail for a long time.

Deviations from 'zero tolerance' suggest that the policy is either resisted by system personnel or is unevenly implemented in Aboriginal communities or in cases involving Aboriginal women. At the same time, women may want immediate protection without bringing the whole system into operation. Their needs and their desires may conflict. The role of police is immediate intervention, prevention of further violence, and the laying of appropriate charges, without moral judgment.

The Lavoie Inquiry (Schulman, 1997) identified similar problems in the execution of the 'zero tolerance' policy, in policing, prosecution, and legal services. Most recommendations have been implemented (Ursel, 1998a).

Designing Alternatives

Respondents were not prepared to discard the justice system. The system has an important symbolic function. It punishes violence, protects the vulnerable, and provides a time of safety by keeping dangerous people in jail. It is not a complete answer. It often fails in its enforcement of its own ideals and does not always give the protection that it seems to promise. It does not reform offenders. Jail terms are not given often enough or for long enough periods to warn or punish abusers or give their victims an adequate period of safety. Yet women in this study did not prefer counselling and mediation, nor did they reject the Anglo-Canadian justice system on cultural grounds. They expressed a belief in the justice system and in incarceration and viewed sentences as far too lenient. They recognized the importance of treatment. While jail does not reform offenders, in the view of respondents, treatment alone was seen as manipulable – *an easy way out* – and an inadequate response to respondents' suffering.

Canadian sentencing generally emphasizes rehabilitation, short sentences, and non-carceral dispositions. Judges are bound by sentencing rules, including limits on length and combination of dispositions set by statutes such as the Criminal Code and by the provincial Court of Appeal. Judicial independence is the cornerstone of the Anglo-Canadian legal system as an assurance of non-partisan treatment. Judges are not accountable to the public or to government, cannot be made to undergo professional upgrading, and cannot be removed except in cases of extreme abuse of power. Provincial policies on charging and prosecution cannot apply to the judiciary. Many judges have voluntarily taken part in judicial education on Aboriginal people and the justice system. Even so, Canadian incarceration rates are among the world's highest.

Respondents viewed community-based dispute resolution as partisan and subject to political manipulation. They would accept diversion only if it guards against manipulation, takes into account the seriousness of the offence, punishes in some way, gives victims safety, respects disclosures of abuse by offenders as well as by victims, offers and enforces treatment, and monitors compliance. Surprisingly, there was division as to whether diversion would work better in the city or on the reserve. The reserve is a favoured site of alternate sentencing because it promises community integration, close surveillance, connectedness, and intimacy. This intimacy may result in shaming. While community shaming was part of traditional First Nations discipline, the victim and her children are now more likely to be shamed than the offender. In some respondents' views, the city offers the victim and her children anonymity and the likelihood that offenders will be held to the terms of diversion. Diversion centres on the offender's reintegration into the community. It is not concerned with the victim's safety or with denouncing the offender's conduct. Those guilty of intimate violence are usually barred from diversion programs by prosecutors or judges (Green, 1998) on the basis of provincial prosecution policy, premised on substantially similar concerns. The strength of a system of diversion lies in its potential for culturally appropriate and community-sensitive disposition of offenders.

Our concern, however, is what would be good for victims of intimate violence. Respondents wanted input into the justice process and saw diversion as easily manipulated by offenders who may 'stack' the process with friends and supporters and avoid responsibility for their actions. Mediation between victim and offender is integral in diversion but is widely recognized as dangerous in domestic violence (Astor, 1994; Shaffer, 1997). The manipulation and control that characterized the abusive relationship can skew mediation, while the mediator or circle may be unaware of the use of such intimate tactics. The strong presence of Aboriginal people as police, lawyers, judges, and support workers might more fairly represent respondents' culture. Some respondents thought that this would be a good idea. Others equated this approach with racism or thought that Aboriginal people might be *too soft* on Aboriginal offenders.

Ensuring that the victim has a strong voice, independent advocacy and support, and continued control over her situation, and that the circle, tribunal, or committee is thoroughly educated in the dynamics of abuse and control, is central in designing alternatives and improving justice response. Support systems in culturally distinct communities are needed to help victims work through issues and find appropriate services. The majority of respondents favour jail because it offered *safety* for them and *punishment* for the offender. Respondents want both stiffer sentences and effective treatment programs.

These findings conflict with those of other Canadian studies. In a 1984 study, Meredith and Conway show that the need most frequently expressed, by 91 per cent of women, is for professional help for the abuser, such as alcohol treatment or programs about wife abuse (cited in McLeod, 1987: 25). 'Most victims do not want their assailant punished so much as they want the abuse to stop and they want their assailants helped.' McLeod concludes that women are more receptive to intervention by the criminal justice system when they perceive it as being preventive and protective, rather than punitive (85). Reports submitted to the Aboriginal Justice Inquiry (Manitoba, 1991) suggest that victims of intimate violence want treatment, not punishment, for abusers. The Alberta Law Reform Institute (1995) concludes: 'Most women felt that incarceration was the appropriate response to criminal sentencing or enforcement of restraining orders. Interestingly, however, their main interest in incarceration seemed not to be related to a desire for punishment for its own sake but rather as a way of giving them an opportunity to rebuild their lives without the destructive intervention of their abusive partners.' This view is reflected by women in this study, but respondents also stressed the symbolic value of jail as punishment for its own sake.

The ambiguity reflects criminal law debates that pit classic justice goals of retribution and denunciation against utilitarian goals of deterrence and rehabilitation. Long jail terms are deterrent, in that they incapacitate offenders and provide safety for victims. Jail also reflects denunciation and retribution – *payback* for victim's suffering. Sentences that combine jail with treatment express both retributive and rehabilitative goals and are in theory most likely to reduce future offending. In practice, however, there are problems. Mandatory 'insight therapy' is a contradiction in terms, as at least some degree of personel commitment to healing is needed. As offenders frequently deny or minimize the significance of their past conduct and continue to blame victims even while in jail, counselling is not always successful. Jail is a stand-in for public denunciation. Jail is also retribution for the victim, who has suffered what the criminal law has since the eleventh century considered the most degrading form of punishment – punishment of the body (McGillivray, 1997b). She has further suffered the degradation of emotional violence inflicted by one who knows her and can exploit what she cares about. She has suffered the pain of leaving, therapy, and self-examination. She wants him to pay. For her, the ideal regime is one that degrades his status, divides him from his family and support systems, and forces him to undergo self-examination. Respondents gave the question of diversion serious attention and suggested important conditions, but there was little support for the idea generally.

The difference between this and other studies may lie in sampling. Respondents had used shelter services, suggesting recent and severe circumstances of intimate violence and readiness to confront the issue. All had been introduced to an agency discourse that stresses treatment and insight. They may accept the *ideal* of abuser treatment even if it does not fit with their experiences or preferences. An interesting research question would be whether preference for treatment and diversion *versus* punishment and jail differs between women who have been exposed to agency discourse and those who have not. Such a study would pose ethical problems, as prior treatment is important to respondents' protection.

Among reforms needed are the expansion and improvement of treatment programs in and outside carceral facilities. If courts and jails are to continue to play the major role in the disposition of intimate violence offenders, then offender treatment programs must be improved and expanded to all carceral facilities, including young offenders' institutions. Studies of the effectiveness of such programs are needed (Proulx and Perrault, 1996; McIvor, 1998), and offender programs need to be approached with caution. Follow-through, protection for women and children during and after disclosure, and improved counselling and support systems for those going to court are essential. Design and analysis of research and policy must be better informed of the dynamics and prevalence of abuse, conflicts underlying the seeking of help, the relationship of community norms to perpetuating and escaping abuse and the intergenerational effect of abuse on victims and abusers.

Chiefs, band councillors, and elders need to recognize the basic human right of children and women to be free of assault and a perfect right to legal protection. Intimate violence is a profound and illegitimate interference with individual self-determination.

For indigenous peoples in colonized nations throughout the world there is another dimension to self-determination. The apparent conflict between group and individual rights is taken up in the next chapter.

6

Rights and Relationships

Until I learned that I had rights as a human being and as a woman, I just accepted what-ever my partners gave to me.

Human Rights and Intimate Violence

The contest is fought out in the larger political arenas of race, feminism, self-determination, and rights, but the ground of the battle is the bodies of children and women. The subject of law that law has created – singular, rational, self-choosing – is challenged by intimate violence. The split and decentred self of victims, deeply conditioned by others, defies this legal construct. Law's focus on the body in cases of intimate violence ignores the subjective, the ways in which the body has intimated its own sensations and an awakening self is speaking. The politicization of women's private struggles and the recognition of wife assault as a crime are hallmarks of second-wave feminism. Criminalization is a symbolic denunciation of intimate violence and promises some real benefits in terms of safety. It has been criticized for failing to provide solutions to the 'real' problems of women – gender inequity and 'the-day-to-day realities of wife battering, rape and assault' – and for increasing the level of punishment of 'populations ... already vulnerable and victimized' (Snider, 1995: 239). The practice of intimate violence is widespread, commonplace, and even encouraged (Straus, Gelles, and Steinmetz, 1980; Stanko, 1985, 1990; Levinson, 1989; Rodgers, 1994). Criminalization was a hard-won feminist and humanitarian goal, the result of nineteenth-century shaming processes in Parliament and the press (Doggett, 1993). Ground was lost in the early twentieth century, when violence against women disappeared from the new professional discourse and from the public agenda. Sexual violators of children were pathologized as 'strangers' with a sexual malfunction (McGillivray, 1992). Rape, battery, and sexual assault lost their familial context. With the return of these issues to public discussion came a rights consciousness that has now taken on international dimensions.

Violence against women *because they are women* is all but universal across states and cultures, whatever form it may take – wife-beating, genital mutilation, claustration, abandonment or infanticide of female infants, child prostitution, slavery, and dowry deaths. Because it is private, within the family, inflicted by individuals rather than by states, it was not seen as a violation of human rights in the international arena. State parties could disclaim responsibility for intervening. When we link it with public discrimination against women in government, workplaces, and schools, we can see clearly that violence against women in all its forms is systemic rather than idiosyncratic. Intimate violence is now becoming the stuff of human rights, implicating state responsibility. Gender-based violence may be a concept new to international human rights but it has long been a women's rights concern, as suggested by the 1632 treatise *The Lawes Resolution of Womens Rights or, The Lawes Provision for Woemen* (Doggett, 1993; Polito, 1994; Goodrich, 1995). This anonymous text warns women of the threat to self and fortune posed by pleasure-seeking violent men and the limited or non-existent legal protection from violent and exploitive husbands available to women under *coverture*.

The women in the current study claim as a basic human right the right to be free from intimate violence. Respondents drew on rights discourse, principles of human dignity and equal worth, and the basic human right to security of the person:

I remember I used to stutter a lot, and my doctor, she says that's from being scared, from having something I didn't tell. You know, that sexual abuse. ... When I was just a little girl I was really kind of shy, too quiet. I guess that's why my uncle ended up abusing me. Now I won't let anyone touch me, touch me the wrong way. And I tell my sons that, too, don't let anyone ever – you know. Everyone has rights.

Until I learned that I had rights as a human being and as a woman, I just accepted whatever my partners gave to me.

I think it takes time to reach someone like an offender. I think it takes time to teach some-

body. I think what's needed is to teach people because people are so unaware ... that they are doing things wrong. People are unaware that they have rights. I think communication is very important because, looking at relationships, my two abuse relationships, I see that if any one of us had been able to communicate, there might have been a different ending.

[I decided to leave] because I was aware that I had rights and did not have to live with it ... I want to teach that, you know. I want to teach my kids it is not the way to live, to be abused or to abuse people. I want them to come to know their rights ... to live free from violence.

Well, I think that a lot of Aboriginal men don't have knowledge of – I know the men and women too – don't have knowledge of the cycle of violence, or their rights.

Respondents' rights in the criminal justice context were not protected, and offenders were seen as having more rights than victims.

'Yeah, you can arrest him and throw him in jail, but he will be back on the street again,' I says. You know as well as I do that the accused have more rights than the victims.

In particular [what is needed is] protecting the victim's rights. For example, if the police officer can refer to their notes, while being cross-examined, why can't the victims have access to their notes too? I feel there is discrimination.

I would like to see justice being done right ... I would like to have the right to a good judge that's going to see what this guy has put us through ..., how we have been affected by what he did. I don't like to have to face him in the courtroom. I don't want to feel victimized by his lawyers or anyone on his side. Because I feel that when women try to protect them-selves, I've noticed that they are always victimized by police and lawyers. Women shouldn't have to go through that. It's bad enough what the partners put them through.

The Women's Advocacy Program does not get involved if a woman's been charged for assault. It is a proven fact, once ... her charges are dealt with, then they do become involved after that. And this is not acceptable. ... They violated the victim's constitu-tion[al] rights, as far as I'm concerned.

I think that a lot of victims are not only – it is not only women that are victims, men are, too – I think a lot of the victims don't know their rights, and the judges and lawyers don't seem to have time to tell people.

What the justice system is for? To protect people, to protect your rights.

Kathleen Mahoney (1992) identifies spousal assault and the response of the Canadian justice system as gender-based discrimination. Wife-battering symbolizes the inequality of women. It also reinforces that inequality. Women's rights to autonomy and to bodily integrity have been recognized recently and incompletely under Canadian law in the adoption of mandatory charging policies by the provinces in the 1980s. Setting intimate violence into the context of human rights in the international arena was a longer process, driven by non-governmental organizations (NGOs) representing grassroots organizations working with abused women in communities all over the world.

In 1948, the United Nations General Assembly adopted the first universal declaration of human rights. In 1979, human rights discourse centred on the condition of women. The United Nations Convention on the Elimination of All Forms of Discrimination against Women (CEDAW) was ratified by 136 member states. The only industrialized nation that did not ratify CEDAW was the United States. CEDAW does not address intimate violence, as private violence was not seen as a state responsibility. Human rights organizations defined violence against women as a private rather than a state matter, as the acts of individuals or the result of cultural and religious practices (Goldberg and Kelly, 1993; Bunch, 1995). Human rights discourse centred on violence committed by public or state actors and on freedom from discrimination in the public sphere. Masculinist conceptions of rights subordinated political, social, and cultural rights to public and political rights (Goldberg and Kelly, 1993).

As one critic notes, 'Until the gendered nature of the human rights system itself is recognized and transformed, no real progress for women can be achieved' (Charlesworth, 1995: 103). Applying the framework and discourse of human rights to violence committed in the private context of the lives of women and girls was first seriously addressed in the international arena at the World Conference of the United Nations Decade on Women in Copenhagen in 1990. In 1992, the Committee on the Elimination of Violence against Women, which oversaw CEDAW and drafted the Declaration on the Elimination of Violence against Women (DEVAW), set out the influential Recommendation 19. This defines gender-based violence as violence directed at women because they are women, or violence that disproportionately affects women, and it states that such violence is a form of discrimination that inhibits women's enjoyment of rights and freedoms on a basis equal to that of men (Commission on the Status of Women, 1995). 'Any act of gender-based violence that results in, or is likely to result in, physical, sexual or psychological harm or suffering to women' is a violation of human rights, both in itself and as an impediment to the enjoyment of other rights and freedoms.

DEVAW encompasses private intimate acts of violence, violence within the community, and traditional practices harmful to women and girls. The World Conference on Human Rights in Vienna in 1993 was the turning-point in acceptance of the new discourse by the international community. On 20 December 1993, the UN General Assembly adopted DEVAW, in the recognition that gender-based violence manifests unequal power relations and is the ultimate social mechanism for maintaining women's subordination to men (Charlesworth, 1995). This discourse appeared in Canada as early as 1986, when the Canadian Council on Social Development (1991) established its Family Violence Program to expand public awareness of the fact of intimate, violence and its impact on women and children. 'It is a basic fundamental right of all people to live in a non-violent environment,' the council states.

Systemic discrimination and chronic conditions of violence affecting women and girls are such that gender discrimination is now recognized as the most pervasive and serious human rights violation in the world, as the 1996 UNICEF *Progress of Nations Report* concludes (1997). Yet the mistreatment and undervaluation of women are for the most part accepted as the norm, 'the way things are,' as the report observes. Population analysis shows that as many as sixty million more women should be alive than are alive today. In the United States, a woman is assaulted by her partner on average every nine seconds. Five thousand women in India each year are victims of dowry death, murdered by husbands and in-laws when extortion attempts against their families fail, and 'countless others' are tortured and disfigured in extortion attempts. The abortion and infanticide of females routinely occurs in India, China, and elsewhere. Each year two million girls, most between the ages of four and ten, are genitally mutilated, causing pain, severe and chronic infection, complications in childbirth, loss of feeling, and often loss of life. Over one million children, mostly female, are forced into prostitution each year. The statistics are low, as under-reporting is the norm. Law in many states stops at the family door, the report concludes, and education and political power for women are central to changing the deep-seated belief that women are less valuable than men.

Although DEVAW is not recognized as an international treaty, it is an important step in recognizing intimate violence against women as a universal concern. A global perspective is essential to appreciating the 'wholeness' of violence against women (Roberts Chapman, 1989). The concept of rights, it is argued, should retain the strength of the legal framework in which it originated and in which rights conflicts continue to be resolved. The vision of rights should be broadened to include law reform, new information on intimate violence and remedies, and local initiatives. The rapid growth of grassroots responses to violence against women in cultures throughout the world has pushed the problem onto the global human-rights agenda.

Children's rights are a less contentious area than that of women's rights, at least on the surface. Childhood is widely constructed as involving a frail and centrally familial population lacking in autonomy and deserving of compassion. Such a population poses no threat to political leaders. Welfare rights of children – to a home and family, to food and shelter, to education, not to be abused – dominate the discussion. Autonomy rights can be read down to token representation in matters affecting children and to token rights of association and information. Even so, the recognition of children as rights-holders under international law is a major step forward, beyond the symbolic (Freeman, 1997). After ten years of work by an international committee representing many of the world's cultures, the UN Convention on the Rights of the Child of 1989 was signed and ratified more quickly by more states than any other UN convention (Cohen, 1990). The United States is one of only two member states, and the only industrialized state, that has not ratified the convention. Juveniles in the United States are placed on death row, and juveniles serving on warships or in potential battle zones will be drawn into armed conflict, breaching convention terms.

The Convention on the Rights of the Child sets out welfare rights, autonomy rights – freedom of thought, expression, information; such political rights as the right to a name and state and to representation in adoption and deportation hearings and other matters affecting the child; separate regimes including limited accountability for prosecuting children for criminal activity; and separate facilities for children's incarceration. Canada, under the leadership of Prime Minister Brian Mulroney, hosted a world summit on the rights of children in 1991. Canada demurred on two articles of the Convention – separate incarceration for juvenile offenders and state-directed adoption, in view of judicial recognition of customary adoptions in northern Canada. Another Canadian law has now come under scrutiny. The UN Committee on the Rights of the Child, overseeing the implementation of the convention, declared section 43 of the Criminal Code – the justification of corporal punishment – to be in breach of the convention (McGillivray, 1997b).

Individualist and masculinist constructions of rights mask the realities of the lives of women and children and render their concerns at once separate and invisible. One way to address the invisibility of women's and children's rights in international discourses on human rights is to problematize the sharp distinction made in law and in rights philosophy between private and public realms (Charlesworth, 1995; Sullivan, 1995). Why should the state tolerate violations of human rights because the place of injury and the relationship between violator and violated are deemed 'private'? Such violations are neither random nor individual. Rather, they are endemic and systemic. Analysing intimate violence as a human rights violation is now possible because of expanded notions of state responsibility.

The human rights vision is essentially a moral one: 'Placing domestic violence within the mainstream of the theory and practice of international human rights draws attention to the extent and seriousness of the problem' (Thomas and Beasley, 1995: 1129). Intimate violence denies the inherent dignity, worth, and equality of all human beings. The essence of discrimination is not the failure to criminalize intimate violence – most aspects of intimate violence are already crimes in most countries – but rather 'the failure to enforce laws equitably across gender lines' (1995: 1129). Discriminatory prosecution violates the right to equal protection of the law and thus constitutes the basis for a human rights claim on prohibited lines of gender discrimination. Although states cannot be held accountable for random acts of private violence, intimate violence presents a special case: it is directed at women, as women, with the intention of preventing them from exercising legal rights. Gender-neutral application of state and international law must yield to gender-specific responses to the abuse of women.

Rights and Culture

There is a second analytical problem to be overcome. This is the apparent conflict between individual rights and the right of the collectivity to self-determination. In the First Nations ethos, reflected in discourses on dispute resolution and self-government, granting women and children rights against the collectivity may be problematic.

Western political philosophy is strongly influenced by John Locke's *Two Treatises of Government* (1690). The work informed the drafting of the U.S. constitution (see chapter 2) and is reflected in thinking in international law about the role of the state. In the Lockean conception of natural rights, human beings are self-owning and the state is guarantor of individual rights – a view that lends support to the extreme individualism and autonomy embedded in dominant rights discourses. The work of liberal rights theorists Hobbes, Locke, and Mill has strongly influenced legal thinking, the construction of nationhood and the limits placed on government interference in such 'private' realms as the family across three and a half centuries. Privacy became a twentieth-century rallying cry of resistance to state interference in familial relations, even though, in Mill's view and that of others, interpersonal violence is never private. The views of these rights theorists have been insufficiently examined in relation to women in the political sphere and to women's status and relations with respect to children, production and reproduction, matrimony and self-determination (Makus, 1996).

It has been argued that the Lockean model of rights and the framework of rights infused with this view are inconsistent with First Nations communitarian values and traditions (Valencia-Weber and Zuni, 1995). Mary Ellen Turpel (1989), legal adviser to the Native Women's Association of Canada, questions the use of rights rhetoric in achieving collective goals of Aboriginal peoples as 'buying into' an individualistic, western liberal view of human rights. Section 35 of the Canadian Charter of Rights and Freedoms, 1982, states, 'The existing aboriginal and treaty rights of the aboriginal peoples of Canada are hereby recognized and confirmed' and 'the aboriginal and treaty rights referred to ... are guaranteed equally to male and female persons.' The Charter as a whole expresses an ethnocentric and dominant culture centred on individualist, property-based claims and ignores the collectivist focus of 'sovereign and distinct (yet entrapped) nations.' The preservation of Aboriginal rights, Turpel suggests, represents a 'conscious strategy of "ignore them and they'll go away"': 'It is difficult to move in a certain direction as a People if individuals can challenge collective decisions based on infringements of their individual rights and if collective goals will not be understood or prioritized ... It makes the preservation of a different culture and the pursuit of collective political goals almost impossible.'

Challenge may come from outside, on the basis that Aboriginal laws fail to conform to Charter standards, or from inside, from a community member arguing that his or her rights are not respected by an Aboriginal government. Turpel quotes the Assembly of First Nations' 1982 presentation to the parliamentary Committee on Aboriginal Affairs: 'As Indian people we cannot afford to have individual rights override collective rights. Our societies have never been structured that way, unlike yours, and that is where the clash comes ... If you isolate the individual rights from the collective rights, then you are heading down another path that is even more discriminatory ... [The Charter] is in conflict with our philosophy and culture.' Internal challenge erodes traditional dispute resolution and collectivist claims: 'Any case which presents a Canadian court with the opportunity to balance or weigh an individual right against a collective right, or Aboriginal collective understanding of community, will be an opportunity to delimit the recognition of Aboriginal Peoples as distinct cultures.' Turpel argues for the establishment of local Aboriginal Human Rights Committees, regional elder councils for dispute resolution, and the development of community codes, to avoid redress of wrongs in foreign (i.e., non-Aboriginal) courts. She does not address the complex issues raised in this context by intimate violence.

When one sector of First Nations – women and children – claims rights against another sector, men who may be part of the problem, who may be in leadership roles or able to obtain protection from leaders, may portray women's and children's right-claims as another form of racism, as an attack from within. The collective interest in self-determination and self-government – and the need to preserve 'face' in negotiations – is threatened by these separate claims. This conflict in part derives from the requirement for group self-determination in international law – that there be an identifiable and distinct population operating and asserting rights as a whole. This view makes no provision for individual claims against the majority of that discrete population. Although the focus on collective rights was inconsistent with the protection of individual rights and women's rights in other United Nations conventions (Valencia-Weber and Zuni, 1995), the United Nations Draft Declaration on the Rights of Indigenous People of 1992 maintained this requirement. The draft declaration was amended in 1993 by the addition of 'indigenous individuals' as a protected class and a guarantee of equal rights to male and female persons. The 1993 amendment did not materially alter the collectivist focus of the document (Valencia-Weber and Zuni, 1995). U.S. First Nations, which have separate courts, lawyers, police forces, and laws, view the guarantee of equal rights set out in CEDAW and the right to be free of intimate violence set out in DEVAW as a challenge to the customary collectivist practices of tribal courts and governments. 'Individualistic principles of gender equality will undoubtedly clash with the Native American legal practice, the foundations of which are premised upon primacy and centrality of the community as a whole' (Valencia-Weber and Zuni, 1995). The vision of human well-being as situated within, but subsidiary to, the collectivity motivates Aboriginal justice reforms in Canada, from peer counselling and circle sentencing to proposed First Nations justice systems. 'The philosophical basis of group rights rests on the primary commitment to the welfare of the community over and above the interests of particular individuals' (Charlesworth, 1995: 109). In discussions in Manitoba on devolution of Indian Affairs powers to First Nations, women do not have a strong voice. Nor, of course, do children.

Women 'are neither purely victims nor purely beneficiaries of cultural politics' (Rao, 1995: 172). Recognizing that women have 'limited access to public defences of cultural practices can help us to contextualize the greater politics of claims against rights on the basis of culture.' Complicating the picture is the fact that First Nations contest the jurisdiction of systems of criminal justice and child protection. Systemic discrimination in child protection and criminal justice, and the devastating impact of both systems on the lives of Aboriginal peoples, constitute a persuasive rationale for developing alternative systems. Yet criminal and child protection systems are the systems most central to response to intimate violence. Invoking either may be seen not only as rejecting one's partner and extended family, but also as denying one's culture and going against the politics of one's people. First Nations are fighting to reject stereotypes of violence. Claims of intimate violence made by Aboriginal women and children against other Aboriginal people may be seen as disloyal.

In the global call to recognize freedom from intimate violence as a human right, diversity among women and the cultures that frame their experiences provide the context in which rights are realized. In colonized nations in which an indigenous population is struggling for cultural rights, women's claims may be silenced as antithetical to the struggle, yet a universal consequence of colonization is the heightened risk and rate of violence against Aboriginal women and children in intimate relationships. Australia, New Zealand, Hawai'i, the continental United States, and Canada are among the nations in which that violence has been identified and addressed. The attempted silencing of respondents in this study is a reflection of these cultural politics. Yet 'culture' can have little (positive) meaning where culture provides the context and the excuse for the assault, rape, and spiritual destruction of women and children. Culture loses significance and respect when it is used to defend what may amount to a form of genocide on an everyday basis.

Historical processes help to explain intimate violence in Aboriginal communities but cannot excuse it or justify its continuation. Women have been doubly disadvantaged by colonial processes, children perhaps triply so, but solutions must be in the present. Women appearing before the Royal Commission on Aboriginal Peoples asserted the right to be free from intimate violence in their communities. The commission summarizes their proposals. 'Don't stereotype all Aboriginal people as violent, but make sure that interventions are targeted at those at risk. Don't make social or cultural excuses for violent actions, but attend to the safety and human rights of the vulnerable. Don't imagine that family violence can be addressed as a single problem; rather, root out the inequality and racism that feed violence in its many forms' (RCAP, 1996b: 64). The commission recommends that 'Aboriginal leaders take a firm, public stance in support of the right to freedom from violence of all members in the community, but particularly of women, children, elders, persons with disabilities and others who may be vulnerable, as well as in support of a policy of zero tolerance of actions that violate the physical and emotional safety of Aboriginal persons.' International treaties and conventions speak to both collective and individual rights of Aboriginal peoples. When First Nations justice systems are established, the balance between collective and individual rights may be better assured for women and children by retention of the overarching authority of the Canadian Charter of Rights and Freedoms (Isaac and Maloughney, 1992). Alternatively, there could be a First Nations Charter broadly based on international human rights conventions, as is the Canadian Charter, and that prohibits practices that discriminate on the basis of age or gender and entrenches the right to equality under the law and to equal treatment by the law.

Two basic approaches have been taken to the question of whether the Charter would apply to Aboriginal governments (RCAP, 1996b: 226 et seq.). The first stresses the anomaly created if Canadians were protected in their relations with every government in Canada except Aboriginal governments. The second accepts the authority of international human rights bodies but rejects the idea that Aboriginal governments can be held accountable in Anglo-Canadian courts. Aboriginal rights to self-government, both inherent and under treaty, are centrally defined in section 35, Part 2 of the Constitution Act, 1982, rather than in the Charter itself, which constitutes part 1 of the act. This suggests that self-government is granted an autonomous constitutional status that is equivalent to the Charter rather than subject to the Charter. However, section 25 of the Charter provides that 'the guarantee in this Charter of certain rights and freedoms shall not be construed so as to abrogate or derogate from any aboriginal peoples of Canada including (a) any rights or freedoms that have been recognized by the Royal Proclamation of October 17, 1763; and (b) any rights or freedoms that now exist by way of land claims agreements or may be so acquired.' Any limitation imposed by the Charter on the powers of Aboriginal governments would derogate from section 25 of the Charter, according to this argument. Section 33 of the Charter gives provincial legislatures the power to declare a law to be operative notwithstanding the fact that the law may be in breach of section 2 or sections 7 to 15 of the Charter. The power has been exercised, for example, in language matters in Quebec. The 'notwithstanding' clause constitutes recognition of localized provincial powers. It is not expressly extended to Aboriginal governments, implying that their right to exercise inherent powers of government is absent from the Charter.

The Royal Commission proposes a halfway house – an intermediate approach embodying three principles. First, all people in Canada in their relations with government are entitled to Charter protection. Second, Aboriginal governments stand equal with federal and provincial governments in their power to use section 33's 'notwithstanding' clause. Any law, rule, or application of a law or rule inconsistent with the Charter can be sustained by section 33, renewable every five years. Third, in applying Charter standards to Aboriginal governments, there must be 'considerable scope for distinctive Aboriginal philosophical outlooks, cultures and traditions,' applying 'with particular force where distinctive Aboriginal perspectives on human rights have been consolidated in Aboriginal charters of rights and responsibilities' (RCAP, 1996b: 230). Aboriginal governments can use the 'notwithstanding' powers of section 33 only in matters falling into the core or centre of Aboriginal jurisdiction, and this core must be seen in the dual context of the Charter and the related provisions of the Constitution Act. The royal commission argues that the fact that only an Aboriginal *Nation* can so derogate means that local Aboriginal communites do not have these powers unless the areas governed by such powers fall into local areas of government. Other powers fall into the periphery.

The question raised by our study is whether Aboriginal governments however constituted can derogate from Charter protections for victims of intimate violence. Women and children can claim protection from the unequal application of law under section 15. Perpetrators can claim rights under sections 7 to 12. First Nations and Aboriginal governments can claim collective rights under both the Constitution Act and the Charter. Can Aboriginal justice systems derogate from the Charter and perhaps inferentially from international convention, in deciding claims made by women and children? Charter rights are equally guaranteed to male and female persons. 'Singly and in combination, these provisions constitute an unshakeable guarantee that Aboriginal women and men have equal access to the inherent right of self-government and that they are entitled to equal treatment by their governments. By their explicit terms, these provisions transcend any other provisions of the Charter, including section 33' (RCAP, 1996b: 233). Yet a certain patronizing tone permeates the Royal Commission's conclusions: 'Where an Aboriginal nation enacts its own charter of rights and responsibilities, private individuals will benefit from its provisions in addition to those of the Canadian Charter. An Aboriginal charter will supplement the Canadian Charter but not displace it. A person subject to the authority of the Aboriginal government will still have direct access to the Canadian Charter. However, in construing the Canadian Charter in the light of section 25, a court may well find the provisions of the Aboriginal charter a useful guide.' The Commission states: 'By virtue of sections 28 and 35(4) of the *Constitution Act*, 1982, Aboriginal women and men are in all cases guaranteed equal access to the inherent right of self-government and are entitled to equal treatment by their governments' (RCAP, 1996b: 234).

Who can exercise these powers? Band councils currently control membership and various policing powers. Should self-government be realized at the band level? On the local level, in such 'core jurisdiction' areas as education and training, local justice initiatives, housing allocations, policing, membership, and residency, band councils exercise considerable self-determination with respect to the local community. Sharon McIvor, speaking for the Native Women's Association of Canada, told the Commission that self-government should be granted to Nations rather than to band councils and be negotiated on a Nation-to-Nation basis. The Commission supports this view, concluding that 'the inherent jurisdiction of Aboriginal peoples can be exercised only through initiatives and treaties at the level of the [Indian] Nation' (RCAP, 1996b: 235).

Aboriginal communities seek identity and solutions in pre-colonial traditions and situate self-determination within these same traditions. If colonialism caused or exacerbated intimate violence, what can the colonizer's contested systems and historically suspect 'solutions' to First Nations problems offer? Yet some traditions are harmful to women and children. 'The challenge is, finally, to ourselves as Native women caught within the burdens and contradictions of colonial history,' Emma LaRocque (1996: 14) writes. 'We are being asked to confront some of our own traditions at a time when there seems to be a great need for a recall of traditions to help us retain our identities as Aboriginal people. But there is no choice – as women we must be circumspect in our recall of tradition. We must ask ourselves whether and to what extent tradition is liberating to us as women ... Culture is not immutable, and tradition cannot be expected to be always of value or relevant in our times. As Native women, we are challenged to change, create, and embrace "traditions" consistent with contemporary and international human rights standards.' International standards in human rights and standards reflected in the Charter thus serve as touchstones for the discovery or rediscovery of cultural practices protective of women.

Rights discourse for children (McGillivray, 1994b; Freeman, 1997) and for women (cf. Smart, 1989) as well as for Aboriginal peoples (Turpel, 1989) has been challenged. Although grassroots feminist groups in Canada, the United States, Australia, New Zealand, and elsewhere lobbied in the 1980s for mandatory charging and prosecution to deal with intimate violence, some feminist theorists questioned this narrow legal terrain, arguing that rights discourse and use of the legal system to assert rights bypass the social restructuring necessary to improve the social and economic status of women. Discrimination by the justice system, and the male privileging and extreme individualism embedded in traditional rights thinking, suggest that rights discourse is inconsistent with women's reality, defined as relational rather than individualist. Feminism is concerned with the analysis and improvement of women's condition and women's self-determination. Collectivist goals of self-determination, within and outside Aboriginal cultures, may be dominated by a male-centrism that denies or even venerates control of women and children. Identifying the interests of women with the collectivity poses problems for both feminist and indigenous movements.

The dissonance between individual and collective rights may not be the extreme disjunction portrayed in self-determination and feminist discourses (McGillivray, 1994b). Rights claims are not a zero-sum game in which one party gains rights at the other's expense or that pits the individual against the collectivity, detracting from its strength. 'Individual' can have meaning only with reference to collectivity. Rights are less claims *against* the collectivity than markers of relationships of equality *in relation to* the collectivity. If individualism is the heart of autonomy, then, as Jennifer Nedelsky (1993) argues, this is a misguided view of auton-

omy. 'What makes autonomy possible is not separation, but relationship. This approach shifts the focus from protection against others to
structuring relationships so that they foster autonomy.' This unseats certain rights notions. Dependence 'is no longer the antithesis of autonomy
but a precondition in the relationship – between parent and child, student and teacher, state and citizen – which provides the security, education, nurturing, and support that make the development of autonomy
possible.' Nor is autonomy a static condition, gained at some arbitrary
point of maturity. Rather, it is 'a capacity that requires ongoing relationships that help it flourish.' The collective is the source of autonomy.
Dependence – on the collectivity, on relationships – does not preclude
either autonomy or rights.

Rights consciousness is not foreign to Aboriginal peoples. The reserve
structure and early Indian Acts removed from First Nations women
important rights enjoyed to a greater or lesser extent within their respective Nations – voting rights and a place in tribal decision-making, property ownership and other economic rights, control of the household and
divorce, control of children and their education in early childhood, a
matrilineal descent that preserved the place of women and children
with the mother's Nation, and, in some Nations, financial opportunities
and status not only equivalent to, but identical with, men's (see chapter
2). These rights were not enjoyed by European women of the day. The
contribution of First Nations women to their economies at least equalled
that of men, while 'women's work' in pre-twentieth-century Europe and
Euro-colonial societies was viewed rather differently.

As LaRocque (1993, 1996) points out, culture is never static. Where
particular myths are injurious to women, she argues, they must be discarded or remade. In this rebuilding of tradition, the rights consciousness of traditional First Nations cultures may re-emerge. Certainly, it is
less alien to these cultures, and to women generally, than has been
depicted by many Aboriginal and feminist writers. First Nations have
embraced a rights framework in self-determination, and legal rights
deriving from treaty are fundamental in settlement of land claims. That
rights claims by women should be opposed on the basis that rights
thinking is not a part of the First Nations psyche or Aboriginal world-
view is not supportable.

Rights, Culture, Holism, and Local Initiatives

Rights discourse has helped to compel state action on behalf of women and children. The larger human rights discourse emergent at the inter-national level is driven by grassroots programs on intimate violence throughout the world. Initiative for change came not from member states – although this might have been expected from states with new laws and strategies on intimate violence – but from non-governmental organizations representing local groups. 'It is local actors and groups which have pushed to bring this issue to global attention' (Merry, 1997: 254). Roberts Chapman (1989) observes that such local initiatives as GABRIELA in the Philippines, Women under Muslim Laws in Bang-ladesh, and Mujeres por la Vida in Chile have driven the 'international machinery' of rights. Globalization of women's rights to be free of inti-mate violence exists outside and beyond the human rights system, and law may be a double-edged sword – a source of protection in some states and of mistreatment and abuse in others.

Initiatives in indigenous and ethnically mixed contexts provide examples of localized interpretations of the emergent global discourse on intimate violence. In her study of response to spousal assault in the ethnically mixed city of Hilo, Hawai'i, anthropologist Sally Merry explores disjunctions and connections between rights as a homogeniz-ing or hegemonic force and rights as 'contextualized within multiple legal orders and resources' (Merry, 1997: 271). Law is used as a form of resistance, and rights have become the discourse of local movements throughout the world. Merry (1997: 250) writes, 'Now, a global legal order offering concepts, rules, and resources is transnationally available to local groups such as indigenous peoples, battered women, or fami-lies of political prisoners. Local actors face a richer and more diverse legal terrain than they did, a terrain which provides new possibilities for using the law as a form of resistance. And local actors are using it extensively. One of the striking developments of the last decade is the extent to which local groups, such as indigenous peoples, wage their struggles on this terrain.' Merry recognizes that the framework of rights is problematic in its preference for certain remedies over others (legal but not economic rights, for example) and embeds concepts of person-hood and responsibility that may not fit with women's subjectivity. While rights provide 'new forms of cultural and coercive capital,' the concept introduces 'categories of identity, conceptions of redress, and modes of defining problems which constrain and channel them' (Merry, 1997: 251). Criminalization emphasizes legal rights and places a specific Euro-cultural frame on intimate violence.

There is irony in the fact that women and children now have the opportunity to appropriate human rights discourse on a grassroots level but may find themselves bounded by law's construction of the rational, autonomous, choosing subject, 'crafted at considerable cost from the sociocultural variability of the world during the Enlightenment in Europe and transplanted through colonial processes' (Merry, 1997: 267). Those who fail to meet law's expectations – women who continue to live with the batterer or themselves engage in violence – are 'redefined as children or "others," often racially and/or gender-coded others. Women become rethought as children.' Even so, the concept of human rights 'is profoundly radical and potentially democratizing' (271). Rights concepts are appropriated in different ways across myriad cultures. Rights in some contexts will have little to do with legal response. In others, there may be reliance on a model of legal rights. 'It is unclear to what extent local communities in different political contexts are, in fact, remote from the cultural categories and systems of meaning embedded in Western law' (258). Research on local interventions into intimate violence will shed light on the extent to which these initiatives both appropriate human rights concepts and culturally reshape them.

The Platform for Action (1995) prepared by the Fourth World Conference on Women in Beijing emerged from local initiatives and reaffirmed the rights discourse. 'Violence against women both violates and impairs or nullifies the enjoyment by women of their human rights and fundamental freedoms. The long-standing failure to protect and promote those rights and freedoms in the case of violence against women is a matter of concern to all States and should be addressed' (section D: 112). The conference in turn inspired new local initiatives through the symbolic power of rights discourse. In this dialectic, the abstract principles of rights discourse, derived from earlier grassroots movements, are reabsorbed at the local level.

The Hamilton Abuse Prevention Project, an urban intervention model in place prior to Beijing, is a case in point. Designed by lawyers, activists, and community members for the ethnically mixed Maori and Pakiha (European) city of Hamilton, New Zealand, the project incorporates intervention and treatment models developed in many parts of the world to provide a holistic response to intimate violence. Like its inspiration and counterpart in Duluth, Minnesota, the Hamilton Project is a community-based, inter-agency, coordinated model of response developed for urban settings. It is designed to reform and reinforce criminal justice response; coordinate agencies and family and criminal courts; and ensure victims' protection through a complex of protocols governing working relationships between agencies, personnel in the justice system, and project programs (Busch and Robertson, 1994). The project's priorities are victims' safety, enhancement of victims' autonomy, and accountability and rehabilitation of offenders. Accountability is seen as central to rehabilitation, which extends through and beyond the justice system into treatment and reintegration. It offsets the perception that abusers can escape penalty or that intimate violence is a 'different' and less important form of violence. Agencies, treatment centres, police, lawyers, and the courts are governed by a series of protocols, closely monitored to ensure consistent implementation of provisions and appropriate consequences for abusers.

Intervention problems prior to the Hamilton Project resonate with those identified in our Winnipeg study – police reluctance to arrest offenders, bail granted without assurance of victims' safety, inadequate sentence, lax enforcement of protection orders, lack of service coordination, and victims' problems in gaining child custody. The development of a shared inter-agency philosophy of the nature of intimate violence and of priorities that must guide response has resulted in the closing of many of these gaps. While the Hamilton Project shares some features with Manitoba policy – mandatory charging and prosecution, victim advocacy – there are deep differences. Most striking is Hamilton's monitoring of individual victims, offenders, and the system itself and the coordination of all response systems. The project takes the position that the justice system colludes in intimate violence if it fails to give an unambiguous message that violence is unacceptable. The discretion of police, lawyers, and judges is limited in all but exceptional cases. Protocols include mandatory arrest in clear cases of assault, notification of the project crisis line to ensure follow-up, and mandatory charging if a male assaults a female partner unless a more serious charge against the female is warranted. Charging for breach of protection orders is mandatory. Victims' requests to have charges withdrawn are always denied. All victims are allocated a court advocate provided by the project. Bail is withheld for a period of time, to reduce the risk of intimidation of victims and give them a chance to get help. A no-contact order is routinely imposed unless the victim specifically requests continued contact. At the district-court level, police evidence of assault can be used in place of the victim's testimony. This is not done in Canada, perhaps because of an archaic or faulty reading of the hearsay rules. Sentencing policy requires that offenders be referred to a project education program and to appropriate treatment programs. Community corrections officers make sentencing recommendations, monitor community-based sentences and parole, and provide information on the victim and a summary of previous incidents of violence.

The Hamilton Project extends to the family courts. Men subject to protection orders issued by these courts must also attend an education program. Women recommended to the women's education program are granted six weeks' delay in the determination of access to children and custody. This enables women to become better able to take part in court-ordered counselling or mediation and negotiate child care options. Central to monitoring, coordination, and service provision is the court advocate. This program supports women who must testify, by demystifying the court process, coordinating child care and transportation, and enforcing protection orders. The advocate's central role is tracking the offender through the justice system and documenting the system's departures from intervention protocol. The advocate works with shelters to operate a joint crisis line and maintain a roster of advocates who can provide immediate support, gather information on the assault, take women to shelters if necessary, and evaluate police response.

Jan Turner (1995:196) writes of a similar holistic response model in Saskatoon, Saskatchewan, a city of 185,000, which, like Hamilton and Winnipeg, has a large Aboriginal population: 'Aboriginal women in particular are often at the fore-front [sic] of finding ways to reduce violence and start the healing process.' Aboriginal women participated in consultations and supported the new legislation which frames the system's response – Saskatchewan's Victims of Domestic Violence Act, SS c. V-6. The act applies to any victim of domestic violence and takes the novel approach of granting jurisdiction to special justices of the peace to issue emergency protection orders subject to any terms that the justice of the peace deems appropriate. Orders must be reviewed by a higher court within a set period. The burden of proving that the order should not be confirmed lies on the person against whom the order is made. Justices of the peace are recruited on the basis of cultural background and sensitivity to intimate violence.

Like the Duluth and Hamilton projects, Saskatoon's coordinates interagency response, provides staff training, improves police and other information systems, and stresses autonomy, healing, and accountability. Unlike them, however, Saskatoon's recognizes that accountability of offenders may not require full involvement with the criminal justice system. Other ways of assuring accountability may permit 'community reintegration in a context more in keeping with Aboriginal tradition.'

Turner notes that most Aboriginal people support mandatory charging and full criminal sanctions for serious offences but 'struggle to find venues to bring more permanent solutions to troubled communities.' This is reflected in Winnipeg respondents' concerns about ensuring punishment, safety, treatment, and alternatives that depend on *how they offend*.

Although the basic philosophy of these projects is shared by Winnipeg agencies and Manitoba justice policy, there are, as noted, many differences. The Winnipeg Victim-Witness Advocacy Program is limited in scope and personnel. There is little or no coordinated systematic management of cases. This should ideally include following up on complaints; tracking cases between jurisdictions; protecting victims in moves between jurisdictions, agencies, and systems; coordinating the actions of family and criminal courts; tracking sentencing and treatment; supplying information to victims; and investigating the training of police, lawyers, and judges. Computer access to protection orders is one step in the right direction.

The Duluth model and its variations have been applied in ethnically mixed centres and in First Nations populations, but other local models have also been developed. In the mid-1970s, a few residents of Manitoba's Hollow Water Reserve, an Ojibwa community of about six hundred, began to turn to traditional approaches to healing (Hollow Water, 1993, 1994; Ross, 1993). Their personal healing journeys and insights gained from social work training became the seed of Hollow Water's holistic community healing project. In 1984, they faced the problem of substance abuse, suicide, vandalism, and truancy among youths. At the problem's core was childhood sexual victimization. Some 75 per cent of residents had been victims of sexual abuse, and 35 per cent have abused others. The Community Holistic Circle Healing Program was created in 1989 to address this problem (Canada, Solicitor-General, 1997). A broad-based team of volunteers and professionals – a child protection worker, the community health representative, the community nurse, a representative of the Royal Canadian Mounted Police and representatives of the school and churches – was established. Most team members are survivors of long-term sexual abuse by family members. Abusers who have completed the healing contract and cleansing ceremony may be invited to join the team. A major step was to break down professional barriers for a partnership model that addresses all aspects of the issue and avoids the 'splintering' of the subject. 'Outside' professionals are welcomed but must agree to the coordinated team approach and to being accompanied at all times by a community team member, for the purposes of mutual learning. A thirteen-step protocol governs all aspects of response. A healing contract requiring an offender to make certain changes is designed by victims and others affected. Thus abusers' denial, manipulation, guilt, self-hatred, injury, and anger are recognized and dealt with in intense, personalized sharing sessions, which strip away pretensions in painful confrontations. Only then can healing and rebuilding begin. After successful completion of the healing contract, a cleansing ceremony is held to honour the offender and mark a new start.

Some cases were seen as 'too serious' for community response, and the criminal justice system was involved. Under the first protocol, charges were laid quickly, and support was available for the offender in the criminal process if he entered a guilty plea. Most chose this route. Sentencing was delayed to allow the team to prepare a full pre-sentence report, which included the impact on, and recommendations of, all others involved, a plan of action based on the healing contract, and an assessment of the sincerity and rehabilitative potential of the offender. Where a jail term was ordered, the team worked with the offender while he was in custody and prepared the community for his release. The project team has since altered its position on the involvement of the justice system for four reasons (Hollow Water, 1993). Support for a criminal response had been motivated by unresolved issues of the originators of the project, as victims – anger, revenge, guilt, and shame. Relatively trivial offences, for which offenders were diverted, may be as damaging as those that the criminal law considers to be more serious. The adversarial nature of the system and the right of an accused to keep silence interfered with early disclosure and healing. The possibility of incarceration inhibited disclosure and drove abusers underground. Diversion and community sentencing, the team asserts, is not an 'easy way out' for the offender but rather establishes 'a very clear line of accountability between the victimizer and his or her community. What follows from that line is a process that we believe is not only much more difficult for the victimizer, but also much more likely to overcome the victimization, than doing time in jail could ever be.' In 1993 the team took its circle into the courtroom or, more accurately, the courtroom into its circle (Hollow Water, 1994). Offenders may now be diverted from the justice system, in accordance with protocols drawn up between the team and personnel of the justice system. The 'boundedness' of the community in terms of culture and geography, the intensive holistic approach, and the high degree of community commitment to the project are central ingredients of what observers agree is a successful initiative in combating sexual abuse of children.

As the Hollow Water project shows, the coordinated, multifaceted response, monitoring, and focus on safety and healing, central to the projects in Duluth, Hamilton, Hawai'i, and Saskatoon are relevant to reserve settings and apply to forms of intimate violence other than spousal assault. Diverting some offenders is possible in such models because of this holistic and victim-centred approach. Respondents' requirements for diversion – censure and safety – seem to be met in these comprehensive projects. However, community sentencing and diversion and such alternate measures as healing circles remain contested. Roberts and La Prairie (1996: 82) question whether sentencing circles will reduce crime and recidivism, lower costs, advance victims' interests, or promote community solidarity. They argue that sentencing circles contradict common law principles of proportionality – the sentence should be proportionate to the gravity of the offence and the degree of responsibility of the offender. Circles further deny parity – similar sentences should be imposed on similar offenders for like offences committed in like circumstances. Circles 'avoid notions of culpability, and pay scant attention to the offence's seriousness' (Roberts and La Prairie, 1996: 75). They 'represent a fracture with the traditions of sentencing and fly in the face of current sentencing reform initiatives in Canada and elsewhere.' This seems an odd claim, in view of the new Criminal Code sentencing provisions and the general tendency of law reform in Canada to seek alternatives to incarceration. The authors argue that disparity must be justified by proof that circles otherwise make a positive contribution to sentencing goals and warn that circles 'may not be the panacea that some of their more enthusiastic advocates would have us believe.'

Sentencing principles set out in the Criminal Code in 1995 require proportionality and sentencing parity, but also support the concept of community sentencing and the sentencing circle. Section 718.2(e) directs the court to consider all sanctions other than imprisonment that may be reasonable in the circumstances, 'with particular attention to the circumstances of aboriginal offenders.' Section 718.2(a) specifies that abuse of a position of trust or authority and, in particular, evidence that an offender abused his or her spouse or child are aggravating factors in sentencing. A 1996 amendment to the Criminal Code – section 742.1, 'Conditional Sentencing' – permits a sentence to be served in the community if the principles set out in section 718 are first considered, the sentence is under two years, and the offender is not a danger to the community. In the circle-sentencing case of *R. v. Manyfingers*, [1996] AJ No. 1025 Alberta Provincial Court, Jacobson Prov. Ct. J., 14 November 1996 (unreported), a conditional sentence of one year followed by two years' probation was ordered for a Blackfoot woman who stabbed her husband in the arm when she found him with another woman. In following the recommendations of the sentencing circle, the Alberta provincial court expressed concerns – case planning was inadequate, the assault was intentional and serious, the accused had problems with alcohol and anger and a history of violence, the assault involved a spouse, and, aside from residing on the reserve, the accused had no particular connection to traditional culture and spirituality. The court awarded the sentence on the grounds that more restrictive sentencing conditions could be imposed at any time and breach would result in immediate incarceration. Conditional sentencing reflects dual goals of punishment and rehabilitation, requiring 'a sound and workable set of reliable methods and procedures to achieve those objectives as part of the proper administration of justice.' The accused must be 'a willing and suitable candidate desirous of change,' 'the community attitude must support the accused and show a commitment to provide adequate resources for her rehabilitation,' and 'there must be no likelihood of violent, dangerous, or aggressive conduct on the part of the accused.' Circle sentencing, like sentencing in the dominant system, is not a panacea but the lesser of two evils, the court opined, with the balance turned by community involvement.

Sentencing amendments to the Criminal Code introduce elements from competing discourses – the justice system's concerns about over-reliance on incarceration of Aboriginal people, Aboriginal concerns about effective community reintegration and return to traditional culture, First Nations' claims of self-government, and concerns about intimate violence focusing on victims' safety, rights, breach of trust, and *payback*. The Hamilton Project is a multi-system approach that relies on and does not centrally challenge criminal justice response. The Hollow Water Project, by contrast, has shifted from support of a criminal justice response towards complete diversion. *Manyfingers* shows that neither breach of trust nor abuse of a spouse – aggravating factors in the code amendments – precludes a conditional sentence. Had it been Mr Manyfingers who assaulted Ms Manyfingers, would the result have been the same? Is gender disparity sufficient to deny sentencing parity or introduce a greater apprehension of dangerousness? The tension between ideas of appropriate response to intimate violence and the role of the justice system is not easily resolvable.

The major themes of this chapter emerge directly or inferentially from the views and experiences of respondents. These themes are holism and rights. Holistic responses developed at grassroots levels and accommodated by the legal system attend to the whole person, in the context of the systems in which he or she is immersed. Such initiatives combine formal and informal responses – prosecution, policing and victims' services, peer counselling and insight therapy, support systems and shelters, case tracking, law reform, and sentencing alternatives that draw together traditional and criminal justice approaches. For Aboriginal communities, responses to intimate violence also may include the assertion or reinvention of cultural approaches to healing, restitution, and reintegration and of traditions that enhance the status and treatment of women and children. Aboriginal women and children should not have to leave their communities for safety and healing.

Tragically, our respondents experienced little or none of this. Left to them was the unhappy residue of colonial processes that stripped away from women their children, their status, and their equality within their communities and that tore from children their mothers, families, and cultures. The breakdown of community ethos and of protective and balancing processes within original systems – women's roles in government, their divorce and property rights, their rights to their children, restitution, the high valuation of children and their social role, and community punishment – led to an onslaught of physical, sexual, and emotional violence by parents, partners, and community members. To save their bodies, spirits, and children, respondents had to flee, abandoning kith and kin, community, and the culture of everyday life. Their communities are the more impoverished for the loss of these women and their children. Failures in the legal system's responses formally or informally dedicated to helping such victims – ranging from police to lawyers through courts to victim support programs – increased their inequality. The services that victims received from Aboriginal agencies in Winnipeg were a saving factor for them.

Throughout the world women's experiences of intimate violence generated a rights-consciousness that is now reflected in international documents on human rights. That intimate violence is a breach of fundamental human rights, and that the state is now implicated under international law in restoring those rights, have in turn influenced local initiatives. This consciousness has created discourses, political spaces, and services for and by Aboriginal women. It has emerged as an important aspect of respondents' realignment of their experiences, from the normalization of violence – and blame heaped on them for this violence by those violating them, by their communities, and by those *who help – supposed to help* them – to a place where they can make choices and judge for themselves.

Rights discourse is the discourse of the dispossesed. It is the symbolic expression of the yearning for autonomy and respect. 'For the historically disempowered,' Patricia Williams (1987: 416) writes, 'the conferring of rights is symbolic of all denied aspects of humanity: rights imply a respect which places one within the referential range of self and others, which elevate one's status from human being to social being.' The elevation from human being to social being lies at the heart of restoring equality to Aboriginal women and children, an equality contested and sometimes denied in Canadian First Nations discourses of self-determination and self-government, as it has been in collective rights discourses of colonized peoples in international law. Rights in Western legal tradition speak to individual relations with the collectivity. Rights discourse lies at the heart of the claims of women and children caught in the self-referencing net of intimate violence, rights now recognized under international human rights law, even under self-determination of colonized or oppressed peoples. *'You don't have to be on the street to be a Skid Row. I was living in a million dollar house,'* she said. *'I was a Skid Row in there.' And even those people who are rich, they suffer.* This sharing of suffering across cultures – and across the great divide of race and socioeconomic status – speaks to a unity between the dispossessed and the fortunate that reinforces the universality of the experience of intimate violence, and the shared difficulty of freeing oneself from it. Rights of women and children in all cultural contexts speak at once to equality in intimate relationships and to equality in relations with the collectivity.

I think it takes time to teach somebody. I think what's needed is to teach people because people are so unaware ... that they are doing things wrong. People are unaware that they have rights. I think communication is very important, because looking at ... my two abuse relationships, I see that if any one of us had been able to communicate, there might have been a different ending.

Appendix: The Winnipeg Study

Intimate violence has been studied over the years with the use of a variety of methods. The literature offers little information on study design, consent issues, or safety measures for respondents. In order to encourage research into intimate violence in ethnically 'othered' communities, we append more detailed information about the design and management of the Winnipeg study.

Background

Original Women's Network approached the Manitoba Research Centre on Family Violence and Violence against Women in the autumn of 1993 for a study that would evaluate the responses of Aboriginal women to a proposed urban diversion project based on the Metro Toronto Aboriginal diversion model. Anne McGillivray agreed to serve as university research partner, a requirement of the centre, and to design a study in consultation with a steering committee to be composed of directors of Winnipeg Aboriginal women's service agencies. The project was a partnership between university and community to explore intimate violence, the system's response, and alternatives from the perspective of Aboriginal women. Brenda Comaskey joined the project to refine and test the research instrument, coordinate sampling, train interviewers, and undertake first-level analysis of data. Her role, going far beyond this, gives her co-authorship of the report and of the present volume.

Participating agencies offer a variety of services to Aboriginal women in Winnipeg and rural Manitoba. The Elizabeth Fry Society of Manitoba serves some 500 women a year, 80 per cent of whom are Aboriginal. The society provides resources to women in conflict with the law or at risk of offending. Almost all clients have experienced intimate violence as children and as adults. Programs include group and individual counselling for women, a family program, community–family liaison, support for accused women in the court process, release planning for incarcerated women, and support for Manitoba women in federal penitentiaries. Ikwe-Widdjiitiwin is a short-term crisis shelter used mainly by Aboriginal women. Its services include twenty-four-hour counselling and housing and resident child care, arrangement of legal appointments, child counselling, toll-free Winnipeg and Manitoba crisis lines, group counselling for family violence, and follow-up support. The Ma Mawi Wi Chi Itata Family Violence Program offers open and closed group counselling services to Aboriginal women, children, and men affected by family violence. Its goals are to provide support and resources within the Aboriginal community that strengthen and empower families, create a safe and supportive environment to help families heal from the effects of violence, and develop and deliver culturally appropriate services (Ma Mawi Wi Chi Itata Centre, n.d.). The centre has developed a counselling program sensitive to Aboriginal tradition for intimate violence offenders at Stony Mountain Penitentiary (Proulx and Perrault, 1996). The Native Women's Transition Centre is a community-based twenty-one-bed women's second-stage housing facility that provides safe housing and culturally appropriate support for Aboriginal women and children affected by family violence. Services include individual counselling, referral and advocacy, sharing circles and group programs on family violence, parenting and assertiveness training, and the Mino-Ayaawin Health and Well-Being Programs for Women and Children. The Original Women's Network provides training and education programs and is a founding member of the Manitoba Coalition Opposing Violence against Women (COVAW).

The first stage in our study was preparation of an annotated bibliography that would draw together relevant research, provide a list of sources for researchers and service providers, assess the need for further research, and base the literature review for new research (McGillivray and Parisienne, 1995). The bibliography currently includes some 150 monographs from Canada, the United States, New Zealand, and Australia and is to be updated from time to time by RESOLVE, formerly the Centre for Research on Family Violence and Violence against Women. The bibliography pointed to major gaps in information on intimate violence in Canadian Aboriginal communities and the need for localized qualitative research. In consultation with the steering committee, we prepared a research plan based on qualitative methodology. Areas to be investigated would include childhood and adult experiences of intimate violence and the response of the justice system and agencies. The study would address research priorities of the research centre – the impact of the state on protecting the vulnerable, creative community initiatives in prevention, and causes and outcomes of violence against women.

Method

In her landmark study *Battered but Not Beaten: Preventing Wife Battering in Canada* (1987), Linda McLeod argues that understanding intimate violence must go beyond incidence into experience. While the prevalence of intimate violence has been widely documented, the voices and experiences of women, and Aboriginal women in particular, are not well represented. Feminist research gives women a chance to break the silence surrounding violence in intimate relationships and to 'name' their own experiences. The goal of Liz Kelly's study *Surviving Sexual Violence* (1989), for example, is to express and validate the experiences and subjective understandings of women. Such research requires qualitative methods sensitive to women's experiences. As Anne Oakley argues, formal survey-based research is not suited to good sociological research on women (Oakley, 1981). The one-on-one 'closed interview' that allows only yes or no responses or short answers to detailed questions imposes external definitions and constraints that reduce completeness and accuracy of accounts. Of particular interest is the concept of community-based participatory research, a method responsive to disempowered communities (St Denis, 1992). Our Winnipeg study is an example of such research, emerging from *within* the Aboriginal community and overseen by Aboriginal women dedicated to finding adequate responses to intimate violence. These women helped to develop the questionnaire, opened agency files, located respondents, helped to set safety limits, and provided safe spaces for interviews.

We chose an open-ended, semi-structured interview format that would balance the need for information with respondents' needs for sharing their views and experiences (DeVault, 1990; Finch, 1984). The conversational dimension of open-ended interviews allows interviewer and respondent to interact on more equal ground. Respondents are invited to tell their histories in their own way, and this requires interviewers to engage with the substance of what is being told to them, follow complex time lines, and recognize points needing clarification. To reduce cultural conflict, we decided that Aboriginal women should conduct the interviews, for reasons stated in chapter 1. Collaboration and the emphasis on women speaking for themselves yield research that is 'for and with' Aboriginal women, rather than 'on or about' them (St Denis, 1992).

Protecting research subjects is of utmost importance in researching sensitive topics. Informed consent, lack of deception, protection of confidentiality, and assurance of physical and emotional safety must be closely considered at every stage – consent and the manner of obtaining consent, place of interview, design of the interview schedule, choice of interviewers, and immediate follow-up support. Rapport between interviewer and interviewee is necessary to ensure comfort and maximize sharing of information. In interviewing women, the first criterion is that the interviewer be a woman. The second is that she be an aware woman of the same culture. Interviewers must be involved and sympathetic, able to pay close attention to detail, to recall things said earlier, and to probe for more detailed response where appropriate in all the circumstances. Interviewers come to understand who they themselves are in relation to the research and become, as do the designers of the study, emotionally implicated in the responses that their questioning elicits.

Consent and Confidentiality

Ethics approval is absolutely essential in research involving human subjects. Such approval is and should be difficult to obtain. Consent must be fully informed and freely given. Confidentiality must be completely protected to guarantee both privacy and safety. There must be no pressure on potential respondents to participate. The potential for overt or subtle agency coercion of potential subjects, covert withdrawal of services should participation be refused, and the 'comfort level' of respondents must be considered. Prior counselling, we felt, would have restored to women a degree of autonomy, and we made this a criterion of the study. A worker from each originating agency made first contact with potential respondents and, after interviews had been arranged by the reserach team, administered the consent form and explained the purpose and nature of the study, the kinds of questions that would be asked, and how their information would be protected and used for the purpose of study and reform. The consent form warned that information indicating that a child might be at risk had to be reported by law. This was explained to respondents with particular care. The consent form reads as follows:

I am willing to take part in a study of Aboriginal women who have experienced abuse, and the criminal justice system.

Time: There will be two interviews scheduled a few days apart, each lasting about an hour. The first interview will have questions about my personal history, my childhood and adult experiences of abuse, and help and support that I have received. In the second interview I will be asked about my experience with the criminal justice system, my opinions of this, and what I would like to see in place to deal with abusers.

Withdrawing: I understand that I may refuse to answer any questions that I am not comfortable with, or to withdraw from the study at any time.

Confidentiality: The interviews will be tape recorded and transcribed. My name will not appear on the computer or anywhere else. When the tape recordings have been transcribed, the tapes will be destroyed. Any identifying information about me on the computer will be destroyed. If my words are used in the reports, it will not be possible to tell who is speaking because identifying information will not be used with these words.

Child in Need of Protection: Everyone in Manitoba must report to Child and Family Services any information regarding a child in need of protection (abuse, neglect, etc.). If I mention such a child, the researcher is under a legal duty to report this.

Use of Information: I give my permission for the information to be used in reports which will be shared with police officers and others in the criminal justice system, service agencies and others who are interested in this subject. I can receive a copy of the interview transcript and final report if I wish.

Expenses: Money for child care and transportation is available if needed.
Please check **one** of the following:

[ ] I would like to review my transcript once the interviews are complete

[ ] I would *not* like to review my transcript once the interviews are complete
Person to contact if I have questions or want to withdraw: [——].

Respondents signed two copies of the consent form, keeping one for their records. Agency workers administering consent witnessed the signature and signed a statement affirming lack of coercion and stating that 'I have read the attached consent form of ___ and have answered any questions that she had.' All participants in the administration of the study – agency workers, interviewers, transcribers, members of the steering committee, and we as researchers – signed a statement of confidentiality:

I, _____, as a member of the research team for the project Intimate Violence, Aboriginal Women and Justice System Response, agree to protect the anonymity and confidentiality of the research subjects at every stage of the project. I understand that I am to refrain from discussing any information from the project with persons outside the research team. I understand that any taped information will be destroyed upon transcription, and that code referents will be destroyed upon study completion. I understand that, in accordance with Canadian law, I am obligated to report any information I may receive regarding a child in need of protection.

Selection and Sampling

The study was set for the summer of 1995. We selected respondents from a sampling frame based on client files from four agencies involved in the research project. We obtained a list of women who met basic criteria and had current addresses from each of the agencies. A complicating factor was introduced by agency record-keeping, which categorized files as open, closed, or inactive and by type of service used. Elizabeth Fry Society files include incarcerated women as well as women in the community. Client files may be open or closed, depending on how long a client has been using agency services. Because of differences in filing systems and problems in contacting clients and former clients, random proportionate sampling was not possible. We excluded files lacking telephone listings or forwarding addresses from the sampling frame. Even so, the majority of women on the initial lists had moved and could not be contacted. We narrowed the sampling frame to women currently using agency services but who were not in crisis, preserving the paramountcy of physical and emotional safety in selection and operational criteria. Women going underground after, as well as before, agency contact is understandable and respected in this context.

To control for changes in justice administration in Manitoba, we included only women who had experienced violence in the five years preceding the study. As respondents' safety was a major concern, we excluded women with very recent experiences of violence. The final sample consisted of nine respondents from Ma Mawi Wi Chi Itata Family Violence Program, seven from Native Women's Transition Centre, six from Ikwe-Widdjiitiwin, and two from Elizabeth Fry. As the study design and questionnaire remained essentially the same after testing, and at the urging of test volunteers, we included two of three test interviews in the data analysis for a total of twenty-six respondents. Although the sample is not random and therefore not generalizable in the strict social sciences sense, the two-stage interview process, with additional opportunities for addition or correction, enhances internal validity. Variation in age, education, and experience of respondents suggests that their views are sufficiently representative to guide policy choice and expand understanding of the nature, dynamics, and effects of intimate violence.

The Research Team

With final ethics approval by the University of Manitoba's Faculty of Law Ethics Review Committee, the research team was formed. Brenda Comaskey was retained as research associate. She refined and tested the interview schedule and trained and supervised the interviewers in the interview schedule, ethics, researching of sensitive topics, probing, note taking, editing and use of audio equipment; trained transcribers; and coordinated sampling of agency files. She managed day-to-day aspects of the study and did original data analysis, working closely with Anne McGillivray. The interviewers were Aboriginal women fluent in Ojibwa. One had been a counsellor with child protection experience, the second had worked in health services, and both were knowledgeable about domestic violence and the criminal justice process. The interviewers were able to account for ambiguities in the transcribed interviews and assure comfort for respondents. They provided feedback from role-playing sessions and from test interviews for refining the interview schedule. Post-interview 'debriefing' sessions were an important part of the process of data collection, necessitated by the painful and sensitive nature of the subject and the practical need to recheck notes and observations. Interviews were taped and transcribed. Notes made by the interviewers on each interview were used where tapes were not audible or clarification or context was needed.

Study Structure

We structured the study around five areas of inquiry – childhood violence and abuse, violence and abuse experienced in adulthood, help and support sought and received, the justice system's response, and changes to the system. The interview schedule was divided into two parts. The schedule format was semi-structured and open-ended in order to allow the women to tell their stories freely. Part I explored demographic information, childhood experiences of abuse, adult experiences of abuse, and support and intervention and was designed to establish a level of ease and familiarity in preparation for the kinds of questions to be asked in Part II. The interviewers probed for information and clarification where needed. We rejected the 'violence checklist' approach as both exclusive and overly suggestive. Part II explored experiences with the justice system and what changes, if any, respondents would like made. Concluding with questions about reform was intended to provide a sense of hope and empowerment.

Twenty-six women completed Part I of the interview, and twenty-five, Part II. Two chose to complete both parts of the interview in one session. Length of Part I interviews ranged from thirty-five minutes to two hours, and Part II, from forty minutes to two hours and fifteen minutes. The average for each part was about one hour. The same interviewer handled both parts of each interview to maintain continuity. Interviews were scheduled as close together in time as was practicable, for this reason. In total, fifty-one interviews were conducted with twenty-six women over a four-week period. Most were concluded within the same week.

Interview Setting and Safety

All but one of the interviews took place on or adjacent to the agency from which the respondent was selected, in order to provide a safe, familiar place and support services should the need arise. One respondent preferred to be interviewed in her home, which had an elaborate security system. Four were interviewed in private suites in a second-stage housing project adjacent to agency offices, with twenty-four-hour support staff. Funds were made available for child care and transportation, and in some cases members of the research team drove women to and from the agency for the interviews. As it is not possible to foresee in every case the consequences of raising painful and sensitive issues, it was the interviewer's job to determine how the woman was feeling and whether she would like to talk to anyone. Only one woman approached for the study declined to participate, a second could not be located for the interviews, and a third dropped out after the first interview. The low attrition rate suggests that women wanted to take part and that the sensitive questions in Part I of the interview had been appropriately handled. Respondents received a resource list of helping agencies at the end of the first interview.

The respondent who dropped out of the study after the first interview was, according to the interviewer's notes, 'not very talkative. Stated she has difficulty sharing problems. Voice very low. No emotional upset, interview went quickly.' Two days later, the interviewer telephoned to confirm the time set for the second appointment, but there was no answer. The respondent returned the call a few minutes later (using 'call-display,' which screens callers) and told the interviewer that she had attempted suicide the night before by trying to jump from a bridge. She had been taken to hospital by a passer-by and discharged that morning. She spoke of the recent miscarriage of her first pregnancy, resulting from her partner's violence. This had not been mentioned in her interview.

The interviewer suggested that they meet at the agency at the arranged time just to talk and have coffee. When she did not come, the interviewer contacted police and agency workers. A worker was able to contact her and confirm that she was 'all right.' The respondent made four more appointments but did not attend another interview. Her transcript showed references to suicidal ideation in childhood and adolescence. In hindsight, she should not have been selected as a candidate. Her abuse was recent, she remained romantically involved with her incarcerated abuser, who continued to control her by telephone from prison, and she had not undergone treatment, having just begun group treatment required by her probation order. Unknown was the fact that her pregnancy had been terminated by her partner's blows.

Two respondents reported that children – their own or those of close relatives – were in need of protection. These children were not living with the respondents. With their consent and assistance, provincial authorities were informed of details by telephone and letter. The file kept to confirm that these reports had been made was destroyed at the close of the project.

Transcription, Analysis, and Reporting

Interviews were audio-taped and transcribed, and interviewers checked transcripts with their notes to ensure accuracy and clarity. A code was assigned to each respondent. Tapes were labelled and enclosed, with consent forms and interview notes, in an envelope initialled first by the transcribers, second by the interviewers after review, and third by the research associate, who then erased the tapes. Respondents were invited to review their transcripts and keep a copy. Transcripts were then analysed to determine categories of response, themes emergent in the data, and counter-views. Categories were coded. Responses were to be directly quoted in the study report to the greatest possible extent, with omissions and clarifications placed in brackets. The information given was disaggregated – separated into units – to ensure that no respondent could be identified. The number of respondents still being harassed by former or current partners justified this decision.

An interim report was prepared for the Beijing conference, and the final research report was given to Aboriginal women and agencies representing them. The report incorporates comments and criticisms from the steering committee. Titled *Intimate Violence, Aboriginal Women and Justice System Response – A Winnipeg Study*, the report has been distributed by member agencies of the steering committee; has been used in workshops given by Aboriginal women to Manitoba police, service agencies, and justice system personnel; and has resulted in the establishment of an Aboriginal diversion project in Winnipeg. Aboriginal Ganootamaage Justice Services of Winnipeg, a three-year trial project that began operations in September 1998, does not divert intimate-violence offenders.

Bibliography

Aboriginal Legal Services of Toronto (1992). 'Community Council Project of Aboriginal Legal Services of Toronto.' The Council, 9 Nov.

Adelburg, Ellen (1993). 'Aboriginal Women and Prison Reform,' in Ellen Adelburg and Claudia Currie, eds., *In Conflict with the Law: Women and the Canadian Justice System*, 76–92. Vancouver: Press Gang.

Alberta Law Reform Institute (1995). *Domestic Abuse: Toward an Effective Legal Response*. Discussion Report No. 15. Edmonton: The Institute.

Armitage, Andrew (1995). *Comparing the Policy of Aboriginal Assimilation: Australia, Canada, and New Zealand*. Vancouver: UBC Press.

Armstrong, Jeannette (1996). 'Invocation: The Real Power of Aboriginal Women,' in Miller and Chuchryk, eds. (1996), ix–xii.

Aron, Raymond (1967). *Main Currents in Sociological Thought II*. New York: Anchor Books.

Astor, Hillary (1994). 'Swimming against the Tide: Keeping Violent Men Out of Mediation,' in Stubbs and Tolme, eds. (1994), 147–73.

Athens, Lonnie (1989). *The Creation of Dangerous Violent Criminals*. London: Routledge.

Bagot, Sir Charles (1845). Report on the Affairs of Indians in Canada (Bagot Report). Legislative Assembly of Upper Canada.

Bala, Nicholas M.C., et al. (1998). *Spousal Violence in Custody and Access Disputes: Recommendations for Reform*. Ottawa: Status of Women Canada.

Bowles, Richard P., et al. (1972). *The Indian: Assimilation, Integration or Separation?* Scarborough, Ont.: Prentice-Hall.

Buckley, H. (1992). *From Wooden Ploughs to Welfare: Why Indian Policy Failed in the Prairie Provinces*. Montreal: McGill-Queen's University Press.

Bull, L.R. (1991). 'Indian Residential Schooling: The Native Perspective,' *Canadian Journal of Native Education* (Supplement) 18: 1–64.

Bunch, Charlotte (1995). 'The Global Campaign for Women's Human Rights: Where Next after Vienna?' *St John's Law Review*, 69: 171–8.

Burt, Sandra, Code, Lorraine, and Dorney, Lindsay, eds. (1993). *Changing Patterns: Women in Canada*. Toronto: McClelland & Stewart.

Busch, Ruth, and Robertson, Neville (1994) '"Ain't No Mountain High Enough (to Keep Me from Getting to You)": An Analysis of the Hamilton Abuse Intervention Pilot Project,' in Stubbs and Tolme, eds. (1994), 34–63.

Canada. Indian Affairs (1983). *Indian Government under Indian Act Legislation 1868–1951*. Ottawa: Department.

– (1989). *Highlights of Aboriginal Conditions, 1981–2001; Part II: Social Conditions*, Ottawa: Department.

Canada. Law Reform Commission of Canada (1991). *Aboriginal Peoples and Criminal Justice*. Report No. 34. Ottawa: Commission.

Canada. Royal Commission on Aboriginal Peoples (RCAP) (1993a). *Exploring the Options: Overview of the Third Round*. Ottawa: Minister of Supply and Services Canada.

– (1993b). *The Path to Healing. The Report of the National Round Table on Health and Social Issues*. Ottawa: Minister of Supply and Services Canada.

– (1995). *Choosing Life: Special Report on Suicide among Aboriginal People*. Ottawa: Minister of Supply and Services Canada.

– (1996a). *Bridging the Cultural Divide: A Report on Aboriginal People and Criminal Justice in Canada*. Ottawa: Minister of Supply and Services Canada.

– (1996b). *Report of the Royal Commission on Aboriginal Peoples*. Ottawa: Minister of Supply and Services Canada.

Canada. Solicitor General (1997). *The Four Circles of Hollow Water*. Ottawa.

Canada. Statistics Canada (1990). 'Conjugal Violence against Women,' *Juristat* 10 no. 7: 1–8.

– (1991). *Adult Corrections Survey*. Ottawa: Canadian Centre for Justice Statistics.

– (1995). *Canadian Crime Statistics 1994*. Ottawa: Canadian Centre for Justice Statistics.

– (1996). *Canadian Crime Statistics 1995*. Ottawa: Canadian Centre for Justice Statistics.

Canadian Bar Association (1989). *Locking up Natives in Canada*. Ottawa: Association.

Canadian Council on Social Development. (1991). *Voices of Aboriginal Women: Aboriginal Women Speak Out about Violence*. Ottawa: Native Women's Association of Canada.

Canadian Panel on Violence against Women (1993). *Changing the Landscape: Ending Violence – Achieving Equality. The Final Report*. Ottawa: Minister of Supply and Services Canada.

Canadian Welfare Council and Canadian Association of Social Workers (1947). *Joint Submission to the Special Joint Committee of the Senate and the House of Commons Appointed to Examine and Consider the Indian Act.* Ottawa: Council.

Cariboo Tribal Council and University of Guelph (1991). 'Faith Misplaced: Lasting Effects of Abuse in a First Nations Community,' *Canadian Journal of Native Education* 18: 161–197.

Carter, Sarah (1996). 'First Nations Women of Prairie Canada in the Early Reserve Years, the 1870s to the 1920s: A Preliminary Inquiry,' in Miller and Chuchryk, eds. (1996), 51–76.

– (1997). *Capturing Women: The Manipulation of Cultural Imagery in Canada's Prairie West.* Montreal: McGill-Queen's University Press.

Caudill, David (1997). *Lacan and the Subject of Law: Toward a Psychoanalytic Critical Legal Theory.* Atlantic Highlands, NJ: Humanities Press.

Certeau, Michel de (1984). *The Practice of Everyday Life.* Trans. Steven Randall, Berkeley: University of California Press.

Charlesworth, Hilary (1995). 'Human Rights as Men's Rights,' in Peters and Wolper, eds. (1995), 103–13.

Chunn, Dorothy (1992). *From Punishment to Doing Good: Family Courts and Socialized Justice in Ontario, 1880–1940.* Toronto: University of Toronto Press.

Clarke, Scott, and Hepworth, Dorothy (1994). 'Effects of Reform Legislation on the Processing of Sexual Assault Cases,' in Julian V. Roberts and Renate M. Mohr, eds., *Confronting Sexual Assault: A Decade of Legal and Social Change,* 113–35. Toronto: University of Toronto Press.

Coalition Opposed to Violence against Women (COVAW) (1995). *Policy Statement.* Winnipeg: Coalition.

Cohen, Cynthia Price (1990). *Children's Rights in America: The United Nations Convention on the Rights of the Child Compared with United States Laws.* Chicago: American Bar Association Center on Children and the Law.

Comack, Elizabeth (1996). *Women in Trouble: Connecting Women's Law Violations to Their Abuse Histories.* Halifax: Fernwood.

Commission on the Status of Women (1995). *Monitoring the Implementation of the Nairobi Forward-Looking Strategies for the Advancement of Women.* New York: Commission.

Criminal Code, RSC 1985, c. C-46.

Daly, Martin, and Wilson, Margo (1988). *Homicide.* New York: Aldine de Gruyter.

DeVault, Marjorie (1990). 'Talking and Listening from Women's Standpoint: Feminist Strategies for Interviewing and Analysis,' *Social Problems* 37 no. 1: 96–116.

Doggett, Maeve E. (1993). *Marriage, Wife-Beating and the Law in Victorian England,* Columbia: University of South Carolina Press.

Dosman, E.J. (1972). *Indians: The Urban Dilemma*. Toronto: McClelland and Stewart.

Dumont, Smith, Claudette, and Labelle, Paulette Sioui (1991). National Family Violence Survey: Phase 1. (Ottawa: Aboriginal Nurses Association of Canada).

Durkheim, Emile (1951). *Suicide*. Trans. John A. Spaulding and George Simpson. New York: Free Press.

Family Violence Professional Education Task Force (1991). *Family Violence: Everybody's Business, Somebody's Life*. Sydney, Australia: Federation Press.

Finch, Janet (1984). '"It's great to have someone to talk to": The Ethics and Politics of Interviewing Women,' in Colin Bell and Helen Roberts, eds., *Social Research-ing: Politics, Problems, Practice*, 70–87. London: Routledge & Kegan Paul.

Fine, Michelle (1994). 'Working the Hyphens: Reinventing Self and Other in Qualitative Research,' in Norman Denzin and Yvonna Lincoln, eds., *Handbook on Qualitative Research*, 70–82. Thousand Oaks, Calif.: Sage.

Fiske, Jo-anne (1991). 'Colonization and the Decline of Women's Status: The Tsimshian Case,' *Feminist Studies* 17 no. 3: 509–35.

Fleras, A., and Elliott, J.L. (1992). *The Nations Within: Aboriginal–State Relations in Canada, the United States, and New Zealand*. Toronto: Oxford University Press.

Fossett, Renee Jones (1990). *Alternatives to Incarceration: Literature Review and Selected Annotated Bibliography*. Report No. 16 to the Aboriginal Justice Inquiry. Ottawa: Inquiry.

Foucault, Michel (1977). *Discipline and Punish: The Birth of the Prison*. Translation of *Surveiller et punir*. New York: Vintage Books.

Frank, Sharlene (1992). *Family Violence in Aboriginal Communities: A First Nations Report*. Victoria, BC: Queen's Printer.

Freeman, Michael (1997). *The Moral Status of Children: Essays on the Rights of the Child*, Dordrecht, The Netherlands: Martinus Nijhoff.

Gelles, Richard (1979). *Family Violence*. London: Sage.

Globe and Mail (9 July 1997). 'More Boys Physically Abused than Girls.'

Giesbrecht, Judge Brian (1992). *The Fatalities Inquiries Act Report: An Inquest Respecting the Death of Lester Norman Desjarlais*. Brandon, Man., 31 Aug.

Goldberg, Pamela, and Kelly, Nancy (1993). 'International Human Rights and Violence against Women,' *Harvard Human Rights Journal* 6: 195–209.

Goodrich, Peter (1995). *Oedipus Lex – Psychoanalysis, History, Law*. Los Angeles: University of California Press.

Gordon, Linda (1988). *Heroes of Their Own Lives: The Politics and History of Family Violence, Boston, 1880–1960*. New York: Viking.

Gowanlock, Theresa, and Delaney, Theresa (1885). *Two Months in the Camp of Big Bear: The Life and Adventures of Theresa Gowanlock and Theresa Delaney*. Parkdale, Ont.: Times Office.

Grant, Agnes (1996). *No End of Grief: Indian Residential Schools in Canada*. Winnipeg: Pemmican Publications.

Green, Ross Gordon (1998). *Justice in Aboriginal Communities: Sentencing Alternatives*. Saskatoon: Purich.

Greer, Pam (1994). 'Aboriginal Women and Domestic Violence in New South Wales,' in Stubbs and Tolme, eds. (1994), 64–78.

Gresko, J. (1979). 'White "Rites" and Indian "Rites": Indian Education and National Responses in the West, 1870–1910,' in David C. Jones, Nancy M. Sheehan, and Robert M. Stamp, eds., *Shaping the Schools of the Canadian West*, 84–106. Calgary: Detselig.

Grevin, Philip (1991). *Spare the Child: The Religious Roots of Physical Punishment and the Psychological Impact of Physical Abuse*. New York: Knopf.

Griffiths, Curt T., and Verdun-Jones, Simon, eds. (1994). *Canadian Criminal Justice*. 2nd ed. Toronto: Harcourt Brace.

Haig-Brown, Celia (1988). *Resistance and Renewal: Surviving the Indian Residential School*. Vancouver: Tillacum Library.

Hale, Sylvia M. (1990). *Controversies in Sociology: A Canadian Introduction*. Toronto: Copp Clark Pitman.

Hall, S. (1991). 'Ethnicity, Identity and Difference,' *Radical America* 3: 9–22.

Hawthorn, H.B., ed. (1966). *A Survey of the Contemporary Indians of Canada: A Report on Economic, Political, Educational Needs and Policies*. Ottawa: Canadian Department of Indian Affairs and Northern Development.

Hollow Water First Nations Community Holistic Circle Healing (1993). *Position Paper*. Hollow Water, Man.: CHCH.

– (1994). *Interim Report*, Appendix 3, 'The Sentencing Circle.' Hollow Water, Man.: CHCH.

Hooper, Carol-Ann (1992). *Mothers Surviving Sexual Abuse*. London: Tavistock/ Routledge.

House of Commons (1991). Sub-Committee on the Status of Women. *War against Women: Report of the Standing Committee on Health, Welfare and Social Affairs*. Ottawa: Minister of Supply and Services Canada.

Ing, N.R. (1991). 'The Effects of Residential Schools on Native Child-Rearing Practices,' *Canadian Journal of Native Education* (Supplement) 18: 65–118.

Isaac, Thomas, and Maloughney, Mary Sue (1992). 'Dually Disadvantaged and Historically Forgotten? Aboriginal Women and the Inherent Right of Aboriginal Self-Government,' *Manitoba Law Journal*, 21: 453–75.

Jensen, Maureen (forthcoming). 'An Analysis of Manitoba Court of Appeal Decisions in Cases Heard in the Winnipeg Family Violence Court, 1990–1992.' MSW thesis, University of Manitoba.

Johnson, Holly (1995a). 'Children and Youths as Victims of Violent Crimes,' *Juristat* 15 no. 15: 1–18.

– (1995b). 'Seriousness, Type and Frequency of Violence against Wives,' in Valverde, McLeod, and Johnson, eds. (1995), 125–47.

Jones, Ann (1994). *Next Time She'll Be Dead: Battering and How to Stop It*. Boston: Beacon Press.

Kelly, Fanny (1872). *Narrative of My Captivity among the Sioux Indians*. Toronto: Maclear.

Kelly, Liz (1988). *Surviving Sexual Violence*. Minneapolis: University of Minnesota Press.

Kimelman, Judge E.C. (1985). Review Commission on Indian and Métis Adoptions and Placements. Final Report. *No Quiet Place*. Winnipeg: Manitoba Community Services.

Kiyoshk, Robert (1990). *Family Violence Research Report: Beyond Violence*. Vancouver: Helping Spirit Lodge.

Klein, Laura F., and Ackerman, Lillian A. , eds. (1995). *Woman and Power in Native North America*. Norman: University of Oklahoma Press.

Kline, Marlee (1993). 'Complicating the Ideology of Motherhood: Child Welfare Law and First Nation Women,' *Queen's Law Journal* 18: 306–342.

Korbin, Jill (1981). *Child Abuse and Neglect: A Cross-Cultural Perspective*. Los Angeles: University of California Press.

Lafitau, Joseph Francois (1724). *Moeurs des sauvages ameriquains, comparés aux moeurs des premiers temps*. Paris, 1724. Translated as *Customs of the American Indians Compared with the Customs of Primitive Times*. Ed and trans. William N. Fenton and Elizabeth L. Moore, Toronto: Champlain Society, 1974.

La Prairie, Carol (1994). *Victimization and Family Violence, Report 3; Seen but Not Heard: Native People in the Inner City*. Ottawa: Department of Justice.

LaRocque, Emma (1993). *Violence in Aboriginal Communities*. Report to the Aboriginal Justice Inquiry. Ottawa: Inquiry.

– (1996). 'The Colonization of a Native Woman Scholar,' in Miller and Chuchryk, eds. (1996), 11–18.

Law Reform Commission of Canada (1991). *See under* Canada.

Law Reform Commission of Manitoba (1997). *Stalking*. Winnipeg: Commission.

Law Society of Manitoba (1992). *Code of Professional Conduct*. Winnipeg: Society.

Levinson, D. (1989). *Family Violence in a Cross Cultural Perspective*. Newbury Park, Calif.: Sage.

Locke, John [1690] (1963). *Two Treatises of Government*, ed. Peter Lazlitt. New York: Cambridge University Press.

Ma Mawi Wi Chi Itata Centre (n.d.). *Family Violence Program* (pamphlet). Winnipeg.

McGillivray, Anne (1986). 'Transracial Adoption and the Status Indian Child,' *Canadian Journal of Family Law* 4: 437–67.

– (1987). 'Battered Women: Models, Policy and Prosecutorial Discretion,' *Canadian Journal of Family Law* 6: 15–45.

– (1990). 'Abused Children in the Courts: Adjusting the Scales after Bill C-15,' *Manitoba Law Review* 19: 549–79.

– (1992). 'Reconstructing Child Abuse: Western Definition and Non-Western Experience,' in M.D.A. Freeman and P. Veerman, eds., *The Ideologies of Children's Rights*, 213–36. London: Martinus Nijhoff.

– (1993). '*R. v. K.(M.)*. Legitimating Brutality,' *Criminal Reports* (4th) 16: 125–32.

– (1994a). 'Intimate Violence and Manly Men,' *Canadian Journal of Law and Society* 9: 233–45.

– (1994b). 'Why Children Do Have Equal Rights: In Reply to Laura Purdy,' *International Journal of Children and the Law* 2: 243–58.

– (1997a). 'Governing Childhood,' in Anne McGillivray, ed., *Governing Childhood*, 1–24. Aldershot: Dartmouth.

– (1997b). '"He'll learn it on his body": Disciplining Childhood in Canadian Law,' *International Journal of Children's Rights* 5: 193–242.

– (1997c). 'Therapies of Freedom': The Colonization of Aboriginal Childhood,' in Anne McGillivray, ed., *Governing Childhood*, 135–99. Aldershot: Dartmouth.

– (1998a). 'A moral vacuity in her which is difficult if not impossible to explain': Law, Psychiatry and the Remaking of Karla Homolka,' in Wesley Pue, ed. (1998), *International Journal of the Legal Profession – Lawyering for a Fragmented World*, 5: 255–88.

– (1998b). '*R. v. Bauder*: Seductive Children, Safe Rapists, and Other Justice Tales,' *Manitoba Law Journal* 25 no. 2: 359–83.

– (1999). 'Capturing Childhood: The Indian Child in the European Imagination,' in Michael Freeman and Andrew Lewis, eds., *Law* and *Literature*. London: Oxford University Press.

McGillivray, Anne, and Comaskey, Brenda (1996). *Intimate Violence, Aboriginal Women and Justice System Response: A Winnipeg Study.* Winnipeg: Manitoba Research Centre on Family Violence and Violence against Women.

– (1997). 'Everybody had black eyes": Intimate Violence, Aboriginal Women and Justice System Response,' in Kevin Bonnycastle and George Rigakos, eds., *Unsettling Truths: Battered Women Policy, Politics and Contemporary Research in Canada*. Vancouver: Collective Press.

McGillivray, Anne, and Parisienne, Joanne (1995). *Intimate Violence, Aboriginal Women and Justice System Response: An Annotated Bibliography.* Winnipeg: Manitoba Research Centre on Family Violence and Violence against Women.

McIvor, Sharon D. (n.d.). *Aboriginal Women: Police Charging Policies and Domestic Violence.* Ottawa: Native Women's Association of Canada.

McIvor, Sharon D., and Nahanee, Teressa A. (1998). 'Aboriginal Women: Invisible Victims of Violence,' in K. Bonneycastle and G. Rigakos, eds., *Unsettling Truths: Battered Women, Policy, Politics and Contemporary Research in Canada*, 63–70. Vancouver: Collective Press.

McLeod, Linda (1987). *Battered but Not Beaten: Preventing Wife Abuse in Canada.* Ottawa: Canadian Advisory Council on the Status of Women.

MacMillan, Harriet L., et al. (1997). 'Prevalence of Child Physical and Sexual Abuse in the Community: Results from the Ontario Health Supplement,' *Journal of the American Medical Association* 278: 131–5.

Mahoney, Kathleen (1992). 'The Legal Treatment of Spousal Abuse: A Case of Sex Discrimination,' *University of New Brunswick Law Journal* 41: 21–40.

Makus, Ingrid (1996). *Women, Politics, and Reproduction: The Liberal Legacy.* Toronto: University of Toronto Press.

Maltz, Daniel, and Archambault, JoAllyn (1995). 'Gender and Power in Native North America,' in Klein and Ackerman, eds. (1995), 230–49.

Manitoba (1991a). *Report of the Aboriginal Justice Inquiry of Manitoba: The Justice System and Aboriginal People.* Vol. I, Commissioners A.C. Hamilton and C.M. Sinclair. Winnipeg: Queen's Printer.

– (1991b). *Report of the Aboriginal Justice Inquiry of Manitoba: The Deaths of Helen Betty Osborne and John Joseph Harper.* Vol. II, Commissioners A.C. Hamilton and C.M. Sinclair. Winnipeg: Queen's Printer.

Manitoba. Justice and Women's Directorate (1996). *Stop the Violence: A Resource Guide for Service Providers on the Processes and Programs Aimed at Combating Domestic Violence.* Winnipeg: Manitoba Justice and Manitoba Women's Directorate.

Manitoba Association of Women and the Law (1991). *Gender Equality in the Courts: Criminal Law.* Winnipeg: Association.

Martin, G. Arthur (1993). *Report of the Attorney General's Advisory Committee on Charge Screening, Disclosure and Resolution Discussion* (The Martin Report). Toronto: Ontario Ministry of the Attorney General.

Merry, Sally (1997). 'Global Human Rights and Local Social Movements in a Legally Plural World,' *Canadian Journal of Law and Society* 12: 247–71.

– (forthcoming). 'Criminalization and Gender: The Changing Governance of Sexuality and Gender Violence in Hawai'i.'

Miller, Alice (1983). *For Your Own Good: Hidden Cruelty in Child-Rearing and the Roots of Violence.* New York: Farrar, Straus, Giroux.

Miller, Christine, and Chuchryk, Patricia, eds. (1996). *Women of the First Nations: Power, Wisdom, and Strength.* Winnipeg: University of Manitoba Press.

Miller, J.R. (1989). *Skyscrapers Hide the Heavens: A History of Indian–White Relations in Canada.* Toronto: University of Toronto Press.

– (1991). 'Owen Glendower, Hotspur, and Canadian Indian Policy,' in J.R. Miller, ed. (1991), 323–32.

– ed. (1991). *Sweet Promises: A Reader on Indian–White Relations in Canada*. Toronto: University of Toronto Press.

– (1996). *Shingwauk's Vision: A History of Native Residential Schools*. Toronto: University of Toronto Press.

Mills, Linda G. (1996). 'On the Other Side of Silence: Affective Lawyering for Intimate Abuse,' *Cornell Law Review* 81 no. 6: 1225–63.

– (1997). 'Intuition and Insight: A New Job Description for the Battered Woman's Prosecutor and Other More Modest Proposals,' *U.C.L.A. Women's Law Journal* 7 no. 2. 183–99.

Monture-Angus, Patricia (1995). *Thunder in My Soul: A Mohawk Woman Speaks*. Halifax: Fernwood.

Monture-Okanee, Patricia A. (1992). 'The Roles and Responsibilities of Aboriginal Women: Reclaiming Justice,' *Saskatchewan Law Review* 56: 237–66.

Nedelsky, Jennifer (1993). 'Reconceiving Rights as Relationship,' *Review of Constitutional Studies* 1: 1–26.

New Democratic Party of Manitoba (1995). Caucus Task Force on Violence against Women. *Ending the Terror: Towards Zero Tolerance*. Winnipeg: Task Force.

Oakley, Anne (1981). 'Interviewing Women: A Contradiction in Terms,' in H. Roberts, ed., *Doing Feminist Research*, 30–61. London: Routledge & Kegan Paul.

Ontario Native Women's Association (1989). *Breaking Free: A Proposal for Change to Aboriginal Family Violence*. Thunder Bay, Ont.: Ontario Native Women's Association.

Payment, Diane P. (1996). '*La Vie en Rose?* Métis Women at Batoche, 1870 to 1920,' in Miller and Chuchryk, eds. (1996), 19–38.

Pedlar, Dorothy (1991). *Domestic Violence Review into the Administration of Justice in Manitoba*. Manitoba. Department of Justice.

Peers, Laura (1996). 'Subsistence, Secondary Literature, and Gender Bias: The Saultaux,' in Miller and Chuchryk, eds. (1996), 39–50.

Peters, Julie, and Wolper, Andrea, eds. (1995). *Women's Rights, Human Rights: International Feminist Perspectives*. London: Routledge.

Platform for Action. 1995. Address, Fourth World Conference on Women, Beijing, 1995.

Polito, Mary (1994). 'Wit, Will and Governance in Early Modern Legal Literature,' *Mosaic* 27 no. 4: 15–34.

Proulx, Jocelyn, and Perrault, Sharon (1996). *An Evaluation of the Ma Mawi Wi Chi Itata Centre Family Violence Program Stony Mountain Family Violence Project*. Winnipeg: Ma Mawi Wi Chi Itata Centre.

Rabin, Bonnie E. (1995). 'Violence against Mothers Equals Violence against Children: Understanding the Connections,' *Albany Law Review* 58: 1109–18.

Rao, Arafi (1995). 'The Politics of Gender and Culture in International Human Rights Discourse,' in Peters and Wolper, eds. (1995).

Roberts, Julian V., and LaPrairie, Carol (1996). 'Sentencing Circles: Some Questions Unanswered,' *Criminal Law Quarterly* 39: 69–83.

Roberts Chapman, Jane (1989). 'Violence against Women as a Violation of Human Rights,' *Social Justice* 17 no. 2: 54–63.

Rodgers, Karen (1994). 'Wife Assault: The Findings of a National Survey,' *Juristat*, 14 no. 9: 1–22.

Ross, Rupert (1993). *Aboriginal Community Healing in Action: The Hollow Water Approach.* Ottawa: Aboriginal Justice Directorate, Department of Justice.

Royal Commission on Aboriginal Peoples (RCAP). *See under* Canada.

St Denis, Verna (1992). 'Community-Based Participatory Research: Aspects of the Concept Relevant for Practice,' *Native Studies Review* 8 no. 2: 51–74.

Schulman, Judge Perry W. (1997). *A Study of Domestic Violence and the Justice System in Manitoba: Commission of Inquiry into the Deaths of Rhonda Lavoie and Roy Lavoie* (Lavoie Inquiry Report). Winnipeg: Queen's Printer.

Shaffer, Martha (1997). 'The Battered Woman Syndrome Revisited: Some Complicating Thoughts Five Years after *R. v. LaVallee*,' *University of Toronto Law Journal* 47: 1–33.

Shakespeare, William (1611). *The Tempest.*

Shaw, Margaret (1990). *Survey of Federally Sentenced Women.* Ottawa: Solicitor General of Canada.

Shoemaker, Nancy, ed. (1995). *Negotiators of Change: Historical Perspectives on Native American Women.* London: Routledge.

Smandych, Russell, and Lee, Gloria (1995). 'Women, Colonization and Resistance: Elements of an Amerindian Autohistorical Approach to the Study of Law and Colonialism,' *Native Studies Review* 10 no. 1: 21–45.

Smandych, Russell, and McGillivray, Anne (1999). 'Images of Aboriginal Childhood: Contested Governance in the Canadian West to 1850,' in Rick Halpern and Martin Daunton, eds., *Empire and Others: British Encounters with Indigenous Peoples,* 238–59. London: University College, London.

Smart, Carol (1989). *Feminism and the Power of Law.* London: Routledge.

Snider, Laureen (1995). 'Feminism, Punishment, and the Potential for Empowerment,' in Valverde, McLeod, and Johnson, eds. (1995), 236–59.

Spotton, Noelle (1998). 'Aboriginal Legal Services of Toronto and the Legal Aid Needs of the Metropolitan Toronto Aboriginal Community,' *Windsor Yearbook of Access to Justice* 16: 296–305.

Stanko, Elizabeth (1985). *Intimate Intrusions: Women's Experiences of Male Violence.* London: Routledge & Kegan Paul.

– (1990). *Everyday Violence: How Women and Men Experience Sexual and Physical Danger.* London: Pandora.

Straus, Murray A. (1994). *Beating the Devil Out of Them: Corporal Punishment in American Families*. New York: Lexington; Toronto: Maxwell Macmillan.

Straus, Murray, Gelles, Richard, and Steinmetz, Suzanne (1980). *Behind Closed Doors: Violence in the American Family*. Garden City, NY: Anchor/Doubleday.

Stubbs, Julie, and Tolme, Julia, eds. (1994). *Women, Male Violence and the Law*. Sydney, Australia: Sydney Institute of Criminology.

Sturtevant, William C., and Quinn, David Beers (1987). 'This New Prey: Eskimos in Europe in 1567, 1576, and 1577,' in Christian F. Feest, ed., *Indians and Europe: An Interdisciplinary Collection of Essays* 61–140. Aachen: Ed. Herodot, Rader-Verlag.

Sullivan, Donna (1995). 'The Public/Private Distinction in International Human Rights Law,' in Peters and Wolper, eds. (1995), 126–34.

Thomas, Dorothy Q., and Beasley, Michele E. (1995). 'Domestic Violence as a Human Rights Issue,' *Albany Law Review* 58: 1119–47.

Thompson Crisis Centre (1988). Presentation to Aboriginal Justice Inquiry, Thompson, Man., 21 Sept.

Thornton, Margaret (1996). *Dissonance and Distrust: Women in the Legal Profession*. Melbourne: Oxford University Press.

Toronto Star (23 June 1998). 'Residential Schools Devastated Indian Society, Lawsuit Claims.'

Titley, Brian (1986). *A Narrow Vision: Duncan Campbell Scott and the Administration of Indian Affairs in Canada*. Vancouver: UBC Press.

Turner, Jan (1995). 'Saskatchewan Responds to Family Violence,' in Valverde, McLeod and Johnson, eds. (1995), 183–97.

Turpel, Mary Ellen (1989). 'Aboriginal Peoples and the Canadian Charter of Rights and Freedoms: Contradictions and Challenges,' *Canadian Woman Studies* 10: 149–57.

– (1991). 'Aboriginal Peoples and the Canadian Charter of Rights and Freedoms: Contradictions and Challenges,' in Elizabeth Comack and Steven Brickey, eds. *The Social Basis of Law*, 223–37. Halifax: Garamond Press.

UNICEF (1997). *Progress of Nations Report 1996*. New York: United Nations Children's Fund.

Ursel, Jane (1991). 'Considering the Impact of the Battered Women's Movement on the State: The Example of Manitoba,' in Elizabeth Comack and Stephen Brickey, eds., *The Social Basis of Law*, 2nd ed., 261–88. Halifax: Garamond.

– (1992). *Private Lives, Public Policy: 100 Years of State Intervention in the Family*. Toronto: Women's Press.

– (1994). 'The Winnipeg Family Violence Court,' in Valverde, McLeod, and Johnson, eds. (1995), 169–82.

– (1998a). *Lavoie Inquiry Implementation Committee: Final Report*. Winnipeg: Committee.

– (1998b). 'Mandatory Charging: The Manitoba Model,' in K. Bonneycastle and G. Rigakos, eds., *Unsettling Truths: Battered Women Policy, Politics, and Contemporary Research in Canada*, 73–81. Vancouver: Collective Press.

Valencia-Weber, Gloria, and Zuni, Christine P. (1995). 'Domestic Violence and Protection of Indigenous Women in the United States,' *St John's Law Review* 69: 69–170.

Valverde, Mariana, McLeod, Linda, and Johnson, Kirsten, eds. (1995). *Wife Assault and the Canadian Criminal Justice System*. Toronto: University of Toronto Centre of Criminology.

Walker, Lenore (1984). *The Battered Woman Syndrome*. New York: Springer.

Weaver, Sally (1993). 'First Nations Women and Government Policy, 1970–92: Discrimination and Conflict,' in Burt, Code, and Dorney, eds., (1993), 92–150.

Williams, Patricia (1987). 'Alchemical Notes: Reconstructing Ideals from Deconstructed Rights,' *Harvard Civil Rights Civil Liberties Law Review* 22: 401–33.

– (1991). *The Alchemy of Race and Rights: Diary of a Law Professor*. Cambridge: Cambridge University Press.

Wilson, Margo, and Daly, Martin (1994). 'Spousal Homicide,' *Juristat* 14 no. 8: 1–15.

Winnipeg Free Press (29 May 1994). 'Crown Error Flayed in Case.'

– (17 Dec. 1995). 'Zero Tolerance Policy Rates an F.'

– (16 Jan. 1996). 'Justice System Failing Women.'

– (7 March 1996). 'Police Admit "Modest" Faults in Lavoie Case'

– (23 July 1997). 'Women, Girls Suffering: Study."

– (8 Nov. 1997). 'Abuse Stats Queried.'

– (29 Sept. 1998). 'Native Healing Circle to Hear First Case.'

– (30 Sept. 1998). 'Thief Told by Healing Circle to Apologize, Get Counselling.'

York, Geoffrey (1990). *The Dispossessed: Life and Death in Native Canada*. Toronto: Little, Brown.

Index

Aboriginal Council of Winnipeg, 18
Aboriginal Ganootamaage Justice
  Services (Winnipeg), 3, 131, 179,
  182
Aboriginal Legal Services (Toronto),
  18, 117
Aboriginal peoples, xiii; Alberta
  Bloods, 39; band council, xiii, 10,
  45–7; Bill C-31 status, 41, 47, 56;
  communities, x, 5, 8, 10–12, 41, 57,
  129, 138, 142–3, 156, 164–70; culture, 46–52, 89, 146, 150, 165; devaluation of, 7, 23–4, 44–5, 50–2, 68,
  131–2, 137, 146; images of, 7, 27, 30–
  2, 39, 47, 156; Key First Nation, 45;
  Mandan, 50; Montana Oglala, 40;
  Ojibwa, 46, 166, 179; Plains, 37–40,
  48, 50; study of, 17–21; Tsimshian,
  30. *See also* discrimination; intimate
  violence; Métis; reserves; residential and industrial schools; rights
Aboriginal Justice Inquiry (Manitoba), 17, 44–6, 92, 115–6, 134, 144
Adelburg, Ellen, 94, 115
Alberta Law Reform Institute, 144
A.N.R. v. L.J.W., 46
Armitage, Andrew, 15, 38, 43

Armstrong, Jeannette, 23, 34, 45–6
Assembly of First Nations, 154
Astor, Hillary, 117, 143
Athens, Lonnie, 5, 11, 16, 72
Awasis Agency (Manitoba), 99

Bagot Report (Report on the Affairs of
  Indians in Canada), 35–7, 42, 49,
  131
British North America Act (1867), 37
Buckley, Helen, 23, 38
Bull, L.R., 27, 38, 43
Busch, Ruth, and Neville Robertson,
  97, 164

Canadian Association of Social Work-
  ers, 45
Canadian Bar Association, 17, 115
Canadian Centre for Justice Statistics,
  14–15
Canadian Council on Social Develop-
  ment, 8; Family Violence Program,
  19
Canadian Panel on Violence against
  Women, 12–13, 15, 18–20, 34, 51, 74,
  92, 105
Canadian Welfare Council, 45

Carter, Sarah, 7, 29, 31–4, 39–40
Certeau, Michel de, 4, 19, 24–5
charging: assault, 12–13, 75, 86–8, 118,
   169; child-related, 86–8, 91–4, 136–
   8, 146, 152; counter-charging, 100,
   103–7; dropping charges, 103–7;
   plea-bargaining, 119, 140; 'zero tolerance,' 89, 91, 100, 103–7, 112, 141–
   2, 150, 160, 164. See also diversion;
   justice system; police
Charlesworth, Hillary, 150–6
Charter of Rights and Freedoms
   (Canada), 154–9
Child and Family Services (Manitoba), 10, 46–7, 56, 62, 75–6, 82, 85,
   111, 132, 136, 140
children and youth: Aboriginal, 7, 12–
   15, 27–8, 38, 41–7, 98, 136–7, 156;
   custody of, 61, 99–100, 109–10, 135–
   6, 164; fostering and adoption of,
   15, 46–7, 59, 62, 147, 152; as offenders, 47, 115, 137, 152; protection of,
   45–7, 57, 61, 71–5, 83–7, 95, 99, 132,
   135–8, 145, 156. See also colonization; intimate violence; residential
   and industrial schools
Children's Aid Societies, 45, 85;
   Ontario research, 14
Clark, Scott, and Dorothy Hepworth,
   87, 91
Clarke Institute for Psychiatry (Toronto), 13
Coalition Opposing Violence against
   Women, Manitoba (COVAW), 91,
   105, 112, 174
colonization and Euro-colonialism:
   ix–xv, 7, 18, 22–41, 137, 161; assimilation, 31–8, 42–4, 47; children, 42–
   8, 132; cultural genocide, 4, 34–5,
   47, 51–2, 156; infantilization and

wardship, 23, 30, 36–8, 51; patriarchy of, 22, 50, 54; sexism of, 30, 34,
   39–41, 52, 170; social policy, 34–41,
   45–7. See also Davin Report; Indian
   Act; intimate violence; residential
   and industrial schools; rights
Comaskey, Brenda, 179
Constitution Act (Canada), 157–9
corporal punishment, 23, 27–8, 115,
   137; defence of moderate correction, 87, 91, 152
coverture and control of women, 53–
   4, 68–72, 84–6, 136–9, 143, 148
Criminal Code (Canada), 54, 75, 86–
   90, 99, 109, 112–15, 136–8, 143, 152,
   168–9

Davin Report, 42–4, 48–9
discrimination: against Aboriginal
   people, 17, 30–41, 100, 137–8, 156;
   gender-based, 33–4, 85, 131, 148–9,
   151, 170–1; justice system and, 156,
   160; othering, xiv, 7, 19, 24–6, 34,
   132; racism, 6, 23, 34, 52, 100, 113,
   137–9, 143–4, 153–6. See also colonization; police; rights
diversion, 3, 6, 125–33, 163–8, 182;
   dispute resolution, 5, 17–18, 114–17,
   132, 143, 155; mediation, 117, 142–4,
   165
Divorce Act (Canada), 85
Doggett, Maeve E., 84–5, 112, 147–8
Donald Marshall Inquiry, 17
Duluth (Minnesota) Domestic Abuse
   Intervention Project, 163, 166–8
Dumont-Smith, Claudette, and Paulette Sioui Labelle, 13, 16, 19, 54

Elizabeth Fry Society, xi, 173, 178
Evidence Act (Canada), 86–7

Family Violence Court (Manitoba), 90–1, 104–6, 113, 124
Family Violence Professional Education Task Force (Australia), 51, 112
Fiske, Jo-anne, 29, 30
Fleras, Augie, and Jean Leonard Elliot, 23, 38
Fossett, Renee Jones, 116
Foucault, Michel, 115
Freeman, Michael, 152, 160

Geneva Convention on the Punishment of Crime and Genocide, 51
Giesbrecht, Brian, 10, 47
Gowanlock, Theresa, and Theresa Delaney, 32–3
Grant, Agnes, 43, 51
Green, Ross Gordon, 18, 114–16, 143
Greer, Pam, 18
Griffiths, Curt, and Simon Verdun-Jones, 17, 115

Hamilton (New Zealand) Abuse Prevention Project, 163–9
Hawthorn Report, 45–6
Hilo (Hawai'i) Family Crisis Shelter, 162, 168
Hollow Water (Manitoba) Community Holistic Circle Healing Program, 116, 166–9
Homolka, Karla, 73–5

Ikwe-Widdjiitiwin, xi, 174, 178
Indian Act (Canada), xiii, 22, 39–41, 44–5, 47, 132, 161
Indian Affairs (Canada), xiii, 39, 45, 156
intervention, 137, 144–5, 152, 174–8; education, 163–9; healing circles, 131, 166–8; help-seeking, 10, 77–83,

135, 138, 145–6. See also diversion; Duluth; Hamilton; Hilo; Hollow Water
intimate violence: Aboriginal peoples and, 8–19, 29, 132, 161; Aboriginal women's experiences of, 5–8, 55–80, 92–3, 133–8, 168, 170–1; assault, 75–7, 88, 135, 151, 171; battered woman syndrome, 73–4; children and, 10–17, 56–64, 71–2, 91, 137, 167–8; colonization and, 4, 52, 156, 159, 162; coping with, 77–80; cycle of violence, 67, 135; emotional abuse, 134–6, 140–5; extent of, 12–17; fighting, 65–6, 139; healing and, 129, 134–7; intergenerational cycle of, 17, 137; isolation and, 13, 23–4, 79–80, 138; justice system and, 6, 18, 54, 77, 84–113, 124, 139–40, 147, 156, 162–7, 170; law reform and, 84–92, 151, 156, 160, 170; leaving the relationship, 73–81, 98–100, 134–7, 141, 171; murder, 53, 59, 73–7, 88, 92, 148, 151; nature of, xiv, 4, 11, 53–4, 67–70, 133–4, 148; normalization of, 8–10, 24, 133, 135, 138, 171; parenting and, 59, 135–8; psychological abuse, 54–5, 67–70; public policy and, 84–9, 150–6, 170; research on, 138, 163, 173; safety and, 83, 99, 124–8, 143–5, 164–6, 170; sexual abuse, 10, 23, 54–5, 64, 79, 85–6, 91, 129; social services and, 45–7, 80–3, 170–1, 173; spiritual abuse, 7, 50–4; stalking, 6, 54–5, 74–5, 88, 99, 101; support systems for, 134, 144–5; treatment, 144–5, 163, 166, 170; victim-witnesses of, 11, 14–16, 58–9, 71–5, 87, 97–9, 107–8, 135–9, 140–9, 163–70; violent partners, 6, 14–17,

53–71, 80, 113–34, 139–41, 156, 171;
women and girls and, xiv, 3–6, 8–
21, 53–83, 84–113, 129, 133–48, 150–
8, 162–71
Isaac, Thomas, and Mary Sue Maloughney, 41, 157

Johnson, Holly, 12, 14, 15
Jones, Ann, 73, 75
judges, 85–6, 91, 113–16, 142–3, 164
justice system: Aboriginal peoples
and, 17–18, 55, 92–5, 113–16, 125,
130, 142, 156–9, 165–9; Anglo-Canadian, 84–113, 140–9, 167, 170;
courts, 90, 103, 111–18, 165–70;
incarceration, 17, 96, 117–30, 142–5,
167, 174–8; restitution, 114, 170;
victim-impact statements and, 92,
109–12. See also charging; discrimination; diversion; Family Violence
Court; intimate violence; judges;
lawyers; Native Courtworker Program; police; sentencing

Kelly, Fanny, 32
Kelly, Liz, 78, 175
Kimelman Report, 23, 44–5, 47
Klein, Laura F., and Lillian K. Acker-
man, 29

La Prairie, Carol, 13, 52, 115
Lacan, Jacques, 25
Lafiteau, Joseph François, 27–8
LaRocque, Emma, xiv, 11, 25, 28–9, 31,
34, 52, 134, 160, 161
Lavoie Inquiry Report, 90–2, 103, 107,
113, 141–3
Law Reform Commission of Canada,
17, 115
lawyers: prosecutors, 17–18, 90–2,

113, 116–18, 125, 140–1, 164; victims
of abuse and, 107, 110, 137, 140–1
Levinson, Diane, 12, 147

McGillivray, Anne, 10–11, 15, 23–8,
31–47, 52–4, 73, 80, 85–90, 112–19,
124, 137, 145, 148, 152, 160, 171–3,
179
McGillivray, Anne, and Brenda
Comaskey, 3
McGillivray, Anne, and Joanne Parisi-
enne, 174
McIvor, Sharon, 112, 138, 145, 159
McIvor, Sharon, and Teressa Nah-
anee, 19, 55, 114
McLeod, Linda, 55, 92, 144–5, 175
McMaster–Clarke Study, 13–14
MacMillan, Harriet, 13
Mahoney, Kathleen, 124, 150
Maltz, Daniel, and JoAllyn Archam-
beault, 29
Ma Mawi Wi Chi Itata Centre, Family
Violence Program (Winnipeg), xi,
174, 178
Manitoba Law Reform Commission,
88
Merry, Sally, 73, 162–3
Métis, xiii; culture, 43–9; images of,
32–6; Métissage, 48–50; Louis Riel,
42, 49, 132; women, 33, 48–9. See
also Davin Report
Miller, James Rodger, 15, 23, 37–9, 43–
4
Miller, Christine, and Patricia
Chuchryk, 31
Mills, Linda, 141
missions, 28–9. See also residential
and industrial schools
Monture-Angus, Patricia, 52
Monture-Okanee, Patricia, 26, 29, 88–9

National Symposium of Aboriginal Women of Canada, 23
Native Courtworker Program, 17–18, 111, 117
Native Women's Association of Canada, 154, 159
Native Women's Transition Centre (Winnipeg), xi, 174, 178
Natural Parents v. Superintendent of Child Welfare, 47
NDP Caucus Report on Violence against Women (Manitoba), 91–2
Nedelsky, Jennifer, 160–1

Oakley, Anne, 175
Ontario Native Women's Association, 13, 18, 118
Original Women's Network (Manitoba), xi, 3, 18, 118, 174

Payment, Diane, 29, 31, 48
Pedlar Report, 90, 109
police: band constables, 92–3, 98, 103, 140; calling, 95–100; charging protocols, 164, 167; discretion, 91, 107, 164; RCMP, 98–100, 103, 110; respondents' fear of, 95–7, 136, 139; response, 6, 59, 63, 73, 83, 88–9, 92–106, 112–13, 125, 133, 137–42, 164–5, 170; Winnipeg Police Service, 91, 92, 103. *See also* protection orders
Proulx, Jocelyn, and Sharon Perrault, 124, 145, 174
protection orders, 6, 90–1, 113, 141, 144, 164–5; computer access to, 103; enforcement of, 101–3

R. v. Czipps, 86
R. v. Jobidon, 89
R. v. Lavallee, 73–4

R. v. Mallot, 74
R. v. Manyfingers, 169
Rabin, Bonnie, 16, 71
reserves, 38–43, 51, 78–83, 92–3, 98, 131–9, 161, 168; reintegration to, 47, 143, 164–5, 170
residential and industrial schools, 15, 22–3, 42–7, 51, 62. *See also* colonization; Davin Report
RESOLVE, xi, 174
rights: Aboriginal peoples', 154–61; children's, 152, 158, 160; collective and group, 151–61; human and individual rights, 146–8, 150–4, 158, 160–3; justice system and, 149, 153; Locke and, 153–4; self-determination, 45, 146, 151, 155–61; women's rights, 147–53, 158, 161–3, 171. *See also* Charter of Rights and Freedoms (Canada); intimate violence; United Nations
Roberts, Julian, and Carol, La Prairie, 168
Roberts Chapman, Jane, 151, 162
Rodgers, Karen, 147
Ross, Janet, 166
Royal Commission on Aboriginal Peoples (RCAP), 8–17, 41–5, 109, 115–16, 156–9; women's input to, 8, 28–9, 44, 52. *See also* intimate violence

St Denis, Verna, 20, 175, 176
Schulman Report. *See* Lavoie Inquiry Report
sentencing, 99, 108, 142, 144–5, 164; Aboriginal peoples and, 155; community-based sentences, 17, 165–8; conditional sentences, 168–9; intimate violence, 113, 118–19, 164;

sentencing circles, 116, 168–9; victim impact statements, 90. *See also* diversion; justice system
Shaffer, Martha, 11, 73, 143
Shakespeare, William, 27
Shaw, Margaret, 94
shelters, 6, 13, 81, 99, 133–4
Shoemaker, Nancy, 50
Smandych, Russell, 4
Smandych, Russell, and Gloria Lee, 30
Smandych, Russell, and Anne McGillivray, 28, 48
Spivak, Gayatri Chakravorty, 19
Spousal Abuse Tracking Project (Manitoba), 91
Stanko, Elizabeth, 147
Straus, Murray, 137
Straus, Murray, Richard Gelles, and Suzanne Steinmetz, 16, 147

Trocme, Nico, 14
Turner, Jan, 165–6
Turpel, Mary Ellen, 154–5, 160

United Nations: Commission on the Status of Women, 150; Convention on the Elimination of All Forms of Discrimination against Women, 150; Convention on the Rights of the Child, 152; Declaration on the Elimination of Violence against Women, 150–1; Draft Declaration on the Rights of Indigenous People (1992), 155; General Assembly (1948), 150–1; UNICEF, 151; World Conference of the Decade on Women (Copenhagen), 150; World Conference on Human Rights (Vienna), 151; World Conference on Women (Beijing), 163
Ursel, Jane, 85, 90–1, 105, 113, 142

Valencia-Weber, Gloria, and Christine P. Zuni, 114, 154–5
Victims of Domestic Violence Act (Saskatchewan), 165
Victim-Witness Advocacy Program (Winnipeg), 166
Violence against Women Survey, 12–13, 16, 88

Weaver, Sally, 40–1
wife-battering. *See* intimate violence
Williams, Patricia, 25, 171
Wilson, Margo, and Martin Daly, 74
Winnipeg Study: design, 3–6, 75, 173–82; repondents' demographics, 20–1, 55–7
Women's Advocacy Program (Manitoba), 107, 111

Young Offenders Act (Canada), 47, 116